Lewis and Clark Trail Guide

Written and Edited by
Bruce W. Smalley

with Special Assistance from
The National Park Service

The Condensed Daily Journals of Lewis and Clark

**Featuring U.S. Department of the Interior
Historic Trail Maps
Showing Locations of Over 400
Campsite Locations**

Written and Edited By
Bruce W. Smalley

With assistance from the National Park Service

Prologue.

What the heck is this? ! I had never seen anything like it. Twenty-five pages printed two-sided showing the Lewis and Clark journey on a map from St. Louis, Missouri to Astoria, Oregon and back. During Lewis and Clark's travels, they made over 400 campsites. Here on this series of maps were shown the approximate locations where they camped each day. Each campsite was illustrated with a small tent and the date and direction of travel. Every book on Lewis and Clark that I had ever read always gave a wonderful verbal description of what the Captains were doing, or what others were doing to them, but never any reference point on a map as to where they were when they wrote about the doings that were taking place.

"Who did this and when?" I frantically searched the old tattered and yellowed pages for some reference. Some detail that would give me a clue as to how old these maps were and who went to all this work. Nothing. Not one single shred of information. I looked closer at the detail…Lewis and Clark campsite locations…Proposed and existing historical sites and parks…And the proposed route of interstate highways, yet un-built. But not one clue who did it.

By the time Steven Ambrose wrote <u>Undaunted Courage</u>, I had already read most everything ever written about Lewis and Clark and was already in the early phase of preparing for a one-year trip via water from St. Louis to Astoria in the summer of 2005. Then William Least Heat-Moon wrote <u>River Horse</u>. It was a great book about his trip via boat up the Hudson River from New York City and through the Erie Canal to Lake Erie, through the Dunkirk Locks to the Allegheny River, down the Ohio River and then up the Missouri and finally the Columbia River to Astoria, Oregon. It was also a revelation, a reality check. The hardest part of his voyage was the Missouri River. In fact his trip up the Missouri was so hard that I have since given up my idea and will only take an excursion via road from Bismarck, North Dakota to the headwaters of the Missouri and then take a boat trip down the Columbia to Astoria.

In June 2002, I was at my father's house in Denver, Colorado. He was 82 and in great health and fitness. My father had collected and saved everything he ever came in contact with that had anything to do with his vocation as a Boy Scout Executive. He called it "memorabilia." Whatever it was called, he had boxes of the stuff and he asked me to go through it all and "see if you want anything." It was a pleasant day so I pulled all the boxes outside the garage and began the long process of opening each box and looking inside. I found more than I wanted to, and I found more than I could have every imagined.

I was going through the last box of "memorabilia" and was much relieved when I came to the last item. It appeared to be some old papers that were in an old plastic bag. After a day of looking into to many old bags at papers that meant nothing to me, I thought for a brief moment that enough was enough. Yet after opening up things all day long, my hand automatically reached in and pulled out just what I had expected…old papers. The tabloid-sized papers were folded so that what was imprinted on them was on the inside, out of view. I fumbled trying to find the center of the pack, and after a brief minute flipped them open.

<u>"Lewis and Clark Expedition Route. 1804 – 1806."</u>

After much research and assistance from people to try and find the source of these documents, it was determined that they were the type of map that a government agency would have produced. I called the Lewis and Clark Trail Heritage Foundation in Great Falls, Montana. They were unaware of any maps fitting the description and they suggested that I call the National Parks Service in Omaha, Nebraska.

Richard Williams, Manager of the Lewis & Clark National Historic Trail, answered the phone. He was responsible for the coordination of all events surrounding the Bicentennial and I had hopes he could help. I described to him what I had found. He was very interested and thought he might be of some assistance. I sent him a copy of the maps so he could see what it was I was describing.

Several days later I called Mr. Williams. He had an answer. Yes, he had identified the maps as the original maps that were sent to Congress as part of the requirement to have the Lewis and Clark Trail established as a Historic Trail. He knew of the existence of only one other set of the maps and the National Park Service had them in their archives. When I asked him how many people might know of the existence of these maps his response surprised me… "Two, you and me." What he meant was the documents were produced by people who were now in their late 70's or older.

What I had found was the map portion of the document, The Lewis and Clark Trail, A Proposal for Development, United States Department of the Interior, 1965. This proposal requested Congress to designate the Lewis and Clark Trail a "Historic Trail." But before Congress could make that designation, the entire Lewis and Clark Trail had to be thoroughly documented. In 1963 and 1964, the Department of Interior and National Park Service in cooperation with other Federal, State, and Local agencies, private organizations and individuals researched and documented everything known about the Lewis and Clark Trail at that time including the approximate locations of the original campsites and other sites of archeological, existing and proposed historic value. The information they gathered was compiled and placed on these trail maps. With this documentation, Congress established the Lewis and Clark Trail Commission, which eventually led to its official designation as a "Historic Trail." How my father got hold of the map portion of this document is still a matter of speculation. It can only be surmised that the link was some joint activity between the Boy Scouts of America and a government agency.

In the vernacular of Captain Clark, *I determined that I would set about* putting together this book and include these maps. The result is Lewis and Clark Trail Guide. These condensed journals were produced as a result of editing the Original Journals of the Lewis and Clark Expedition, Reuben Gold Thwaites, 1904. It was my intent to provide the layman with a daily moving story rather than a finely detailed study and to retain the accuracy of the events and the flavor of the original writing style. The serious student will find the maps a piece of essential history. I am pleased to include this article submitted by Mr. Richard N. Williams on how the Lewis and Clark Trail became designated a "Historic Trail" and eventually its designation as a "National Historic Trail."

A Brief History of the Lewis and Clark Trail
By Richard N. Williams
Manager, Lewis and Clark National Historic Trail
National Park Service
United States Department of the Interior

"The Lewis and Clark Expedition did not occur in 1804 – 1806 and then become history. Instead, it fired a national spirit of adventure which yet persists." These are the words of Stuart Udall, Secretary of Interior in 1965. Udall continued, "We can preserve vital parts of the Lewis and Clark Trail and remind ourselves and generations to come, of the heritage we derive from the expedition. We can also provide an inviting and stimulating chain of historic and recreational areas along the entire Lewis and Clark Trail." Of course, Secretary Udall was not the first to envision or follow the Lewis and Clark Trail. John Colter, a member of the expedition, was probably the first to retrace parts of the trail when he turned back to the Rocky Mountains from the Mandan Villages in 1806. Just as many modern day travelers, Colter detoured off the trail and discovered the Yellowstone Park area.

In 1904, Olin D. Wheeler followed the entire Lewis and Clark Trail and published "The Lewis and Clark Trail, 1804 -1904. Ruben Gold Thwaites published a new edition of the Lewis and Clark journals in 1904 and centennial celebrations were held in cities along the route such as St. Louis and Portland.

As early as 1948 the National Park Service recommended a "Lewis and Clark Touring Route." By the 1960's, conservationist J. N. "Ding" Darling, an editor from Des Moines, Iowa, was suggesting a "recreation ribbon" of historic sites and conservation areas following the Lewis and Clark route. In 1965, Congress established the Lewis and Clark Trail Commission. The Bureau of Outdoor Recreation, at the direction of the Secretary of the Interior, moved to study the Lewis and Clark Trail concept. The federal commission lasted five years and made several important recommendations. The commission recommended that all of the eleven trail states from Wood River, Illinois, to the mouth of the Columbia River, mark highways with Lewis and Clark signs. Thus was born the now ubiquitous "pointing finger" silhouette of Lewis and Clark. The commission also recommended that a citizen's organization be formed to further the work of the commission after 1969. The Lewis and Clark Trail Heritage Foundation was formed in St. Louis in 1969. The final recommendation was that the Lewis and Clark Trail be sanctioned as a national scenic trail under the National Trails System Act of 1968.

In the 1970s the Bureau of Outdoor Recreation continued to study the concept of a Lewis and Clark Trail. People like Stephen Ambrose and Dayton Duncan were picking up their copies of the Lewis and Clark journals and following the trail. The Lewis and Clark Trail Heritage Foundation was holding annual meetings along the trail. By 1975, 51 persons attended the meeting in Seaside, Oregon. In 1978, the Bureau of Outdoor Recreation determined that the Lewis and Clark Trail did not qualify as a scenic trail, given the criteria in the National Trails System Act. Congress amended the Act and added the new category of National Historic Trail. The Lewis and Clark National Historic Trail was established for the purpose of protection of the historic route, remnants, and artifacts for the benefit and enjoyment of the public. Congress realized that National Historic Trails were much different than national scenic trails. National Historic Trails are not continuous overland routes but may have water components, hiking trails and motor routes. These historic trails are not wholly located on federal property but are to be managed though partnerships with federal agencies, local and state agencies, non-profit organizations and even private landowners. The act provides for inclusion of nonfederal sites and sections of trail as official parts of the trail through a process of "certification." Today there are more than 90 certified nonfederal sites and segments on the trail. For example, the longest hiking section of the Lewis and Clark National Historic Trail is the 160 miles of the KATY Trail State Park in Missouri.

By the 1980s Professor Gary Moulton of the University of Nebraska began work on a new edition of the journals of Lewis and Clark. The National Park Service had been delegated administration of the Lewis and Clark National Historic Trail and a Comprehensive Management Plan was developed. The NPS assigned administrative duties to one individual in the Midwest Regional Office who also administered two national scenic trails, and several other "rivers and trails" programs. The Lewis and Clark Trail had no budget and the NPS struggled with defining the administrative responsibilities. This nebulous, loosely defined "partnership" program was new and unlike the more traditional land management known to the NPS. By the end of the decade, the Lewis and Clark National Historic Trail would have an annual operating budget of $80,000. New interpretive centers were being built at Fort Clatsop and at other nonfederal sites. The NPS had published a Lewis and Clark Trail map and brochure and the Lewis and Clark Trail Heritage Foundation established a Bicentennial Committee.

The decade of the 1990s saw more and swifter change on the Lewis and Clark Trail than any period in history. Dr. Ambrose published the extremely popular "Undaunted Courage," followed by the Ken Burns' Public Television documentary of the Lewis and Clark Expedition. Public awareness of the Lewis and Clark Trail exploded. The Bicentennial Committee of the Foundation was incorporated as a separate nonprofit organization, the National Lewis and Clark Bicentennial Council. Federal agencies expanded their Lewis and Clark interpretive and educational activities. The Lewis and Clark National Historic Trail Interpretive Center, administered by the US Forest Service, was built in Great Falls, Montana. The Bureau of Land Management purchased Pompey's Pillar National Historic Landmark from a private landowner. State and private organizations developed interpretive centers in Washburn, North Dakota; St. Charles, Missouri; Pasco, Washington and others were being planned.

In 1997, federal agencies began a new partnership resulting in federal Memorandum of Understanding for cooperation on the Lewis and Clark Bicentennial. The signing ceremony in 1998 took place in the Library of Congress and was attended by three Cabinet Secretaries, numerous agency heads and members of Congress. Public interest had transformed into political interest. Congress formed a Lewis and Clark Caucus in the House and Senate, later combined in to one organization, which now has 82 members. The NPS and Bicentennial Council facilitated the organization of the Circle of Tribal Advisors (COTA) and the Circle of State Advisors (COSA) as advisor to Bicentennial activities. As many as 17 states legislated Bicentennial Commissions and Committees. Major events and activities were being planned at literally hundreds of locations along the trail. The National Park Service and other federal agencies began planning a Corps of Discovery II, a traveling education center to follow the trail during the Bicentennial.

The Lewis and Clark story continues to fire the imagination of the American people. The Bicentennial will bring more public attention to the trail. Most of the Bicentennial events will have the goal of educating people about all aspects of the Lewis and Clark story, from the American Indian perspectives to scientific discoveries of flora and fauna. Stephen Ambrose once said that every generation rediscovers the Lewis and Clark story. He is surely correct. Through their volunteer service and dedication, the American people, their government and private sector partners, will ensure that the legacy of the Lewis and Clark Expedition will be preserved and enjoyed by many, many, future generations. **END.**

Forward

For the two centuries prior to the Lewis and Clark Expedition, Indians told stories to white men about the Western regions of the continent..."long rivers and a mighty range of mountains...a river that ends in a salt lake...Indians with flat-heads and pointed hats...large fish spouting water." These tales along with the search for the fabled Northwest Passage sparked an incurable desire to explore such a land.

In 1786 while serving as U. S. Minister to France, a young Thomas Jefferson asked John Ledyard, an adventurer from Connecticut who had been to the Pacific Ocean with Captain Cook, to explore North America (from Alaska to the Mississippi) by way of Russia and Siberia. Thomas Jefferson negotiated with the Russian government regarding the trip, but Queen Catherine of Russia would not grant her permission. In 1792 Alexander Mackenzie began to realize his dream to find an overland route to the Pacific Ocean. He and several voyageurs in a 25-foot birch-bark canoe successfully made their way across Canada and arrived at the Pacific Ocean, above present day Vancouver, British Columbia. It was Mackenzie's book of his overland voyage to the Pacific Ocean that caused President Thomas Jefferson to conceive the more famous Lewis and Clark Expedition. In 1793, Thomas Jefferson, backed by the American Philosophical Society, hired a French botanist, Andre Michaux, to make a trip to the Pacific Ocean. It turned out that Mr. Michaux was a French spy and President Washington put an end to it.

From the Lewis and Clark Trail, A Proposal for Development, United States Department of the Interior, 1965:
The Lewis and Clark Expedition of 1804- 1806 is considered by many historians as the single most important event in the development of the western United States. Politically it secured the recent American purchase of the Louisiana Territory and extended American claims to the Pacific. Economically, it provided the first knowledge of the resources which eventually led to the opening of the western lands for development and settlement.

In 1804 the United States was a young nation of 17 states. Although having won independence from Great Britain, it was still dependent on rivalry among the three great powers – Great Britain, France and Spain – for its survival.

Of the three, Spain was the weakest. In 1762 as its booty for helping Great Britain win the French and Indian War, Spain had been ceded the interior of the Continent west of the Mississippi River along with the key French city of New Orleans. The new lands merely added to Spain's already vast American holdings. So even after control of most lands east of the river passed to the United States in 1783, Spain continued to exploit her more immediately lucrative holdings in Mexico, Peru and the Caribbean. She appears to have failed completely to grasp the significance of the fertile and temperate Mississippi Valley in the balance of world power.

Conquered by Napoleon early in the 19th Century, Spain made peace by returning all of the Louisiana Territory to France.

President Thomas Jefferson was at once alarmed. He knew the global political and economic significance of the rich Mississippi Valley, and he suspected that Napoleon did too. Dealing with a deteriorating and incompetent Spanish colonial administration had given the American government no real worries. The ferment of revolutions for independence was stirring across all of Spanish America. When the revolutions came and the Spanish empire collapsed, Louisiana could be expected to fall easily into American hands. There was no occasion to join the push until Spain was actually at the brink.

Napoleon was a different matter. The most brilliant and effective of European military and political leaders in a millennium, he had conquered virtually the entire continent and possessed both the military might and the organizational genius to take real control of his possessions.

Jefferson correctly saw French control of New Orleans as an iron gate across the main artery of internal American commerce. Despite his own feelings about the limited powers of the national government, he boldly sent representatives to Paris to buy New Orleans.

They found Napoleon facing another war with Great Britain and embroiled in a hapless adventure in the Caribbean. Moreover, he was in debt and in need of money. If the French leader knew the global value of the western half of the Mississippi Valley, he was also realist enough to know that the Americans would take it sooner or later, for without a navy he could not hold it by force of arms against them. Should he sell New Orleans, he would have no way to exploit the rest of the continent. So, Napoleon gracefully startled the American negotiators by offering to sell all of the Louisiana Territory for $15 million.

Jefferson seized his opportunity and consummated the bargain, brushing aside any questions about the French title to the land.

On October 25, 1803, the United States Senate ratified the Louisiana Purchase Treaty. The following May 14, with the firing of cannon shot, the Lewis and Clark Expedition set forth from their winter camp at the mouth of Wood River, Illinois, to nail down the American claim to Louisiana and to extend American claims to the Pacific. Jefferson saw the 13 colonies for whom he had written a Declaration of Independence only 28 years earlier as a continental power which could some day be first in the world if her leaders were bold enough to act decisively when opportunity knocked.

The timing of the Treaty and the Expedition was fortuitous. Jefferson actually had planned the Expedition long before Napoleon made his offer and had proposed the appropriation of $2,500 for the journey in his address to Congress on January 18, 1803. Indeed, Congress had appropriated the money before it adjourned that March.

The need for such an expedition was clear. A route across the continent to the Oregon country was needed. Relations with Great Britain were strained and British fur traders were entrenched along the Missouri River. War with Great Britain could bring hordes of Indians attacking the frontier settlements. It was important that the United States Government know as much about the area as possible.

Few similar excursions were so well managed and so free from errors in judgment, miscalculations and tragedy. The trip lasted two years, four months and nine days. The expedition traveled about 7500 miles through a wilderness inhabited by war-like, hostile Indians and wild animals. **END.**

Table of Contents:

1. Preparing the Way. February 1801 – May 13, 1804.   10

2. St. Louis to Fort Mandan. May 13 to November 2, 1804.   17

3. Wintering at Fort Mandan. – November 2, 1804 – April 7, 1805.   32

4. Fort Mandan to Fort Clatsop. April 7 to December 8, 1805.   36

5. Wintering at Fort Clatsop. December 8, 1805 – March 22, 1806.   61

6. Homeward Bound. March 24 to September 26, 1806.   64

7. Maps and Charts 1-25   88

1. Preparing the Way. February 1801 – May 13, 1804.

In February 1801, President Jefferson requested Meriweather Lewis to be his personal secretary. Lewis immediately accepted. The President's prime objective was to have Lewis mount an expedition to explore the "Western Ocean." After giving Lewis intensive schooling on "all matters of necessity," Jefferson and Lewis were ready. President Jefferson had asked and received of Congress $2,500 to fund an Expedition.

On July 4, 1803, President Thomas Jefferson presented this letter to Captain Lewis outlining his expectations of, and procedures for the Expedition.

"To Meriwether Lewis, esquire, captain of the first regiment of infantry of the United States of America:

"Your situation as secretary of the president of the United States, has made you acquainted with the objects of my confidential message of January 18, 1803, to the legislature; you have seen the act they passed, which, though expressed in general terms, was meant to sanction those objects, and you are appointed to carry them to execution.

"Instruments for ascertaining, by celestial observations, the geography of the country through which you will pass, have already been provided. Light articles for barter and presents among the Indians, arms for your attendants, say from ten to twelve men, boats, tents, and other traveling apparatus, with ammunition, medicine, surgical instruments and provisions, you will have prepared, with such aids as the secretary at war can yield in his department; and from him also you will receive authority to engage among our troops, by voluntary agreement, the attendants abovementioned; over whom you, as their commanding officer, are invested with all the powers the laws give in such a case.

"As your movements, while within the limits of the United States, will be better directed by occasional communications, adapted to circumstances as they arise, they will not be noticed here. What follows will respect your proceedings after your departure from the United States.

"Your mission has been communicated to the ministers here from France, Spain, and Great Briton, and through them to their governments; and such assurances given them as to its objects, as we trust will satisfy them. The country of Louisiana having ceded by Spain to France, the passport you have from the minister of France, the representative of the present sovereign of the country, will be a protection with all its subjects; and that from the Minister of England will entitle you to the friendly aid of any traders of that allegiance with whom you may happen to meet.

"The object of your mission is to explore the Missouri River, and such principal streams of it, as, by its course and communication with the waters of the Pacific Ocean, whether the Columbia, Oregon, Colorado, or any other river, may offer the most direct and practicable water-communication across the continent, for the purposes of commerce.

"Beginning at the mouth of the Missouri, you will take observations of latitude and longitude, at all remarkable points on the river, and especially at the mouths of rivers, at rapids, at islands, and other places and objects distinguished by such natural marks and characters, of a durable kind, as that they may with certainty be recognized hereafter. The courses of the river between these points of observation may be supplied by the compass, the log-line, and by time, corrected

10

by the observations themselves. The variations of the needle, too, in different places, should be noticed.

"The interesting points of the portage between the heads of the Missouri, and of the water offering the best communication with the Pacific ocean, should also be fixed by observation; and the course of that water to the ocean, in the same manner as that of the Missouri.

"Your observations are to be taken with great pains and accuracy; to be entered distinctly and intelligibly for others as well as yourself; to comprehend all the elements necessary, with the aid of the usual tales, to fix the latitude and longitude of the places at which they were taken; and are to be rendered to the war-office, for the purpose of having the calculations made concurrently by proper persons within the United States. Several copies of these, as well as of your other notes, should be made at leisure times, and put into the care of the most trust worthy of your attendants to guard, by multiplying them against the accidental losses to which they will be exposed. A further guard would be, that one of these copies be on the cuticular membranes of the paper-birch, as less liable to injury from damp than common paper.

"The commerce which may be carried on with the people inhabiting the line you will pursue, renders knowledge of those people important. You will therefore endeavor to make yourself acquainted, as far as a diligent pursuit of your journey shall admit, with the names of the nations and their numbers:

> *"The extent and limits of their possessions;*
> *"Their relations with other tribes or nations;*
> *"Their language, traditions, monuments;*
> *"Their ordinary occupations in agriculture, fishing, hunting, war, arts, and the implements for these;*
> *"Their food, clothing, and domestic accommodations:*
> *"The diseases prevalent among them, and the remedies they use;*
> *"Moral and physical circumstances which distinguish them from the tribes we know;*
> *"Peculiarities in their laws, customs, and dispositions;*
> *"And articles of commerce they may need or furnish, and to what extent.*

"And, considering the interest which every nation has in extending and strengthening the authority of reason and justice among the people around them, it will be useful to acquire what knowledge you can of the state of morality, religion, and information among them; as it may better enable those who may endeavor to civilize and instruct them, to adapt their measures to the existing notions and practices of those on whom they are to operate.

> *"Other objects worthy of notice will be;*
> *"The soil and face of the country, its growth and vegetable productions, especially those not of the United States;*
> *"The animals of the country generally, and especially those not known in the United States;*
> *"The remains and accounts of any which may be deemed rare or extinct;*
> *"The mineral productions of every kind, but more particularly metals, lime-stone, pit-coal, and salt-peter; salines and mineral waters, noting the temperature of the last, and such circumstances as may indicate their character;*
> *"Volcanic appearances;*
> *"Climate, as characterized by the thermometer, by the proportion of rainy, cloudy, and clear days; by lightning, hail, snow, ice; by the access and recess of frost; by the winds prevailing at different seasons; the dates at which particular plants put forth, or lose their flower or leaf; times of appearance of particular birds, reptiles or insects.*

"Although your route will be along the channel of the Missouri, yet you will endeavor to inform yourself, by inquiry, of the character and extent of the country watered by its branches, and especially on its southern side. The North river, or Rio Bravo, which runs into the gulf of Mexico, and the North river, or Rio Colorado, which runs into the gulf of California, are understood to be the principal streams heading opposite to the waters of the Missouri, and running southwardly. Whether the dividing grounds between the Missouri and them are mountains or flat lands, what are their distance from the Missouri, the character of the intermediate country, and the people inhabiting it, are worthy of particular inquiry. The northern waters of the Missouri are less to be inquired after, because they have been ascertained to a considerable degree, and are still in a course of ascertainment by English traders and travelers; but if you can learn any thing certain of the most northern source of the Mississippi, and of its position relatively to the Lake of the Woods, it will be interesting to us. Some account too of the path of the Canadian traders from the Mississippi, at the mouth of the Ouisconsing to where it strikes the Missouri, and of the soil and rivers in its course, is desirable.

"In all your intercourse with the natives, treat them in the most friendly and conciliatory manner which their own conduct will admit; allay all jealousies as to the object of your journey; satisfy them of its innocence; make them acquainted with the position, extent, character, peaceable and commercial dispositions of the United States; of our wish to be neighborly, friendly, and useful to them, and of our dispositions to a commercial intercourse with them; confer with them on the points most convenient as mutual emporiums, and the articles of most desirable interchange for them and us. If a few of their influential chiefs, within practicable distance, wish to visit us, arrange such a visit with them, and furnish them with authority to call on our officers on their entering the United States, to have them conveyed to this place at the public expense. If any of them should wish to have some of their young people brought up with us, and taught such arts as may be useful to them, we will receive, instruct, and take care of them. Such a mission, whether of influential chiefs, or of young people, would give some security to your own party. Carry with you some matter of the kine-pox; inform those of them with whom you may be of its efficacy as a preservative from the small-pox, and instruct and encourage them in the use of it. This may be especially done wherever you winter.

"As it is impossible for us to foresee in what manner you will be received by those people, whether with hospitality or hostility, so is it impossible to prescribe the exact degree of perseverance with which you are to pursue your journey. We value too much the lives of citizens to offer them to probable destruction. Your numbers will be sufficient to secure you against the unauthorized opposition of individuals, or of small parties; but if a superior force, authorized, or not authorized, by a nation, should be arrayed against your further passage, and inflexibly determined to arrest it, you must decline its further pursuit and return. In the loss of yourselves we should lose also the information you will have acquired. By returning safely with that, you may enable us to renew the essay with better calculated means. To your own discretion, therefore, must be left the degree of danger you may risk, and the point at which you should decline, only saying, we wish you to err on the side of your safety, and to bring back your party safe, even if it be with less information.

"As far up the Missouri as the white settlements extend, an intercourse will probably be found to exist between them and the Spanish post of St. Louis opposite Cahokia, or St. Genevieve opposite Kaskaskia. From still further up the river the traders may furnish a conveyance for letters. Beyond that you may perhaps be able to engage Indians to bring letters for the government to Cahokia, or Kaskaskia, on promising that they shall there receive such special compensation as your shall have stipulated with them. Avail yourself of these means to communicate to us, at

seasonable intervals, a copy of your journal, notes and observations of every kind, putting into cypher whatever might do injury if betrayed.

"Should you reach the Pacific ocean, inform yourself of the circumstances which may decide whether the furs of those parts may not be collected as advantageously at the head of the Missouri (convenient as is supposed to the waters of the Colorado and Oregon or Columbia) as at Nootka Sound, or any other point of that coast; and that trade be consequently conducted through the Missouri and United States more beneficially than by the circumnavigation now practiced.

"On your arrival on that coast, endeavor to learn if there be any port within your reach frequented by the sea vessels of any nation, and to send two of your trusty people back by sea, in such way as shall appear practicable, with a copy of your notes; and should you be of opinion that the return of your party by the way they went will be imminently dangerous, then ship the whole, and return by sea, by the way either of Cape Horn, or the Cape of Good Hope, as you shall be able. As you will be without money, clothes, or provisions, you must endeavor to use the credit of the United States to obtain them; for which purpose open letters of credit shall be furnished you, authorizing you to draw on the executive of the United States, or any of its officers, in any part of the world, on which draughts can be disposed of, and to apply with our recommendations to the consuls, agents, merchants, or citizens of any nation with which we have intercourse, assuring them, in our name, that any aids they may furnish you shall be honorably repaid, and on demand. Our consuls, Thomas Hewes, at Batavia, in Java, William Buchanan, in the Isles of France and Bourbon, and John Elmslie, at the Cape of Good Hope, will be able to supply your necessities, by draughts on us.

"Should you find it safe to return by the way you go, after sending two of our party round by sea, or with your whole party, if no conveyance by sea can be found, do so; making such observations on your return as may serve to supply, correct, or confirm those made on your outward journey.

"On reentering the United States and reaching a place of safety, discharge any of your attendants who may desire and deserve it, procuring for them immediate payment of all arrears of pay and clothing which may have incurred since their departure, and assure them that they shall be recommended to the liberality of the legislature for the grant of a soldier's portion of land each, as proposed in my message to congress, and repair yourself, with your papers, to the seat of government.

"To provide, on the accident of your death, against anarchy, dispersion, and the consequent danger to your party, and total failure of the enterprise, you are hereby authorized, by any instrument signed and written in your own hand, to name the person among them who shall succeed to the command on your decease, and by like instruments to change the nomination, from time to time, as further experience of the characters accompanying you shall point out superior fitness; and all the powers and authorities given to yourself are, in the event of your death, transferred to, and vested in the successor so named, with further power to him and his successors, in like manner to name each his successor, who, on the death of his predecessor, shall be invested with all the powers and authorities given to yourself. Given under my hand at the city of Washington, this twentieth day of June, 1803." President Thomas Jefferson.

Meriwether Lewis' first decision was to gain additional leadership. He found it in William Clark, an old friend, Indian fighter and former Army officer whose disposition would not clash with his own.

"If therefore there is anything...in this enterprise which would induce you to participate with me in its fatigues, its dangers and its honors, believe me there is no man on earth with whom I should feel equal pleasure in sharing them as with yourself." Meriwether Lewis to William Clark.

"I will chearfully join you - and partake of the dangers, difficulties, and fatigues, and I anticipate the honors & rewards of the result of such an enterprise, should we be successful in accomplishing it. This is an undertaking fraited with many difeculties, but My friend I do assure you that no man lives whith whome I would perfur to undertake Such a Trip &c. as your self." William Clark to Meriwether Lewis, July 18, 1803.

In July 1803, Lewis left President Jefferson and the Capitol and thus began the Expedition.

At Harpers Ferry, West Virginia, Lewis' first stop, he oversaw the construction of a collapsible iron boat frame of his own design. The dimensions of the frame were 30 feet long, 4 ½ feet wide and 2 feet deep. The frame was lightweight, 99 pounds, and could be carried in sections for easy transport. It was to be assembled on site for use at the Great Falls of the Missouri River and then covered with animal skins and sealed with pine tree pitch. Lewis tested the finished boat and found it could hold 8,000 pounds of cargo. Lewis also acquired rifles, powder horns, bullet molds, ball screws, tomahawks and large knives. Captain Lewis departed Harpers Ferry for Philadelphia on July 8, 1803.

Government expeditions at the time of Lewis and Clark were outfitted by the "purveyor of public supplies" located in Philadelphia at the Schuylkill Arsenal. When Lewis left the Arsenal he had over 3,500 pounds of supplies and required two wagons to transport it to Pittsburgh. It was at Pittsburgh where the Keel Boat, which would take him to St. Louis and subsequently up the Missouri to Fort Mandan, was being built. Here is a sampling of essentials excluding Indian trade goods.

Arms & Ammunition
Pocket & Horseman's Pistols – 1 pair each
Rifles - 15
Powder - 226 lbs.
Sheet lead - 420 lbs.
Flints - 625
Powder Horns -15
Gun Slings-15
Ball Screws - 15
Bullet Molds - 15 pairs
Tomahawks - 18
Oiled Knapsacks - 15
Cartouch Box Belts - 15 **NOTE:** A Cartouch is a paper gun cartridge.
Leaden canisters for gun powder - 52
Scalping Knives & Belts - 15
Clothing
Coats with Hoods - 15
Woolen Overalls - 15
Socks - 36 pair
Hunting Shirts - 30
Strong Linen Shirts - 30
Shoes – 20 pair

Blankets - 15, 3 Point. **NOTE:** First offered for trade in 1670 by the Hudson Bay Company, Point Blankets were so highly prized by Native Americans that they became important articles of trade - each short line or "point" woven into the edge of the blanket indicated the number of beaver pelts to be exchanged for the blanket. The highest quality was a Four Point blanket.

Camp Equipment
Copper kettles - 6
Falling axes - 25
Drawing knives, short & strong - 4
Files, chisels, nails, hand vice, handsaw, cord and line
Whetstone for sharpening
Corn Mill
Oiled linen for wrapping articles - 20 yards.
Tin Trumpets - 4
Steels (30) and flints (100) for fire making
Iron Spoons - 24
Tin Cups - 24
Mosquito Curtains
Large Awls & Needles
Oilcloth bags - 15
Common tent - 1

Writing Supplies
Brass Ink Stands - 6
Ink Powder Paper - 6
Sealing Wax - 1 lb.
Quills - 100
India Ink - ¼ lb.
Paper

Recruitment

Lewis and Clark wanted no "Favorite Sons." They wanted men who had learned to be resourceful. Lewis made the decision to expand his cadre of men to include both Army and civilian. In a letter to Clark, Lewis addresses the need for the best possible recruitment of civilians. "It shall be my duty to find out and engage some good hunters, stout, healthy, unmarried, accustomed to the woods and capable of bearing bodily fatigue to a considerable degree; should any young men answering this description be found in your neighborhood I would thank you to give information of them on my arrival at the falls of the Ohio; and if possible learn the probability of their engaging in this service . . ."

At the same time, Secretary of War, Henry Dearborn informed all members of the Army, "all the aid in your power in selecting suitable men . . . If any non-commissioned officer or private in your company should be disposed to join Capt. Lewis, whose characters for sobriety, integrity and other necessary qualifications render them suitable for such service, you will detach them accordingly."

Clark wrote to Lewis of his success in procuring "the best woodsmen and hunters...of the country." Lewis responds: "I am much pleased with the measures you have taken relative to the engaging the men you mention, as men of that description only will answer our purposes; I scarcely suppose that such that you have conceived not fully qualified for this service will by any means meet my approbation; your ideas in the subject of a judicious selection of our party perfectly comport with my own."

William Clark was waiting with the young Kentuckians he had selected. They were John Shields, George Gibson, Charles Floyd, Nathaniel Pryor, William Bratton, and the brothers Reuben and Joseph Fields, Shannon and Colter. They have been referred to as the "nine young men from Kentucky." Lewis picked up Clark and the recruits in Louisville. At Fort Massac at the location of present Paducah, Kentucky, on the 11th of November 1803, they chose privates Joseph Whitehouse and John Newman and recruited a civilian interpreter at the fort, George Drouillard. (**NOTE:** Drouillard was spelled "Drewyer" by Lewis and Clark. Historians have proclaimed him the most important person on the Expedition after Lewis and Clark.) On December 12, 1803, the Corps arrived at the mouth of the Dubois (Wood) River about 18 miles above St. Louis on the present day Illinois side of the Mississippi River. The men immediately began building huts for the winter.

The Detachment. The following is the generally accepted list of members of the expedition as verified by the official payroll at the close of the venture: Captains Meriwether Lewis and William Clark. Sergeants: John Ordway, Nathaniel Pryor, Charles Floyd, Patrick Gass. Privates: William Bratton, John Colter, John Collins, Peter Cruzatte, Rueben Fields, Joseph Fields, Robert Frazier, George Gibson, Silas Goodrich, Hugh Hall, Thomas P. Howard, Francis Labiche, Hugh McNeal, John Potts, George Shannon, John Shields, John B. Thompson, William Werner, Joseph Whitehouse, Alexander Willard, Richard Windsor, Peter Wiser. Interpreters: George Drewyer [Drouillard], and Trussaint Charbonneau and his wife Sacajawea and son Jean Baptiste Charbonneau or "Pomp". Also accompanying the expedition was York, Captain Clark's slave. Two soldiers, John Newman and M.B. Reed, who had set out with the Expedition, were punished for misconduct and sent back to St. Louis on April 7, 1805. Jean Baptiste Lepage was enlisted in Newman's place at Fort Mandan.

Note: Here is the explanation of the vocabulary and editing marks used to condense The Original Journals of Lewis and Clark.

Each day's edited Journal entry is but a part of what they wrote. Not every day was filled with drama. The less important text entries of each day's events have been edited out. When read in its entirety, the complete story and a feel for the times, style and manner of communicating is compelling and complete. The spelling of most words has been corrected for the reader's convenience. The run-on sentences are in-style with the original Journals.

Reading through the editing marks may seem awkward at first but the reader will quickly learn to read through them. Note the word Mark and its relation to quote marks and the three periods.

"Mark	Shows that "Mark" is the first word of a sentence.
"...mark	Shows that "mark" is not the first word of the sentence. The preceding copy of the sentence has been edited out.
mark...	Shows that "mark is not the last word of the sentence. The copy following the word has been edited out.
mark."	Shows that "mark' is the last word of the sentence.
mark...Mark	Shows that "mark" is the last word of an edited, or whole sentence and that "Mark" is the first word of a sentence.
mark...mark	Shows that copy between "mark" and "mark" has been edited out. Neither "marks" are at the beginning or end of sentences.

2. St. Louis to Fort Mandan. May 13 to November 2, 1804.

The following Journal entries refer to map 1.

May 13, 1804. River Dubois. **Captain Clark.** "I dispatched an express this morning to Captain Lewis at St. Louis. All our provisions, goods, and equipage on board...Men complete with powder cartridges and 100 balls each, all in health and readiness to set out. Boats and everything complete, with the necessary stores of provisions and such articles of merchandize as we thought ourselves authorized to procure-though not as much as I think necessary for the multitude of Indians through which we must pass on our road across the continent."

May 14, 1804. Crossed the Mississippi to the Missouri River. **Captain Clark.** "Rained the fore part of the day. I determined to go as far as St. Charles...7 leagues up the Missouri, and wait at that place until Captain Lewis could finish the business which he was obliged to attend to at St. Louis and join me by land...I set out at 4 o'clock, p.m., in the presence of many of the neighboring inhabitants, and proceeded on under a gentle breeze up the Missouri...and camped on the island."

May 15, 1804. Captain Lewis. "It rained during the greater part of last night...The barge ran foul...on logs... the barge was several minutes in imminent danger. This was caused by her being too heavily laden in the stern. Persons accustomed to the navigation of the Missouri, and the Mississippi also, below the mouth of this river, uniformly take the precaution to load their vessels heaviest in the bow when they ascend the stream, in order to avoid the danger incident to running foul of the concealed timber, which lies in great quantities in the beds of these rivers." **Captain Clark.** "...proceeded on 9 miles passed two Islands and encamped...saw a number of Goslings today on the shore, the water excessively rapid, and banks falling in."

May 16 - 20, 1804. Captain Clark. "We arrived at St. Charles at 12 o'clock...This village contains...about 450 inhabitants, chiefly French." **Orderly Book.** "Note the Commanding Officer is fully assured that every man of his Detachment will have a respect for their own dignity and not make it necessary for him to leave St. Charles for a more retired situation." **May 17. Captain Clark.** "...compelled to punish for misconduct...George Drewyer arrived." **Orderly Book.** "A sergeant and four men of the party...formed themselves into a court-martial, to hear and determine the evidences adduced against William Warner and Hugh Hall, for being absent last night without leave, contrary to orders; and John Collins, first for being absent without leave; second, for behaving in an unbecoming manner at the ball last night; third, for speaking in a language last night after his return tending to bring into disrespect the orders of the commanding officer." **May 18. Captain Clark.** "...had the loading in the boat and pirogue...changed so as the bow of each may be heavier loaded than the stern...(**NOTE:** By placing a heavier load in the front, or bow of the boat, it will navigate easier when going into the current or wind.) Sent George Drewyer with a letter to Captain Lewis." **May 19. Captain Clark.** "R. Fields killed a Deer today. (**NOTE:** The first of about 1,000 Deer killed on the Expedition.) George Drewyer returned from St. Louis...he lost a letter from Captain Lewis to me." **May 20. Captain Lewis.** " As I had determined to reach St. Charles this evening and knowing that there was now no time to be lost, I set forward in the rain...arrived at half after six and joined Captain Clark. Found the party in good health and spirits." **Captain Clark.** "The letter George (Drewyer) lost yesterday found by a country man."

May 21, 1804. Captain Clark. "All the forepart of the day arranging our party and procuring the different articles necessary...we set out today a hard wind...accompanied with a hard rain."

May 22, 1804. Captain Clark. "...camp of Kickapoo (Indians)...told me they would have some provisions for us...we camped in a Bend...the Indians arrived with 4 Deer...we gave them two quarts of Whiskey."

May 23, 1804. Captain Clark. "Captain Lewis near falling from the pinnacles of rocks 300 feet, he caught at 20 feet." **NOTE:** The Corp stopped briefly at Femme Osage Creek to pay respects to Daniel Boone. In 1799, he and his wife Rebecca moved here to build their final home. During this day, Captain Lewis climbed 300-foot high cliffs over a large cave called the Tavern whose mouth hangs out over the water. During his exploration of the cave he slips off the 300-foot ledge and barely catches hold.

May 24, 1804. Captain Clark. "...very bad part of the river called the Devils Race Ground...Current sets projecting against rocks...attempted to pass up under the bank which was falling in so fast that obliged to cross...The swiftness of the current wheeled the boat, broke our tow rope, and was nearly oversetting the boat."

May 25, 1804. NOTE: The Corp passed the small town of La Charette, the last white mans settlement they would see in over two years.

May 26, 1804. Orderly Book. "The day after tomorrow lye corn and grease will be issued to the party, the next day pork and flour, and the day following Indian meal and pork...no pork is to be issued when we have fresh meat on hand."

May 27, 1804. Captain Clark. "...two canoes loaded with fur and peltries came to from the Mahar (Omaha) nation...they informed nothing of consequence."

May 28, 1804. Captain Clark. "Rained hard all night."

The following Journal entries refer to map 2.

May 29, 1804. Captain Clark. "Rained...the Mosquitoes are very bad."

May 30 - 31, 1804. Captain Clark. "Rained...the river continued to rise." **May 31.** "Rained...the wind from the West raised and blew with great force until 5 o'clock p.m. which obliged us to lay by...Several *rats* of considerable size caught in the woods today." **Captain Lewis** describing the Eastern Wood Rat... "The distinguishing trait of possessing a tail covered with hair like other parts of the body..."

NOTE: During the "break-in" period, Captains Lewis and Clark established a routine among the men and themselves that served the expedition well. The men were split into two groups; those who served the boats and those who replenished the meat supply. In the swift current of the Missouri, navigation of the big boats was strenuous and constant. Those men serving the boats spent most days straining on oars and poles, and were too often in the water pulling the big boats against the current. The only relief came when they could use their sail. Those who hunted for the expedition faired little better. Their business was hard and dangerous. They spent all of their time in unknown and potentially hostile territory. They never knew what the next hill or draw might hold. While they were hunting, were they being hunted? Furthermore they hunted miles from the Corp and if they ran into trouble they were on their own. They were responsible for stalking, killing, dressing and transporting everything they harvested to the rivers edge. Many times they stayed out overnight away from the main party and left their kill where the boatmen would find it. Captains Lewis and Clark split their duties also. Lewis being more introverted loved the solitude of walking the shore and exploring the hills above the river. He was the better hunter and President Jefferson gave him the best training available as a naturalist. Clark loved the companionship of the men and spent most of his time on the water with the party in their boats mapping the river.

June 1 - 2 1804. NOTE: The Corp reached the Osage River and camped for two days taking observations. **Captain Clark.** "Set up until 12 o'clock taking observations." **June 2.** "George Drewyer and John Shields, who we had sent with the Horses by land on the North side, joined us this evening...Those men gave a flattering account of the country..."

June 3, 1804. Captain Clark. "We made other observations in the evening after the return of Captain Lewis from a walk of three or four miles...proceeded on...saw sign of war parties of Indians."

June 4, 1804. Captain Clark. "…ascended a hill of about 170 feet to a place where the French report that Lead ore has been found, I saw no mineral of that description…our hunters killed 7 Deer today."

June 5, 1804. Captain Clark. "…our scout discovered the fresh sign of about 10 Indians. I expect that those Indians are on their way to war, against the Osage nation probably they are the Sauk."

June 6, 1804. The Salt River. Captain Clark. "…the water of the spring in this lick is strong as one bushel of the water is said to make 7 lb of good Salt…saw some Buffalo sign today."

June 7, 1804. Captain Clark. " Passed…rock of Limestone inlaid with white, red, and blue flint, of a very good quality…we landed and…found it a den of Rattle Snakes…our hunters brought in three Bear this evening." **NOTE:** The Expedition kills its first Black Bear. The first of about 25 killed on the Expedition.

June 8, 1804. Captain Clark. "Camped…Island of Mills…found canteens, axes, pummel stone and peltry…this day met 3 men from the Sioux River…had been hunting 12 months and made about $900 in pelts and furs. They were out of provisions and out of powder."

June 9, 1804. NOTE: The Corp wrestled with their boats all day. Getting snagged, then almost losing the keelboat to the current and logs. They finally camped on an island rather than on land because the riverbanks were continually falling in and too dangerous to be near.

June 10-11, 1804. Captain Clark. "I saw great numbers of Deer in the prairies, the evening is cloudy, our party in high spirits." **June 11.** "The N. W. wind blew hard and cold as this wind was immediately a head, we could not proceed…we took the advantage of this delay and dried our wet articles…"

June 12, 1804. Captain Clark. (From passing trappers) "…we purchased 300 lbs of grease (Buffalo grease and tallow) and finding that old Mr. Durion was of the party we questioned him…Concluded to take old Durion back as far as the Sioux nation with a view to get some of their Chiefs to visit the President of the United States (this man being a very confidential friend of those people, he having resided with the nation 20 odd years.)" **NOTE:** Pierre Dorion was born in Quebec City in 1740. He was married to a Yankton Indian woman. He joined the Expedition at this point as an interpreter and was sent back to St. Louis with chiefs of the Yankton, Omaha, Oto & Missouri tribes after having spent the winter near Yankton, South Dakota.

June 13, 1804. Captain Clark. "…in the open prairie we caught a Raccoon." **NOTE:** Because Raccoons were well know to Lewis and Clark they only mention this animal a total of five times in their Journals.

June 14, 1804. NOTE: George Drewyer giving an account to Captain Clark of a snake. "…making gobbling noises like a Turkey. He fired his gun and the noise was increased…"

June 15, 1804. Captain Clark. "…next to the river is an elegant bottom plain which extends several miles…our hunters did not come in this evening…"

June 16, 1804. Captain Clark. "Came to…old French fort…could see no traces." **NOTE:** The fort referred to was probably the post of Fort Orleans, which had been established in 1723 by Bourgmont. It was the first military post ever built on the Missouri river and located about 5 miles below the mouth of Grand River, near the mouth of the Osage. The French government of Louisiana established this fort as a means of holding the allegiance of the Indians and guarding against Spanish invasion.

June 17, 1804. Captain Clark. "Came to, to make oars, and repair our cable and tow rope…men to get ash timber for oars…make a tow rope out of the cords of a cable which had been provided by Captain Lewis at Pittsburgh…this crossing place for the war parties against (Osage)…party is much afflicted with boils, and several have the dysentery…tick and mosquitoes are very troublesome."

June 18, 1804. Captain Clark. "…party to work at the oars, make rope, and jerk meat all day. Dry our wet sails in the evening…"

The following Journal entries refer to map 3.

June 19, 1804. Captain Clark. "We set out under a gentle breeze...leaving J. Shields and one man to go by land with the Horses..."

June 20, 1804. Captain Clark. "Some very swift water today...a beautiful night but the air exceedingly damp, and the mosquitoes very troublesome."

June 21, 1804. Captain Clark. "The river rose 3 inches last night...presented a most unfavorable prospect of swift water..."

June 22, 1804. Captain Clark. "River rose 4 inches last night...proceeded on under a gentle breeze..."

June 23, 1804. Captain Clark. "...wind blew hard...river fell 8 inches last night…Peeled some bark to lay on and gathered wood to make fires...at dark, Drewyer came to me with the Horses, one fat Bear and a Deer." **NOTE:** Clark spent the night on land as the main party was stranded on an island due to the wind and could not cross to meet him.

June 24, 1804. Captain Clark. "...I lay on the sand waiting for the boat...a large snake swam to the bank immediately under the Deer...I found that he was determined on getting to the meat. I was compelled to kill him...immense herds of Deer is seen"

June 25, 1804. Captain Clark. "The river is still falling, last night it fell 8 inches."

June 26-27-28, 1804. At the confluence of the Kansas and Missouri Rivers. **Captain Clark.** "I observed a great number of Parroquets this evening." **NOTE:** Naturalist Nathaniel Wyeth led an expedition to the Rocky Mountains and the Columbia River in 1834. During this expedition he was accompanied by a young ornithologist, John Kirk Townsend. They too recorded seeing Parroquets in this general vicinity. **June 27.** "...we determined to delay at this place three or four days to make observations..." **June 28.** "Missouri has raised...about 2 foot...This river (Kansas) receives its name from a nation which dwells at this time on its banks...those Indians are not very numerous at this time, reduced by war with their neighbors...I am told that they are a fierce and warlike people…this nation is now out in the plains hunting Buffalo...waters of the Kansas is very disagreeably tasted to me."

June 29, 1804. Orderly Book. "A Court Martial for two men (John Collins and Hugh Hall) who were charged by Sergeant Floyd with getting drunk on their post. John Collins plead guilty and received 100 lashes on his bare back and Hugh Hall plead guilt and received 50 lashes."

June 30, 1804. Expedition saw their first Gray Wolf on a sand bar. **Captain Clark.** "A very large Wolf came to the bank and looked at us this morning..."

July 1, 1804. Captain Clark. "Deer and Turkeys in great quantities on the bank."

July 2, 1804. Captain Clark. "...passed a large Island on the S. S." **NOTE:** Starboard Side. This island is now called Kickapoo Island and is above Fort Leavenworth, Kansas.

July 3, 1804. Expedition saw Beaver for the first time.

The following Journal entries refer to map 4.

July 4, 1804. Captain Clark. "Ushered in the day by a discharge of one shot from our bow piece, proceeded on...Fields got bit by a Snake, which was quickly doctored with bark by Captain Lewis...we closed by a discharge from our bow piece, an extra Gill of whiskey." **NOTE:** Joseph Fields had a "poultice" made of bark and gunpowder applied to his bite.

July 5, 1804. Captain Clark. "Deer is not so plenty as usual, great deal of Elk sign."

July 6, 1804. Captain Clark. "I observe that the men sweat more than is common from some cause, I think the Missouri's water is the principal cause..."

July 7, 1804. Captain Clark. "Saw a large rat on the bank. Killed a Wolf. ...one man very sick, struck with the sun... bled him and gave Niter (soda) which has revived him much."

July 8, 1804. Orderly Book. "In order to insure a prudent and regular use of all provisions...*Superintendents of Provision*, are held immediately responsible to the Commanding Officers for a judicious consumption...in such a manner as is most wholesome and best calculated to afford the greatest proportion of nutriment..."

July 9, 1804. Captain Clark. (Viewing an unknown party on the opposite bank and wanting to warn his men on shore) "...not answering our signals caused us to suspect the persons camped opposite to us was a war party of Sioux, we fired the bow piece to alarm the party on shore, all prepared to oppose if attacked."

July 10, 1804. Captain Clark. "Set out this morning and crossed the river with a view to see who the party was that camped on the other side, we soon discovered them to be our men, proceeded on..."

July 11-12, 1804. Captain Clark. "I observed a fresh Horse track...pursued the track and found him on a sand beach. This Horse probably had been left by...hunters who wintered or hunted in this quarter last fall or winter." **July 12.** "Concluded to delay here today with a view of taking equal altitudes and making observations as well as refreshing our men who are much fatigued."

Orderly Book. "A Court Martial for Alexander Willard who was charged with "lying down and sleeping on his post while a sentinel." **NOTE:** Willard confessed that he was "Guilty of Lying Down, and not Guilty, of Going to Sleep." While the usual punishment for such an offense was the shooting of the negligent soldier, Willard was graced with the less severe punishment of 100 lashes for just "lying down." Willard died at the age of 87 near Sacramento, CA. He bore the scars of the lashings all his life.

July 13, 1804. Captain Clark. "Set out at sunrise, and proceeded on under a gentle breeze...In the first bend to the left is situated a beautiful and extensive plain...This plain also abounds in grapes   of   different   kinds,   some   nearly   ripe."

July 14, 1804. Captain Clark. "...this morning...the atmosphere became suddenly darkened by a black and dismal looking cloud...the storm, which passed over an open plain from the N.E. struck the boat on the starboard quarter, and would have thrown her up on the sand island dashed to pieces in an instant, had not the party leaped out on the Leeward Side, and kept her off with the assistance of the anchor and cable...when the storm suddenly ceased and the river became instantaneously as smooth as glass... Several men unwell with *Boils...*"

July 15, 1804. Captain Clark. "A heavy fog this morning prevented our setting out before 7 o'clock...The high prairies are...entirely void of timber, except what grows on the water."

July 16-17, 1804. Captain Clark. "...proceeded on under a gentle breeze...an extensive prairie on the L. S." (Larboard Side). **July 17.** "We concluded to lay by at this place today to fix the Latitude and Longitude of this place...Several of the party much inflicted with *tumors* of different kinds...and difficult to cure."

July 18, 1804. Captain Clark. "...saw a Dog nearly starved on the bank, gave him some meat, he would not follow..."

The following Journal entries refer to map 5.

July 19, 1804. Captain Clark. "...We approach this great River Platte the sand bars much more numerous and the quick or moving sands much worse..."

July 20, 1804. Captain Clark. "It is worthy of observation to mention that our party has been much healthier on the voyage than parties of the same number is in any other situation...From this evenings encampment a man may walk to the Pawnee village on the S. bank of the Platte River in two days, and to the Oto in one day...as those Indians are now out in the Prairies following and hunting the Buffalo, I fear we will not see them."

July 21, 1804. The Corp reached the Platte River. **Captain Clark.** "...we found great difficulty in passing around the sand at the mouth of this river...a great number of Wolves about us this evening." **NOTE:** The Platte River has been an important east-west corridor throughout history. The Oregon, Mormon and California trails, the Pony Express route, the Union Pacific Transcontinental Railroad, and the first transcontinental paved highway (U.S. Highway 30) all follow it West to its headwaters in the Rocky Mountains.

July 22-26, 1804. Captain Clark. "This being a good situation and much nearer the Oto town...we concluded to delay at this place a few days and send for some of the Chiefs of that nation, to let them know of the change of government, the wishes of our government to cultivate friendship with them, the objects of our journey, and to present them with a flag and some small presents." **July 23.** "...sent off George Drewyer and Peter Cruzatte with some tobacco to invite the Oto if at their town and Pawnee if they saw them, to come and talk with us at our camp...Prairies being on fire near their towns induce a belief that they...have returned..." **July 24.** "This evening Goodrich caught a White Catfish, its eyes small and tail much like that of a dolphin." (**NOTE:** Captain Clark named this site White Catfish Camp. It is 10 miles above the Platte River.) **July 25.** "...Drewyer and Peter returned from the Oto village, and informs that no Indians were at their towns..." **July 26.** " I opened the tumor of a man, on the left breast, which discharged half a pint."

July 27, 1804. Captain Clark. "...we set sail under a gentle breeze...Mosquitoes so thick and troublesome that it was disagreeable and painful to continue a moment still."

July 28, 1804. Captain Clark. "...our party on shore...informs that they heard firing to the S.W....Drewyer brought in a Missouri Indian which he met with hunting in the prairie...his camp about 4 miles from the river, his party was small consisting only of about 20 Lodges...Miles further another camp where there was a Frenchman, who lived in the nation..."

July 29, 1804. Captain Clark. "Sent a Frenchman, La Liberty, with the Indian to Oto camp to invite the Indians to meet us on the river above...Caught three very large Catfish...very fat, a quart of oil came out...of one of those fish."

July 30, 1804. Captain Clark. "Proceeded on to a clear open prairie...formed a camp...From the bluff...above our camp, the most beautiful prospect of the river, up and down...which I ever beheld...Fields killed and brought in an animal called by the French *blaireau.*" **NOTE:** What they killed was a Badger, the first anyone in the Expedition had ever seen. Captain Clark's description placed it in the Bear family however it is part of the Weasel family. It was stuffed and sent back to President Jefferson aboard the Keelboat from Fort Mandan.

July 31, 1804. Captain Clark. "The Indians not yet arrived. Caught a young Beaver alive, which is already quite tame. Caught a Buffalo Fish. The evening very cool, the mosquitoes are yet troublesome." **SPECIAL NOTE:** Sergeant Charles Floyd writes in his diary, "I am very sick and has been for sometime, but have recovered my health again."

August 1, 1804. Captain Clark. "...(sent) one man back to the place from which the messenger was sent for the Oto (Indians), to see if any Indians were, or had been, there since our departure. He returned and informed that no person had been there since we left it...The Indians not yet arrived we fear something amiss..." **NOTE:** Captain Clark's Birthday.

August 2, 1804. Captain Clark. "At Sunset...a party of the Oto and Missouri nation came to camp, among those Indians, six were Chiefs. Captain Lewis and myself met those Indians and informed them we were glad to see them, and would speak to them tomorrow, Sent them some roasted meat, pork, flour and meal. In return, they sent us watermelons. Every man on his guard and ready for anything."

August 3, 1804. Captain Clark. "Made up a small present for those people in proportion to their consequence; also a package with a medal to accompany a speech for the Grand Chief. After breakfast, we collected those Indians under an awning of our mainsail. In presence of our party, paraded, and delivered a long speech to them, expressive of our journey, the wishes of our Government, some advice to them, and directions how they were to conduct themselves...Those Chiefs all delivered a speech, acknowledging their approbation to the speech and promising to pursue the advice and directions given them, that they were happy to find that they had fathers which might be depended on...After Captain Lewis' shooting the air gun a few shots, we set out, and proceeded on..."

August 4, 1804. Captain Clark. "Set out early...one Buck killed today...Reed, a man who went back to camp for his knife, has not joined us."

August 5, 1804. Captain Clark. "...in every bend the banks are falling in from the current...Great quantities of grapes on the banks. I observe three different kinds, at this time ripe; one of the number is large and has the flavor of the purple grape...the Mosquitoes very troublesome. The man who went back after his knife has not yet come up, we have some reasons to believe he has deserted."

August 6, 1804. Captain Clark. "...Reed has not yet come up. Neither has...the Frenchman whom we sent to the Indian Camps a few miles below the Council Bluffs.

The following Journal entries refer to map 6.

August 7, 1804. Captain Clark. "...dispatched Drewyer, R. Fields, Bratton, and Labiche back after the deserter, Reed, with order if he did not give up peaceably to put him to Death...Proceeded   on..."

August 8, 1804. NOTE: The boat passed above what is today called the Little Sioux River. **Captain Clark.** "...the mosquitoes so bad in the prairies that with the assistance of a bush I could not keep them out of my eyes...On the upper point of... island, some hundreds of Pelicans were collected, they left three fish on the sand which was very fine. Captain Lewis killed one and took his dimensions...worthy of remark that snakes are not plenty in this part of the Missouri."

August 9, 1804. Captain Clark. "The fog being thick detained us."

August 10, 1804. Captain Clark. "Set out early...much Elk and Beaver Sign."

August 11, 1804. Captain Clark. "...ascended the hill...to the top...where the (Chief of the Mahar, Black Bird) was buried 4 years ago. A mound of earth about 12 feet is raised over him..." **NOTE:** This Chief gained power over the tribes of that region by his possession of some arsenic, from which he threatened death against anyone who opposed him. He was buried upon his Horse, thus the size of the mound that Captain Clark described.

August 12, 1804. Captain Clark. "...a Prairie Wolf came near the bank and barked at us this evening, we made an attempt but could not get him, the animal barks like a large fierce Dog...Beaver is very plenty on this part of the river."

August 13-19, 1804. Captain Clark. "Dispatched (a party) to the Mahar village with a flag and some tobacco to invite the nation to see and talk with us tomorrow." **August 14.** "The men sent to the Mahar town...Could not find the Indians, nor any fresh sign...The ravages of the Small Pox...has reduced this nation not exceeding 300 men and left them to the insults of their neighbors..." **August 15.** "I went with ten men to a creek dammed by the Beavers...made a drag...caught 318 fish...a shrimp precisely of shape, size, and flavor of those about New Orleans...The men sent to the Oto and in pursuit of the deserter Reed, has not yet returned or joined our party." **August 16.** "...Caught upwards of 800 fine fish...the party sent to the Oto not yet joined us..." **August 17.** "...informed that the party was behind with one of the Deserters (Reed)...Set the prairies on fire to bring the Mahar and Sioux if any were near, this being the usual signal." **August 18.** "The party with the Indians arrived...after a short talk we gave them provisions to eat and proceeded to the trial of Reed. He confessed that he "deserted and stole a public rifle, shot-pouch, powder and ball, and requested that we would be as favorable with him as we could, consistently with our oaths, which we were, and only sentenced him to run the gauntlet four times through the party, and that each man with switches should punish him, and for him not to be considered in future as one of the party. The three principal Chiefs petitioned for pardon for this man. After we explained the injury such men could do them by false representations, and explained the customs of our country, they were all satisfied with the propriety of the sentence, and were witnesses to the punishment. After which we had some talk with the Chiefs about the origin of the war between them and the Mahas. The evening was closed with an extra gill of whiskey, and a dance until 11 o'clock." **NOTE:** Captain Lewis's birthday. **August 19.** "Sergeant Floyd is taken very bad all at once with a *bilious colic*. We attempt to relieve him without success as yet. He gets worse and we are much alarmed at his situation. All attention to him."

August 20, 1804. Captain Clark. "…Sergeant Floyd as bad as he can be no pulse, and nothing will stay a moment on his stomach or bowels. Passed two islands on the S.S. ...at the first bluff...Sergeant Floyd died with a great deal of composure. Before his death, he said to me, "I am going away-I want you to write me a letter." We buried him on the top of the bluff a half mile below a small river to which we gave his name. He was buried with the honors of war, much lamented."

August 21, 1804. Captain Clark. "...passed the Sioux River...is navigable to the falls 70 or 80 Leagues (located at present day Sioux Falls, South Dakota) and...still further...heads with the St. Peter (now the Minnesota River)...passes through cliffs of red rock which the Indians make pipes of and when the different nations meet at those quarries all is peace." **NOTE:** The red rock refers to the Pipestone Quarry in Pipestone County, Minnesota.

August 22, 1804. Captain Clark. "Ordered a vote for a sergeant to choose one of three which may be the highest number. The highest numbers are P. Gass (had 19 votes)…"

August 23, 1804. NOTE: The expedition killed its first Buffalo. The first of about 225 Buffalo killed on the Expedition. **Captain Clark.** "J. Fields sent out to hunt. Came to the boat and informed that he had killed a Buffalo in the plain ahead. Captain Lewis took 12 men and had the buffalo brought to the boat…"

August 24, 1804. Captain Clark. "In a northerly direction from the mouth of this creek, is an immense plain, a high hill is situated, and appears of a conic form, and by the different nations of Indians in this quarter, is supposed to be the residence of devils: that they are in human form with remarkable large heads, and about 18 inches high, that they are very watchful, and are armed with sharp arrows with which they can kill at a great distance… So much do the Mahar, Sioux, Oto, and other neighboring nations, believe this fable, that no consideration is sufficient to induce them to approach the hill."

August 25, 1804. Captain Clark. "Captain Lewis and myself concluded to go and see the mound…The only remarkable characteristic of this hill, admitting it to be a natural production, is that it is insulated or separated a considerable distance from any other, which is very unusual in the natural order or disposition of the hills…We set the prairies on fire as a signal for the Sioux to come to the river."

August 26, 1804. Captain Clark. "...after jerking the meat killed yesterday and preparing the Elk skins for a tow rope, we set out leaving Drewyer and Shannon to hunt the Horses which was lost with directions to follow us keeping on the high lands."

August 27, 1804. Captain Clark. "G. Drewyer came up and informed that he could neither find Shannon nor Horses. We sent Shields and J. Fields back to hunt Shannon and the Horses…At 2 o'clock passed the mouth of the James River…one Indian at the mouth of this river swam to us…informed (us) that a large camp of Sioux were on the James River near the mouth…We sent Sergeant Pryor…Mr. Durion…to the camp with directions to invite the principal Chiefs to council with us at Bluff above called Calumet."

August 28, 1804. Captain Clark. "J. Shields and J. Field, who were sent back to look for Shannon and the Horses, joined us and informed that Shannon had the Horses ahead and that they could not overtake him. This man not being a first-rate hunter, we determined to send one man in pursuit of him, with some provisions."

August 29, 1804. Captain Clark. "Sent on Colter with provisions in pursuit of Shannon…Dorion, with five (Sioux) Chiefs and about 70 men and boys, arrived on the opposite side. …informed the Chiefs that we would speak to them tomorrow... A fat Dog was presented as a mark of their great respect for the party, of which they partook heartily, and thought it good and well flavored." **NOTE:** The Expedition eats its first Dog. About 190 Dogs were consumed by the party, most of them west of the Rocky Mountains. **Sergeant Pryor** informs Clark, "The Sioux's camps are handsome-of a conic form, covered with Buffalo robes painted different colors, and all compact and handsomely arranged, covered all around. An open part in the center for the fire, with Buffalo robes. Each lodge has a place for cooking, detached. The lodges contain from ten to fifteen persons."

August 30, 1804. Captain Clark. "...at 12 o'clock we met (with the Indians), and Captain Lewis delivered the speech...The Sioux is a stout, bold looking people...the greater part of them make use of bows and arrows...the warriors are very much decorated with paint, Porcupine quills and feathers, large leggings and moccasins, all with Buffalo robes of different colors. The squaws wore petticoats and a White Buffalo robe with the black hair turned back over their necks and shoulders."

August 31, 1804. Captain Clark. "After the Indians got their breakfast, the Chiefs met and arranged themselves in a row, with elegant pipes of peace all pointing to our seats, we came forward, and took our seats. The great Chief, The Shake Hand, rose, and spoke at some length, approving what we had said, and promising to pursue the advice...Last night the Indians danced until late..."

September 1, 1804. Captain Clark. "...set out under a gentle breeze...proceeded on past the (Calumet) bluffs...170 or 180 feet high...numbers of Catfish caught, those fish is so plenty that we catch them at any time and place in the river."

The following Journal entries refer to map 7.
September 2, 1804. Captain Clark. "I went out and made a survey of the ancient works which is situated in a level plain about 3 miles from the hills which are high." **NOTE:** Later exploration revealed that these "Works" were the result of natural formations made by the drifting sands, but appeared to be man-made.

September 3, 1804. Captain Clark. "The white banks appear to continue on both sides of the river. Grapes plenty and finely flavored."

September 4, 1804. Private Whitehouse. "Drewyer killed a Turkey. We looked for tracks of Shannon but could not see whether he had passed or not." **NOTE:** Private Joseph Whitehouse was one of only two privates that kept a journal. The other Private was Robert Frazer whose diary was never published and its whereabouts are unknown. Private Joseph Whitehouse kept a journal from May 14, 1804 to April 2, 1806. Although it was never published during his lifetime, his journals were eventually obtained and finally published in Rueben G. Thwaites' 1904 edition of the Original Journals of the Lewis and Clark Expedition. Whitehouse was born in Virginia and enlisted in the army in 1798. He came to the Corp of Discovery in late autumn 1803 at Kaskaskia, Illinois. Whitehouse was a member of the larger detachment and was a skin dresser. His greatest contribution was his skill at tailoring leather clothing. Following the Expedition Whitehouse left the army but re-enlisted in 1807 and served through the War of 1812. A few of Private Whitehouse's journal entries are mentioned as a tribute to the workingmen of the Expedition.

September 5, 1804. Private Whitehouse. "We took a cedar mast on board. We passed handsome mineral springs...hunters killed 2 Elk and a Deer."

September 6, 1804. Private Whitehouse. "...Colter joined us had not found Shannon."

September 7, 1804. NOTE: The Expedition discovered the Prairie Dog which resulted in a day of trying to capture one by flooding them out of its borrow. For their effort, they eventually killed one and captured one. **Captain Clark...**"we poured into one of the holes 5 barrels of water without filling it."

September 8, 1804. Private Whitehouse. "...we set off early...passed an old trading house..." **Captain Clark.** "...passed the house of Troodo where he wintered in 96..." **NOTE:** Jean Baptiste Trudeau, (1713-1827,) schoolmaster, trader, traveler, traveled up the Missouri River and wrote of the life and manners of the Indian tribes. See "Journal of Jean Baptiste Trudeau among the Arekara Indians in 1795," Missouri Historical Society, *Collections* 4 (1922-1923): 9-48.

September 9, 1804. Captain Clark. "...I saw at one view near the river at least 500 Buffalo, those animals have been in view all day feeding in the plains...every copse of timber appear to have Elk or Deer..."

September 10, 1804. NOTE: The Expedition appeared to have stumbled across some Dinosaur bones. **Private Whitehouse.** "A foggy morning. We set off early proceeded on. We saw a ruck of bones on the bank which appeared to be the bones of a monstrous large fish the back bone is 45 feet long..."

September 11, 1804. Private Whitehouse. "...Saw a man coming down to the bank on Horseback...we came to shore and found it was Shannon...He had been absent 16 days and 12 of them he had eat nothing but Grapes." **Captain Clark.** "This man supposing the boat to be ahead pushed on as long as he could, when he became weak and feeble determined to lay by and wait for a trading boat, which is expected...thus a man had like to have starved to death in a land of plenty for the want of bullets or something to kill his meat..."

September 12, 1804. Clark reported seeing a great numbers of Grouse.

September 13, 1804. Captain Clark. "A dark drizzly day..."

September 14, 1804. Captain Clark writing about the Pronghorn Antelope. "...his nostrils large, his eyes like a Sheep he is more like the Antelope or Gazelle of Africa than any other species of Goat...Captain Lewis measured the length of leap of the Jack Rabbit and found it to be about 20 feet." **NOTE:** About 60 Pronghorn Antelope were consumed during the Expedition. They were hard to stalk and kill and were the last choice of red meat the men wanted to eat.

September 15, 1804. Noted a great number of Rabbits, probably the Desert Cottontail.

The following Journal entries refer to map 8.

September 16-17, 1804. Discovered the Black-Billed Magpie and Mule Deer. **Captain Clark.** "Could not proceed with the present load (due to sand bars) for this purpose we concluded to detain ...I gave out a flannel shirt to each man, and powder to those who had expended theirs...Dried all our wet articles this fine day....I killed a curious kind of Deer..." **NOTE:** Captain Lewis' first recorded Journal entry since leaving St. Louis. **Captain Lewis.** "...I do not think I exaggerate when I estimate the number of Buffalo which could be comprehended at one view to amount to 3,000...We found the Antelope extremely shy and watchful, insomuch that we had been unable to get a shot at them; when at rest they generally select the most elevated point in the neighborhood... it is almost impossible to approach them within gunshot. In short, they will frequently discover, and flee from you at the distance of three miles."

September 18, 1804. NOTE: Discovered the Coyote or Prairie Wolf. **Captain Clark.** "I Killed a Prairie Wolf, about the size of a Gray Fox...what has been taken heretofore for the Fox was those Wolves, and no Foxes has been seen..."

September 19, 1804. NOTE: They had arrived at the Big Bend in the Missouri where 30 miles of river loops back on itself with less than two miles separating the narrow neck. The Expedition ran into the Prickly Pear Cactus for the first time. While little is mentioned of this plant now, it was to be one of the major "pains" of the Expedition.

September 20. 1804. Private Whitehouse. "...we proceeded on passed a long range of bluffs...this earth melts like sugar (in the current), and...keeps continually mixing through the water all the way to the mouth of the Mississippi."

September 21 1804. Captain Lewis. "... the sand bar on which we camped began to undermine and give way, ...We had pushed off but a few minutes before the bank, gave way..."

September 22, 1804. Captain Lewis. "...our hunters joined us...They complain much of the mineral substances in the barren hills, over which they passed, destroying their moccasins."

September 23, 1804. Captain Clark. "...three Sioux boys came to us and informed that the Band of Sioux called the (Tetons) of 80 lodges, were camped at the next creek above; we gave those boys two carrots of tobacco to carry to their Chiefs, with directions to tell them that we would speak to them tomorrow." **NOTE:** Lewis and Clark had been informed by traders that the Teton

Sioux could be troublesome. And at times exhibit piracy and bribery in exchange for safe passage.

September 24-25, 1804. Captain Clark. "Set out early...prepared all things for action in case of necessity...Soon after, (our men) on shore ran up the bank and reported that the Indians had stolen the Horse...(**NOTE:** Captains Lewis and Clark very forcefully told a party of five Sioux that they were not afraid and demanded the Horse, which was a gift for their Grand Chief, be returned before they would speak to the Indians. That evening they invited some of the Chiefs to have a short smoke.) All well, we prepare to speak with the Indians tomorrow, at which time, we are informed, the Indians will be here. Two-thirds of our party camped on board, the remainder with the guard on shore." **September 25.** "A fair morning. All well. Raised a flagstaff and made ... shade on a sand bar in the mouth of Teton River, for the purpose of speaking with the Indians. About 11 o'clock, the 1st and 2nd Chiefs came. We gave them some of our provisions to eat. Met in council...and, after smoking agreeable to the usual custom, Captain Lewis proceeded to deliver a speech, which we (were) obliged to curtail for want of a good interpreter. All our party paraded. Gave a medal to the Grand Chief. (Black Buffalo) Invited those Chiefs on board (the Keelboat) to show them our boat...we gave them 1/4 glass of whiskey, ...one the 2nd Chief, assuming drunkenness as a cloak for his rascally intentions. I went with those Chiefs, in one of the pirogues...As soon as I landed the pirogue, three of their young men seized the cable of the pirogue (in which we had presents.) The Chiefs' soldier hugged the mast, and the 2nd Chief was very insolent, both in words and gestures declaring I should not go on, stating he had not received presents sufficient from us, his gestures were of such a personal nature, I felt myself compelled to draw my sword, (and made a signal to the boat to prepare for action) at this motion Captain Lewis ordered all under arms in the boat, those with me also showed a disposition to defend themselves and me, the Grand Chief (Black Buffalo) then took hold of the rope and ordered the young warriors away, I felt myself warm and spoke in very positive terms. Most of the warriors appeared to have their bows strung, and took out their arrows from the quiver. As I (being surrounded) was not permitted (by them) to return, I sent all the men except two interpreters to the boat. The pirogue soon returned with about 12 of our determined men ready for any event. This movement caused a number of the Indians to withdraw at a distance...Their treatment to me was very rough and I think, justified roughness on my part. They all left my pirogue...I turned off and went with my men on board the pirogue...We proceeded on about one mile, and anchored out off a willow island...placed a guard on shore to protect the cooks and a guard in the boat. Fastened the pirogues to the boat, I called this island Bad Humored Island, as we were in a bad humor." **Note:** Had it not been for Black Buffalo ordering his warriors away, the Expedition would probably have fought the Sioux and, being badly outnumbered, would have perished.

September 26-27, 1804. Captain Clark. "Captain Lewis and 5 men went on shore with the Chiefs, who appeared disposed to make up and be friendly...We determined to remain. I was received on an elegant painted Buffalo robe, and taken to the village by 6 men, and was not permitted to touch the ground until I was put down in the grand council house, on a white dressed robe... A large fire was near, in which provisions were cooking. In the center, about 400 pounds of excellent Buffalo beef as a present for us...Soon after they set me down, the men went for Captain Lewis. Brought him in the same way... In a few minutes an old man rose and spoke, approving what we had done, and informing us of their situation, requesting us to take pity on them and which was answered. The great Chief ... took up the pipe of peace and, after pointing it to the heavens, the four quarters of the globe and the earth, he made some dissertation, lit it and presented the stem to us to smoke... A large fire made ... men began to sing and beat on the tambourine... proceeded to dance the War Dance which they did with great cheerfulness...returned to our boat...All the men on board...All in spirits this evening." **September 27.** "...we continued until we were sleepy and returned to our boat. The 2nd Chief and one principal man accompanied us...Captain Lewis, with a guard, still on shore. The man who steered, not being much accustomed to steer, passed the bow of the boat, and the pirogue came broad side against the cable and broke it, which obliged me to order, in a loud voice, all hands up and at their oars. My preemptory order to the men, and the bustle of their getting to their oars, alarmed the Chiefs...The Chief hollered and alarmed the camp informing them that the Mahar was about, attacking us. In about 10 minutes the bank was lined with men armed... About 200 men appeared...This alarm I, as well as Captain Lewis, considered as the signal of their intentions (which was to stop our proceeding on our journey and, if possible, rob us)... We show as little signs of knowledge of their intentions as possible. All prepared on board for anything, which might happen. We kept a strong guard all night. No sleep."

September 28, 1804. Captain Clark. "Made many attempts in different ways to find our anchor, but could not, the sand had covered it... With great difficulty, got the Chiefs out of our boat, and when we were about setting out, the class (of Indian) called the Soldiers took possession of the cable. The 1st Chief, who was still on board, intended to go a short distance with us. I told him the men of his nation sat on the cable. He went out and told Captain Lewis, who was at the bow, the men who sat on the rope were soldiers and wanted tobacco. Captain Lewis would not agree to be forced into anything. The 2nd Chief demanded a flag and tobacco, which we refused to give... nearly reduced us to the necessity for hostilities, I threw a carrot of tobacco to 1st Chief...The Chief gave the tobacco to his soldiers, and he jerked the rope from them, and handed it to the bowman. We then set out under a breeze from the S.E. proceeded on about two miles higher up, and came to a very small sand bar in the middle of the river, and stayed all night. I am very unwell for want of sleep. Determined to sleep tonight if possible. The men cooked, and we rested well."

September 29,1804. Captain Clark. "We substitute large stones for anchors in place of the one we lost. All in high spirits…"

September 30, 1804. Captain Clark. "Sand bars are so numerous that it is impossible to describe them, and think it unnecessary to mention them." **NOTE:** Lewis and Clark found themselves followed by the Teton Sioux who wanted handouts. They were always prepared for the threat that the Tetons would make another attempt at preventing them from continuing up river. Thankfully, by early October, the Tetons disappeared. Fall was fully in the air as winter approached. Large flocks of migrating birds were recorded.

October 1, 1804. Captain Clark. "We passed the River Cheyenne...so called from the Cheyenne Indians who live on the head of it...Continued on...(**NOTE:** Lewis and Clark met French traders.) Mr. Jon Vallié informs us that he wintered last winter 300 leagues up the Cheyenne River under the Black Mountains. (The Black Hills.) The Black Mountains, he says, are very high, and some parts of them have snow on them in the summer. Great quantities of pine grow on the mountains...On the mountains great numbers of Goats, and a kind of animal with large circular horns; this animal is nearly the size of a small Elk. White Bears are also plenty." **NOTE:** The animals described were the Big Horn Sheep and the Grizzly Bear.

October 2, 1804. Captain Clark. "The wind changed to the N.W., and rose very high, and cold, which continued. The current of the Missouri is less rapid and contains much less sediment…"

The following Journal entries refer to map 9.

October 3, 1804. Captain Clark. "We attempted several channels and could not find water to ascend. Landed on a sand bar and concluded to stay all night and send out and hunt a channel."

October 4, 1804. Captain Clark. "Several Indians on the shore viewing of us, called to us to land. We paid no attention. Proceeded on … The day very cool."

October 5, 1804. Captain Clark. "Frost this morning. We set out early and proceeded on. Saw three Indians of the Teton band. Begged some tobacco. We answered them as usual…"

October 6, 1804. Captain Clark. "Found an abandon Arikara village of about 80 lodges. The men help themselves to squash that were left growing. Captain Lewis saw a large number of Prairie Hens." **NOTE:** The expedition observed a "Bull Boat" for the first time. This is a large, round leather-covered tub that requires more than one person to navigate it in a straight line of travel.

October 7, 1804. Captain Clark. "Found the remains of another Arikara village... of about 60 lodges...killed a Black Tail Deer, the largest doe I ever saw."

October 8, 1804. Captain Clark. "Two of our men discovered the Arikara village (on an island)...The Island is covered with fields, where those people raise their corn, tobacco, beans. Great numbers of those people came on the island to see us pass. We passed above the head of the island, and Captain Lewis, with two interpreters and two men, went to the village...A pleasant evening. All things arranged, both for peace or war."

October 9, 1804. Captain Clark. "Windy, rainy...cold. So much so we could not speak with the Indians today...Many came to view us all day, much astonished at my black servant, who did not lose the opportunity of displaying his powers and strength. This nation never saw a black man before."

October 10, 1804. Captain Clark. "The Chiefs all assembled, and after some little ceremony, the council commenced. We informed them what we had told the others before, i.e., Oto and Sioux. After the council was over, we shot the air gun, which astonished them, much. They then departed, and we rested secure all night. Those Indians were much astonished at my servant...All flocked around him and examined him from top to toe. He carried on the joke and made himself more terrible than we wished him to do."

October 11, 1804. Captain Clark. "...we met the Grand Chief in council...set out for the upper villages...the Grand Chief...on board...Those people gave us to eat bread made of corn and beans, also corn and beans boiled: a large bean of which they rob the mice of the prairie who collect and discover it-which is rich and very nourishing; also squashes. All tranquility."

October 12, 1804. Captain Clark. "...the council commenced. This man...requested us to take a Chief of their nation and make a good peace with Mandans and nations above..."

October 13, 1804. Captain Clark. "One man, J. Newman, confined for mutinous expression...the brother of the Chief we have on board...we proceeded on under a fine breeze...We tried the prisoner Newman last night by 9 of his peers. They did sentence him 75 lashes and disbanded (from) the party." (**NOTE:** Newman was charged with insubordination: "having uttered repeated expressions of a highly criminal and mutinous nature." Newman pleaded with Captain Lewis to allow him to continue as a permanent member of the Corp and he worked hard to earn atonement for his crime. However Captain Lewis thought it "impolitic to relax from the sentence" and sent Newman home from Fort Mandan. Newman saved the Keelboat from certain disaster on several occasions during the return trip to St. Louis. After the Expedition, Lewis wrote a letter to Secretary of War Henry Dearborn commending Newman for "highly meritorious...zeal." J. Newman became a fur trader and was killed by the Yankton Sioux in 1838.)

October 14, 1804. Captain Clark. "The punishment of (J. Newman) this day alarmed the Indian Chief very much. He cried aloud, or affected to cry. I explained the cause of the punishment and the necessity for it. He also thought examples were necessary, and he himself had made them by death."

The following Journal entries refer to map 10.

October 15. 1804. Clark. "Rained all last night...about 30 of the Indians came over in their canoes of skins. We ate with them. They gave us meat. In return, we gave fish hooks, and some beads...Those people are much pleased with my black servant. Their women very fond of caressing our men..."

October 16, 1804. NOTE: In the fall vast migrations of herd animals, Buffalo, Elk, and Antelope moved from their summer to their winter grounds near the Black Hills. When they crossed the various rivers they became easy prey for Man, Wolves and Bear. Here Clark refers to an instance of the Indians preying on the Antelope (Goats). **Captain Clark.** "I discovered great numbers of

Goats in the river, and Indians on the shore on each side. As I approached, or got nearer, I discovered boys in the water killing the Goats with sticks and hauling them to shore. Those on the banks shot them with arrows, and as they approached the shore, would turn them back. Of this gang of Goats I counted 58 which they had killed on the shore."

October 17, 1804. Captain Clark. "Saw Buffalo, Elk and great numbers of Goats (Antelope)...and this is about the season they cross from the east of the Missouri to go to the mountain." (Referring to the Black Hills.)

October 18. 1804. Captain Clark. "Met two Frenchmen in a pirogue, descending from hunting, and complained of the Mandan's robbing them of four traps, their furs, and several other articles. They turned and followed us."

October 19, 1804. NOTE: Captain Clark described some rounded top hills that the Indians said were home to the "Calumet Bird." This bird, which turned out to be the Golden Eagle, was called Calumet because it's tail feathers were used to decorate the Calumet pipes of the Indians. The Calumet pipe was named by the French and consisted of a long, feathered stem, with a pipe bowl. Calumet pipes were considered sacred and were smoked at peace treaties and spiritual ceremonies.

October 20, 1804. Captain Clark. "Our hunters killed 10 Deer and a goat today, and wounded a White Bear. I saw several fresh tracks of those animals which are 3 times as large as a man's track..."

October 21, 1804. Captain Clark. "A very cold night." **NOTE:** Clark recorded the temperature at 31 degrees at sunrise and only 34 degrees by 4 o'clock in the afternoon. Lewis and Clark and their men had never experienced the depth of cold weather they were about to encounter.

October 22, 1804. Captain Clark was attacked in middle of the night by what he described as a "Rheumatism in the neck." Captain Lewis applied a warm stone wrapped in flannel, which "gave me some temporary ease."

October 23, 1804. Captain Clark. "A cloudy morning. Some snow. Set out early. Passed five lodges, which were deserted, the fires yet burning. We suppose those were the Indians who robbed the 2 French trappers a few days ago. Those 2 men are now with us, going up with a view to getting their property from the Indians, through us. Cold and cloudy."

The following Journal entries refer to map 11.

October 24, 1804. Captain Clark. "On this island, we saw one of the Grand Chiefs of the Mandans...this Chief meets the Chief of the Arikara who accompanied us, with great cordiality and ceremony."

October 25, 1804. Captain Clark. "...several Indians came to see us this evening, among others, the son of the late great Chief of the Mandan's, this man has his two little fingers off. On inquiring the cause, was told it was customary for this nation to show their grief by some testimony of pain...it was not uncommon for them to take off 2 smaller fingers..."

October 26, 1804. Captain Clark. "...we proceeded on to the camp of two of their Grand Chiefs...at this camp saw a Mr. McCracken, Englishman from the N.W. Company. This man came nine days ago to trade for Horses and Buffalo robes." **NOTE:** Lewis and Clark reached the Mandan villages at the mouth of the Knife River. The Mandan and Hidatsa Indians in the vicinity were very familiar with white men. Their first contact was in 1738 when a French trader, Pierre Gaultier Verendrye, led a trading expedition of voyageurs from the Assiniboine River in what is now Canada to the Missouri River. In 1913 some school children discovered a Lead plate near Fort Pierre, South Dakota, which had been left by Verendrye's two sons on a later expedition. The words, engraved translate: "In the 26th year of the reign of Louis XV, the most illustrious Lord, the Lord Marquis of Beauharnois, 1741, Pierre Gaultier De La Verendrye placed this." Scratched on the back: "Placed by the Chevalier Verendrye [his brother] Louis [and] La Londette and A. Miotte. 30 March 1743." They were among the first newcomers to see the Dakota plains and may have explored the Black Hills and Eastern Wyoming. This Lead plate is on exhibit at the South Dakota State Historical Society in Pierre, South Dakota.

October 27, 1804. Captain Clark. "We…came to a village…situated…about 50 feet above the water in a handsome plain…smoked a pipe with the Chief of the village they were anxious that I would stay and eat with them…a fine warm day…we met a Frenchman by the name of Jessome which we employ as an interpreter."

October 28, 1804. Captain Clark. "The Black Cat Grand Chief of the Mandans, Captain Lewis and myself with an interpreter, walked up the river…to examine the situation and timber for a fort. We found the situation good but the timber scarce."

October 29, 1804. Captain Clark. "We collected the Chief and commenced a council…We delivered a long speech the substance of which was similar to what we had delivered to the nations below…We at the end of the speech, mention the Arikara who accompanied us to make a firm peace. They all smoked with him…we presented him with a certificate of his sincerity and good conduct…After the council, we gave the presents with much ceremony and put the medals on the Chief…shot the air gun which appeared to astonish the natives…The Arikara Chief came to me this evening and tells me that he wishes to return to his village… the prairie was set on fire…the fire went with such velocity that it burned to death a man and woman."

October 30, 1804. Captain Clark. "I took 8 men…up the river…to see if a situation could be got on it for our winter quarters…wood was scarce as well as game."

October 31, 1804. Captain Clark. "…the Chief of the Mandans sent a 2nd Chief to invite us to his lodge…the Chief spoke…some brave men will accompany the Arikara Chief…to his village and nation to smoke with that people…he put before me 2 of the steel traps which was robbed from the French (traders)."

3. Wintering at Fort Mandan – November 2, 1804 – April 7, 1805.

Lewis and Clark spent over five months at Fort Mandan. They began to build their wintering fort immediately, using the only material available, Cottonwood. The weather was getting very cold and the men needed shelter quickly. They began building November 3rd and the Fort was officially completed on November 30th, at which time there was over six inches of snow on the ground. The walls were thick with a fireplace in each of the eight adjoining rooms. Going outside in the below zero cold to hunt and complete chores was an experience the young men from Virginia and Kentucky would want to forget.

The business that winter was preparation for the next leg of the journey. Lewis and Clark met with the various local Indian nations and visiting traders gathering as much information on the geography and the other Indian tribes that lay ahead. They rewrote their journals and notes and prepared the large quantities of specimens they had collected for shipment on the keelboat back to President Jefferson in the spring. But the big task was gathering enough food to feed the 44 men during the winter. They had to travel many miles from the villages to gather fresh meat, and in the dead of winter the hunters had the hardest job. Lewis and Clark also bartered for additional food from the Indians.

During the winter of 1804-05 Captains Lewis and Clark met Charbonneau and his wife Sacajawea. On February 11, 1805, she gave birth to a baby boy that was named Baptiste. The members of the expedition quickly named him "Pomp," for his pompous "little dancing boy" personality. Charbonneau was hired for his guide and interpreter skills. As it would turn out, Sacajawea would also prove a most valuable addition to the Expedition.

Because the keelboat was going to return to St. Louis with the specimens and manuscripts collected on the voyage to Fort Mandan, the Corp built six dugout canoes from large Cottonwood trees to transport the men, trade goods and other supplies up the Missouri River.

Excepts from the Journals while encamped at Fort Mandan.
November 2, 1804. Captain Clark. "I went down the river with 4 men to look for a proper place to winter…found a place well supplied with wood…Our Arikara Chief set out (for home) accompanied by one Chief of the Mandans and several brave men…"
November 3, 1804. Captain Clark. "We commence building our cabins."
November 4, 1804. Captain Clark. "We continued to cut down trees and raise our houses. A Mr. Charbonneau, interpreter for the Gros Ventre nation came to see us…this man wished to hire as an interpreter."
November 6, 1804. Captain Clark. "We were awoke by the Sergeant of the Guard to see a Northern light…(The) 2 French boys who came with us, set out in a small canoe on their return to the Illinois…Continued to build the huts out of Cotton timber."
November 11, 1804. Captain Clark. "A cold day. Continued at work at the fort. Two men cut themselves with an ax."
November 13, 1804. Captain Clark. "Ice began to run in the river…rose early and unloaded the boat…stored away in a store house.
November 15, 1804. Captain Clark. "All hands work at their huts until 1 o'clock at night."
November 20, 1804. Captain Clark. "Captain Lewis and myself move into our hut."
November 25, 1804. Captain Clark. "We completed our huts…Captain Lewis with Charbonneau and Jessome set out to visit the Indian hunting camps."

November 27, 1804. Captain Clark. "Seven traders arrived from the fort on the Assiniboin from the N.W. Company. One of which, Lafrance, took upon himself to speak unfavorable of our intentions. The principal, Mr. Larocque was informed of the conduct…and the consequences if they did not put a stop to unfavorable and ill founded assertions."

December 7, 1804. Captain Clark. "The Big White Grand Chief…informed us that a large drove of Buffalo was near…Captain Lewis took 15 men out and joined the Indians…killing the Buffalo on Horseback with arrows which they did with great dexterity. His party killed 10 Buffalo, five of which we got to the fort…three men frost bit badly today."

December 18, 1804. Captain Clark. "Sent 7 men to hunt…they found the weather too cold and returned."

December 25, 1804. Captain Clark. "…the men merrily disposed…permitted 3 cannon fired."

January 1, 1805. Captain Clark. "The day was ushered in by the discharge of 2 cannon. We suffered 16 men with their music to visit the (Mandans) for the purpose of dancing, by, as they said, the particular request of the Chief of that village…I found them (the Indians) much pleased at the dancing of our men. I ordered my black servant to dance, which amused the crowd very much. And somewhat astonished them that so large a man should be active."

January 5, 1805. Captain Clark. "…a Buffalo Dance…a curious custom. The old men arrange themselves in a circle and after smoking a pipe which is handed them by a young man…the young men who have their wives back of the circle go to one of the old men with a whining tone and request the old man to take his wife…and the girl then takes the old man and leads him to a convenient place for the business…all this is to cause the Buffalo to come near so they may kill them."

January 7, 1805. Captain Clark. "The Big White Chief of the Lower Mandan village dined with us and gave me a sketch of the country as far as the high mountains, and on the south side of the River Rejone. **NOTE:** An imperfect spelling of the French name for the river Roche-Jaune, meaning Yellowstone.)

January 10, 1805. Captain Clark. "Last night was excessively cold. The mercury this morning stood at 40 degrees below 0, which is 72 degrees below the freezing point…about 10 o'clock, a boy…came to the fort with his feet frozen…we had his feet put into cold water and they are coming too…a man came in who had also stayed out without fire and very thinly clothed. This man was not the least injured. Customs and the habits of those people has annealed them to bear more cold than I thought it possible for man to endure."

January 15, 1805. Captain Clark. "This morning, we had a total eclipse of the Moon."

January 16, 1805. Captain Clark. "About thirty Mandans came to the fort today…One of the 1st War Chiefs…gave us a chart…of the Missouri."

January 27, 1805. Captain Clark. "A fine day. Attempt to cut our boat and canoes out of the ice…Captain Lewis took off the toes of one foot of the boy who got frost bit some time ago."

January 28, 1805. Captain Clark. "Attempt to…get our boat and canoes out without success."

NOTE: From February 4th to the 12th , the Journal was written by Captain Lewis. Clark was absent on a hunting trip.

February 4, 1805. Captain Lewis. "Our stock of meat, which we procured in the months of November and December, is now nearly exhausted…Captain Clark therefore determined to continue…down the river (to hunt)…the men transported their baggage on a couple of small wooden sleighs drawn by themselves, and took with them 3 pack Horses which we had agreed should be returned with a load of meat to Fort Mandan as soon as they could procure it."

February 11, 1805. Captain Lewis. "About five o'clock this evening one of the wives (Sacajawea) of Charbonneau was delivered of a fine boy. It is worthy of remark that this was the first child this woman had borne, and as is common in such cases, her labor was tedious and the pain violent. Mr. Jessome informed me that he had frequently administered a small portion of the rattle of the Rattle Snake, which he assured me had never failed to produce the desired effect, that of hastening the birth of the child. Having the rattle of a snake by me I gave it to him and he administered two rings of it to the woman broken in small pieces with the finger and added to a small quantity of water. Whether this medicine was truly the cause or not I shall not undertake to determine, but I was informed that she had not taken it more than ten minutes before she brought forth." **NOTE:** It was later discovered that a Rattlesnake's rattle does contains a chemical that induces labor. Today a similar product is manufactured and called Pitocin.

February 12, 1805. Captain Lewis. "The only food of the Horse consists of a few sticks of the Cottonwood from the size of a man's finger to that of his arm. The Indians are invariable severe riders, and frequently have occasion for many days together through the whole course of the day to employ their Horses in pursuing the Buffalo or transporting meat to their villages during which time they are seldom suffered to taste food. At night the Horse returned to his stall where food is what seem to me a scanty allowance of wood...A little after dark this evening Captain Clark arrived with the hunting party...killed forty Deer, three Buffalo and sixteen Elk."

February 13, 1805. Captain Clark. "I returned last night...much fatigued having walked 30 miles on the ice and through point of woodland in which the snow was nearly knee deep."

February 14, 1805. Captain Clark. "Dispatched George Drewyer and 3 men, with two sleighs drawn by three Horses for the meat left below."

February 15, 1805. Captain Clark. "At 10 o'clock P.M. last night the men that were dispatched yesterday for the meat, returned and informed us that as they were on their march down at a distance of about 24 miles below the Fort...about 105 Indians which they told to be Sioux rushed on them and cut their Horses from the sleighs, two of which they carried off in great haste...We dispatched two men to inform the Mandans, and if any of them chose to pursue those robbers, to come down in the morning and join Captain Lewis who intended to set out with a party of men...Captain Lewis set out at sunrise with 24 men to meet those Sioux. Several Indians accompanied him. The thermometer stood at 16 below 0."

February 16, 1805. Captain Clark. "One man (Howard) returned with his feet frosted and informed that the Indians who committed the robbery...was so far ahead that they could not be overtaken."

February 18, 1805. Captain Clark. "Our store of meat is out today."

February 21, 1805. Captain Clark. "Captain Lewis returned with 2 sleighs loaded with meat. After finding that he could not overtake the Sioux...determined to proceed on...he hunted two days. Killed 36 Deer and 14 Elk...amounting to 3,000 lbs."

February 27, 1805. Captain Clark. "A few Indians visit us today. One, the largest Indian I ever saw, and as large a man as ever I saw."

March 6, 1805. Captain Clark. "Smokey all day from the burning of the plains...for an early crop of grass as an inducement for the Buffalo to feed on."

March 18, 1805. Captain Clark. "Mr. Toussaint Charbonneau enlisted as interpreter this evening."

March 26, 1805. Captain Clark. "The ice began to break away this evening."

March 27, 1805. Captain Clark. "The river choked up with ice...all employed preparing to set out."

March 28, 1805. Captain Clark. "Ice running...had all canoes calked, pitched."

March 30, 1805. Captain Clark. "I observe extraordinary dexterity of the Indians in jumping from one cake of ice to another, for the purpose of catching the Buffalo as they float down." **NOTE:** As the ice breaks up, Buffalo are stranded on ice floes as they try to cross the River. The Indians kill these animals as well as harvest the dead and decaying drowned Buffalo which float down the river. The Mandan Indians eat the rotten, jelly-like meat of the floating Buffalo and think it a delicacy.

March 31, 1805. Captain Clark. "Generally healthy except venereal complaints which is very common among the natives and men catch it from them."

April 3, 1805. Captain Clark. "Some ice on the edge of the water, a fine day. Pack up and prepare to load…packing up articles to be sent to the President of the United States."

April 5, 1805. Captain Clark. "We have our 2 pirogues and six canoes loaded with our stores and provisions."

4. Fort Mandan to Fort Clatsop. April 7 to December 8, 1805.

April 7, 1805. Captain Lewis. "At the same moment that the barge departed from Fort Mandan, Captain Clark embarked with our party and proceeded up the river. As I had used no exercise for several weeks, I determined to walk on shore as far as our encampment of this evening... Our vessels consisted of six small canoes and two large pirogues. This little fleet, although not quite so respectable as that of Columbus or Captain Cook, was still viewed by us with as much pleasure as those deservedly famed adventurers ever beheld theirs, and, I daresay, with quite as much anxiety for their safety and preservation. We were now about to penetrate a country at least two thousand miles in width, on which the foot of civilized man had never trod. The good or evil it had in store for us was for experiment yet to determine, and these little vessels contained every article by which we were to expect to subsist or defend ourselves. However, as the state of mind in which we are, generally gives the coloring to events, when the imagination is suffered to wander into futurity, the picture that now presented itself to me, was a most pleasing one. Entertaining as I do the most confident hope of succeeding in a voyage which had formed a darling project of mine for the last ten years, I could but esteem this moment of my departure as among the most happy of my life. The party are in excellent health and spirits, zealously attached to the enterprise, and anxious to proceed. Not a whisper or murmur of discontent to be heard among them, but all act in unison and with the most perfect harmony." **NOTE:** From this point, thirty-three members of the Expedition continued the journey. Eleven men returned to St. Louis aboard the Keel Boat with the specimens and manuscripts, and to pick up several Indian chiefs who were to meet with President Jefferson.

April 8, 1805. Captain Lewis. "One of the small canoes filled with water and all her cargo including some rifle powder got wet. The men immediately spread this powder out to dry."

April 9, 1805. NOTE: Both Lewis and Clark commented about the vast striations of coal located in the huge bluffs above the river. **Captain Lewis.** "Many of them (hills) have the appearance of having been on fire at some former period."

April 10, 1805. Captain Lewis. "The bluff is now on fire and throws out considerable quantities of smoke..."

April 11, 1805. NOTE: The Expedition found the rifle powder they were drying "appeared to be restored so we put it up."

April 12, 1805. NOTE: Arrived at the Little Missouri River. Lewis wrote with remarkable accuracy as to its origins based on the good information provided by both the Indians and the French traders. **Captain Lewis.** "This river passes through the northern extremity of the Black Hills where it is very narrow and rapid. It takes its rise in a broken country west of the Black Hills...the country through which it passes is generally broken and the highlands possess but little timber."

April 13, 1805. Captain Lewis. "Saw...many tracks of the White Bear of enormous size, along the river shore. We have not as yet seen one of these animals...The men...are anxious to meet with some of these Bear. The Indians give a very formidable account of the strength and ferocity of this animal, which they never dare to attack but in parties of six, eight, or ten persons; and are even then frequently defeated with the loss of one or more of their party. The savages attack this animal with their bows and arrows and the indifferent guns with which the traders furnish them. With these they shoot with such uncertainty and at so short a distance that, unless shot through head or heart wound not mortal, they frequently miss their aim and fall a sacrifice to the Bear."

April 14, 1805. NOTE: The Expedition passes the farthest known assent of the Missouri River by a white man. **Captain Lewis.** "Passed an island above which two small creeks fall in on the larboard side...This was the highest point to which any white man had ever ascended..." **NOTE:**

Lewis killed a Montana Horned Owl. He reported it identical to an eastern owl but "more booted (feathered legs) and thickly clad with feathers."

April 15, 1805. Captain Lewis. "… I heard the frogs crying for the first time this season."

April 16, 1805. Captain Lewis. "There was a remarkably large Beaver caught...last night. These animals are very abundant...several trees which have been felled by them (are) 20 inches in diameter."

The following Journal entries refer to map 12.

April 17, 1805. Captain Lewis. "...saw some track of Indians who had passed about 24 hours; they left four rafts of timber...we supposed them to have been a party of the Assiniboins who had been to war against the Rocky Mountain Indians, and then on their return."

April 18-19, 1805. Captain Lewis. "...found a species of Pea bearing a yellow flower...resembles that of the common garden Pea. Captain Clark went out for a walk with Charbonneau, Sacajawea and 'Little Pomp' and killed an Elk and a Deer."

April 19. NOTE: The wind blew so hard that the Expedition was laid up for the day.

April 20, 1805. NOTE: The wind continues to blow hard. The Expedition was at risk all day and made only 6.5 miles. Lewis describes an Indian burial site. **Captain Lewis** "...a small scaffold of about 7 feet high...a human body was lying, well rolled in several dressed Buffalo skins and near it a bag of the same materials consisting (of) sundry articles belonging to the deceased...moccasins, some red and blue earth, Beaver's nails, instruments for dressing the Buffalo skin, some dried roots, several plats of the sweet grass, and a small quantity of Mandan tobacco...saw the carcass of a large Dog...it is customary…to sacrifice the favorite Horses and Dogs of their deceased relations…I have never heard of any instances of human sacrifices…"

April 21, 1805. NOTE: The wind abated a little and the Expedition made 16.5 miles.

April 22, 1805. Captain Lewis. "Set out at an early hour this morning; proceeded pretty well until breakfast, when the wind became so hard ahead that we proceeded with difficulty even with the assistance of our tow lines…I ascended to the top of the cut bluff this morning, from whence I had a most delightful view of the country… I met with a Buffalo calf which attached itself to me, and continued to follow close at my heels...the wind blows with astonishing violence."

April 23, 1805. Captain Lewis. "Set out at an early hour…about nine A.M. the wind arose, and shortly after became so violent that we were unable to proceed."

April 24, 1805. Captain Lewis. "The wind blew so hard during the whole of this day, that we were unable to move."

April 25, 1805. Captain Lewis. "…the water froze on the oars this morning as the men rowed. About 10 o'clock A.M. the wind began to blow so violently that we were obliged to lie too." **NOTE:** Even though they quit early in the morning, the wind later abated and they were able to continue.

April 26, 1805. NOTE: The Expedition arrives at the confluence of the Yellowstone and Missouri Rivers. **Captain Lewis.** "Captain Clark measured these rivers just above their confluence: found the bed of the Missouri 520 yards wide... It's channel deep. The Yellowstone River, including its sand bar, 858 yards…The deepest part, 12 feet…The Indians inform that the Yellowstone River is navigable for pirogues and canoes nearly to its source in the Rocky Mountains, and that in its course, near these mountains, it passes within less than half a day's march of a navigable part of the Missouri. Its extreme sources are adjacent to those of the Missouri, River Platte, and I think probably with some of the south branch of the Columbia River."

April 27, 1805. Captain Lewis. "Beaver are very abundant. The party kills several of them every day. The Eagles, Magpies, and Geese have their nests in trees adjacent to each other. The Magpie particularly appears fond of building near the Eagle, as we scarcely see an Eagle's nest unaccompanied with two or three Magpie's nests within a short distance. The Bald Eagles are more abundant here than I ever observed them in any part of the country."

April 28, 1805. Captain Lewis. "…the wind was favorable and we employed our sails to advantage…coal is in great abundance…the woods are now green…"

April 29, 1805. NOTE: The Expedition kills its first Grizzly Bear. The first of over 40 Grizzly Bears killed. **Captain Lewis.** "About 8 A.M. we fell in with two brown or yellow Bear, both of which we wounded. One of them made his escape; the other after my firing on him, pursued me seventy or eighty yards but fortunately had been so badly wounded that he was unable to pursue so closely as to prevent my charging my gun. We again repeated our fire, and killed him. It was a male, not fully grown. We estimated his weight at 300 pounds…the Indians may well fear this animal equipped as they generally are with their bows and arrows or indifferent fuzees (cheap trade guns) but in the hands of skillful riflemen they are by no means as formidable or dangerous as they have been represented…We took the flesh of the Bear on board and proceeded."

April 30, 1805. NOTE: The Expedition once again experienced winds but were determined to proceed. They made 24 miles.

May 1, 1805.   Private Whitehouse. "…clear, pleasant morning but cold…we sailed some…about 12 o'clock the wind rose so high that we were obliged to halt in a bottom of timber…one canoe lay on the opposite shore and could not cross. I and one more was in the canoe and were obliged to layout all night without any blanket. It being very cold, I suffered very much." **NOTE:** The wind blew all night and it began to snow. Clark recorded the temperature at 28 degrees the next morning.

May 2, 1805. Captain Lewis. "…on our way this evening we also shot three Beaver along the shore. These animals in consequence of not being hunted are extremely gentle. Where they are hunted they never leave their lodges in the day. The flesh of the Beaver is esteemed a delicacy among us. I think the tail a most delicious morsel. When boiled it resembles in flavor the fresh tongues and sounds of the Codfish…" **NOTE:** The "sounds" referred to here are the air-bladders of the Codfish and the "tongues" are not really the tongue but the meaty throat. Both are prized tidbits. The tongues are rolled in corn meal and fried, and the sounds are broiled and then served with spicy brown gravy.

May 3, 1805. Captain Lewis. "…we saw an unusual number of Porcupines, from which we determined to call the river after that animal, and accordingly denominated it Porcupine River."

May 4, 1805. Captain Lewis. "I saw immense quantities of Buffalo in every direction, …They are extremely gentle; the bull Buffalo, particularly, will scarcely give way to you. I passed several in the open plain within fifty paces."

The following Journal entries refer to map 13.

May 5, 1805. NOTE: Captain Lewis describes a Grizzly Bear. **Captain Lewis.** "Captain Clark and Drewyer killed the largest brown Bear we have yet seen. It was a most tremendous-looking animal, and extremely hard to kill. Notwithstanding he had five balls through his lungs and five others in various parts, he swam more than half the distance across the river, to a sandbar, and it was at least twenty minutes before he died. He did not attempt to attack, but fled, and made the most tremendous roaring from the moment he was shot. We had no means of weighing this monster. Captain Clark thought he would weigh 500 pounds. For my own part, I think the estimate too small by 100 pounds. He measured 8 feet 7 1/2 inches from the nose to the extremity of the hind feet; 5 feet 10 1/2 inches around the breast; 1 foot 11 inches around the middle of the arm; and 3 feet 11 inches around the neck. His talons, which were five in number on each foot, were 4 3/8 inches in length…This Bear differs from the common black Bear in several respects: its talons are much longer and more blunt; its tail shorter; its hair, which is of a reddish or bay brown, is longer, thicker, and finer than that of the black Bear, his liver, lungs, and heart are much larger, even in proportion with his size. The heart, particularly, was as large as that of a large ox. His maw was also ten times the size of black Bear, and was filled with flesh and fish…This animal also feeds on roots and almost every species of wild fruit."

May 6, 1805. Captain Lewis. "Saw a brown Bear swim the river above us. He disappeared before we can get in reach of him. I find that the curiosity of our party is pretty well satisfied with respect to this animal. The formidable appearance of the male Bear killed on the 5^{th,} added to the difficulty with which they die when even shot through the vital parts, has staggered the resolution of several of them. Others however, seem keen for action with the Bear. I expect these gentlemen will give us some amusement shortly."

May 7, 1805. Captain Lewis. "...one of the most beautiful plains we have yet seen, it rises gradually from the river bottom to the height of 50 or 60 feet, then becoming level as a bowling green extends back as far as the eye can reach..."

May 8, 1805. NOTE: At the entrance of the Milk River. **Captain Lewis.** "The water of this river possesses a peculiar whiteness, being about the color of a cup of tea with the admixture of a tablespoonful of milk...we called it Milk River...wild Liquorice is found on the sides of these hills, in great abundance...we saw where an Indian had recently grained, or taken the hair off of a goatskin; we do not wish to see those gentlemen just now as we presume they would... be troublesome to us."

May 9, 1805. NOTE: Charbonneau cooks Boudin Blanc. **Captain Lewis.** "...this white pudding we all esteem one of the greatest delicacies of the forest...6 feet of the large gut of the Buffalo is the first morsel that the cook makes love to...(He squeezes out the crap and then chops the meat of the front shoulder and the tenderloin)...these are kneaded up with a good portion of kidney suet...to this... added...salt and pepper and a small portion of flour. (NOTE: Charbonneau then stuffs this mixture into the gut and ties off each end.)...It is then baptized in the Missouri with two dips and a flirt, and bobbed into the kettle from whence, after it be well boiled it is taken and fried with Bears oil until it becomes brown when it is ready to assuage the pangs of a keen appetite or such as travelers in the wilderness are seldom at a loss for."

May 10, 1805. Captain Clark. "We proceeded on but a short distance e're the wind became so violent we could not proceed..." **NOTE:** 4.5 miles traveled.

May 11, 1805. Captain Lewis. "These Bears, being so hard to die, rather intimidate us all. I must confess that I do not like the gentlemen and had rather fight two Indians than one Bear. There is no other chance to conquer them by a single shot but by shooting them through the brains, and this becomes difficult in consequence of two large muscles which cover the sides of the forehead, and the sharp projection of the center of the frontal bone, which is also of a pretty good thickness."

May 12, 1805. Captain Lewis. "I walked on shore this morning for the benefit of exercise...In these excursions, I most generally went alone armed with my rifle and Espontoon." (**NOTE:** Espontoon is a form of walking stick with a sharp metal point on one end. During this period, most Army Officers carried them.) "Thus equipped I feel myself more than an equal match for a brown Bear provided I get him in open woods or near the water, but feel myself a little diffident with respect to an attack in the open plains. I have therefore come to a resolution to act on the defensive only, should I meet these gentlemen in the open country."

May 13, 1805. Captain Lewis. "The wind continued to blow so violently this morning that we did not think it prudent to set out...At 1 P.M. the wind abated...the current rather stronger than usual and the water continues to become rather clearer, from both which I anticipate a change of country shortly."

May 14-15, 1805. NOTE: The men take on this monster Grizzly Bear. **Captain Lewis.** "...Two of them reserved their fires as had been previously concerted; the four others fired nearly at the same time...In an instant, this monster ran at them with open mouth. The two who had reserved their fires discharged their pieces at him as he came toward them. Both of them struck him-one only slightly, and the other, fortunately, broke his shoulder. This, however, only retarded his motion for a moment. The men, unable to reload their guns, took to flight. The Bear pursued, and had very nearly overtaken them before they reached the river. Two of the party betook themselves to a canoe, and the others separated and concealed themselves among the willows, and reloaded their pieces; each discharged his piece at him as they had an opportunity. They struck him several times again, but the guns served only to direct the Bear to them. In this manner he pursued two of them, separately, so close that they were obliged to throw away their guns and pouches, and throw themselves into the river, although the bank was nearly twenty feet perpendicular. So enraged was this animal that he plunged into the river only a few feet behind the second man he had compelled to take refuge in the water. When one of those who still remained on shore shot him through the head and finally killed him." **NOTE:** They almost lose the white pirogue. **Captain Lewis.**"...This is the upsetting and narrow escape of the white pirogue. It happened, unfortunately for us this evening that Charbonneau was at the helm of this pirogue instead of Drewyer, who had previously steered her. Charbonneau cannot swim, and is perhaps the most timid waterman in the world. Perhaps it was equally unlucky that Captain Clark and myself were both on shore at that moment, a circumstance which rarely happened, and though we were on the shore opposite to the pirogue, were too far distant to be heard, or to do more than remain spectators of her fate. In this pirogue were embarked our papers, instruments, books, medicine, a great part of our merchandise-and, in short, almost every article indispensably necessary to further the view or ensure the success of the enterprise in which we are now launched to the distance of 2,200 miles. Suffice it to say that the pirogue was under sail when a sudden squall of wind struck her obliquely and turned her considerably. The steersman, alarmed, instead of putting her before the wind, lufted her up into it. The wind was so violent that it drew the brace of the square sail out of the hand of the man who was attending it, and instantly upset the pirogue and would have turned her completely topsy-turvy had it not have been for the resistance made by the awning against the water. In this situation, Captain Clark and myself both fired our guns to attract the attention, if possible, of the crew, and ordered the halyards to be cut and the sail hauled in, but they did not hear us. Such was their confusion and consternation at this moment that they suffered the pirogue to lie on her side for half a minute before they took the sail in. The pirogue then righted but had filled within an inch of the gunwales. Charbonneau, still crying to his God for mercy, had not yet recollected the rudder, nor could the repeated orders of the bows man, Cruzatte, bring him to his recollection until he threatened to shoot him instantly if he did not take hold of the rudder and do his duty. The waves by this time were running very high, but the fortitude, resolution, and good conduct of Cruzatte saved her. He ordered 2 of the men to throw out the water with some kettles that fortunately were convenient, while himself and two others rowed her ashore, where she arrived scarcely above the water. We now took every article out of her and laid them to drain as well as we could for the evening, bailed out the canoe, and secured her...After having all matters arranged for the evening as well as the nature of circumstances would permit, we thought it a proper occasion to console ourselves and cheer the spirits of our men, and accordingly took a drink of grog, and gave each man a gill of spirits." **NOTE:** It was during this incident that Sacajawea, who was also in the boat, saved the manuscripts and medicine from floating away. Some historians write that after this incident, Captain Lewis' opinion of Sacajawea changed and he began to show her more respect. **May 15.** The Corp took the day off to dry their instruments, manuscripts and medicine before proceeding.

May 16, 1805. NOTE: The Expedition saw its' first Mountain Lion. **Captain Clark.** "Two of our men fired at a Panther a little below our camp. This animal had caught a Deer and eat half and buried the balance."

May 17, 1805. NOTE: Captain Clark narrowly escapes being bitten by a rattlesnake and during the night a tree catches fire and falls onto the Captains lodge a few minutes after they had moved. The tree was ignited from the campfire.

May 18, 1805. NOTE: The wind blew hard. But because the river bottom was becoming more solid, it allowed for better footing and they were able to use the towline to make 21 miles.

May 19, 1805. NOTE: Departure was delayed several hours due to a very heavy fog. Captain Lewis' Dog was badly bitten by a wounded Beaver.

May 20, 1805. NOTE: The Expedition passes the entrance of the Muscle Shell River. **Captain Clark.** Writes about Blow Flies being so bad that they "gather on our meat in such numbers that we are obliged to brush them off what we eat."

May 21, 1805. Captain Lewis. "...immense quantities of the Prickly Pear (cactus)...country...crowned with some scrubby pines...wind...increase(d) in the evening...found ourselves so enveloped with clouds of dust and sand that we could neither cook, eat, nor sleep..."

The following Journal entries refer to map 14.

May 22, 1805. NOTE: Clark reported that the surrounding soil was sticky and produced Prickly Pear Cactus and little grass. **Captain Clark.** "game not so abundant as below."

May 23, 1805. Captain Lewis. "The mosquitoes troublesome this evening."

May 24, 1805. Captain Lewis. "Game is becoming more scarce."

May 25, 1805. Captain Clark. "In my walk of this day, I saw mountains on either side of the river at no great distance. Those mountains appeared to be detached...I also think I saw a range of high mountains at a great distance to the south-southwest but am not certain, as the horizon was not clear enough to view it with certainty." **NOTE:** Expedition killed their first Big Horn Sheep. The first of about 35 total Big Horn Sheep killed on the Expedition.

May 26, 1805. Captain Clark. "...ascended the high country... could plainly see the mountains on either side, which I saw yesterday...On one, the most southwesterly of those mountains, there appeared to be snow...I beheld the Rocky Mountains for the first time, with certainty...Whilst I viewed those mountains, I felt a secret pleasure in finding myself so near the head of the - heretofore conceived - boundless Missouri. But when I reflected on the difficulties which this snowy barrier would most probably throw in my way to the Pacific Ocean, and the sufferings and hardships of myself and party in them, it in some measure counterbalanced the joy I had felt in the first moments in which I gazed on them. But, as I have always held it little short of criminality to anticipate evils, I will allow it to be a good, comfortable road until I am compelled to believe otherwise."

May 27, 1805. Captain Clark. "Wood for cooking and warmth is becoming a problem as the banks and surrounding area is almost devoid of trees."

May 28, 1805. Captain Lewis. "Found a new Indian lodge pole ...A football also, and several other articles... These are strong evidences of Indians being on the river above us, and probably at no great distance."

May 29, 1805. Captain Lewis. "Last night we were all alarmed by a large Buffalo bull which swam over from the opposite shore and coming along the side of the white pirogue, climbed over it to land. He... ran up the bank in full ...and was within 18 inches of the heads of some of the men who lay sleeping...my Dog saved us by causing him to change his course...We were happy to find no one hurt...I counted the remains of the fires of 126 Indian lodges which appeared to be of very recent date, perhaps 12 or 15 days...passed... the remains of...mangled carcasses of Buffalo, which had been driven over a precipice of 120 feet by the Indians...They created a most horrid stench... no appearance of even wood enough to make our fires...gave each man a small dram...several of them were considerably affected by it. Such is the effect of abstaining for some time the use of spirituous liquors. They were all very merry."

May 30, 1805. Captain Clark. "No timber of any kind on the hills. We discover old encampment of large bands of Indians, a few weeks past..."

May 31, 1805. Captain Lewis. "...the men are compelled to be in the water even to their armpits, and the water is yet very cold...the banks and bluffs along which they are obliged to pass are so slippery, and the mud so tenacious, that they are unable to wear their moccasins, and in that situation, dragging the heavy burden of a canoe, and walking occasionally for several hundred yards over the sharp fragments of rocks which tumble from the cliffs and garnish the borders of the river. In short, their labor is incredibly painful and great, yet those faithful fellows bear it without a murmur."

June 1, 1805. NOTE: With the mountains ever in view, the Expedition travels 23 miles into a wind.

June 2, 1805. Captain Lewis. "Charbonneau is ambushed by a Grizzly Bear and hides very securely in bushes until Drewyer finally killed it by a shot in the head."

June 3, 1805. Captain Lewis. "This morning early we passed over and formed a camp…by the junction of the two large rivers. Here in the course of the day I continued my observations…An interesting question was now to be determined; which of these rivers was the Missouri? To mistake the stream at this period of the season…and then be obliged to return and take the other stream would not only lose us the whole of this season, but would probably so dishearten the party that it might defeat the expedition…an investigation of both streams was the first thing to be done…we dispatched two light canoes with three men in each up those streams…to penetrate…as far as they conveniently can permitting themselves time to return this evening…The north fork is deeper…but it's current not so swift…it's waters are of a whitish brown color…also characteristic of the Missouri…south fork is perfectly transparent, runs very rapid…it's bottom composed of stones like most rivers issuing from a mountainous country…the party pronounced the North fork to be the Missouri. Myself and Captain Clark…have not yet decided…what astonishes us a little is that the Indians who appeared to be so well acquainted with the geography of this country should not have mentioned this river on right hand if it be not the Missouri, *the river that scolds at all others*…our cogitating faculties been busily employed all day…the parties…returned…Their accounts were by no means satisfactory…Captain Clark and myself concluded…I should ascend the right hand…he the left…made all matters ready for an early departure…is the first time in my life that I had ever prepared a (burden) of this kind, and I am fully convinced that it will not be the last."

June 4-5-6-7, 1805. NOTE: Both men ascended their rivers to gather valuable information from which to make a decision. **Captain Clark. June 5.** "…river runs west of south a long distance and has a strong current…continued its width, depth and rapidity and the course west of south, going up further would be useless. I determined to return." **Captain Lewis. June 6.** "I now became well convinced that this branch…had its direction too much to the North for our route to the Pacific…determined to return…"

June 8, 1805. Captain Clark. "Captain Lewis arrived with the party much fatigued and informed me that he had ascended the river about 60 Miles." **NOTE:** Lewis named this river Maria's River after his sweetheart.

June 9, 1805. NOTE: The first order of business this day was to direct the men to prepare the red pirogue and all heavy baggage, which could be left behind and deposited in a hole or cellar in which it would keep until the Expedition returned. The most important business was to decide which branch of the river to take. After Lewis and Clark conferred and discussed all they had learned from their advances up both rivers, they determined that the South Fork was the Missouri River. Information from the Indians about the clarity of the water at the Great Falls plus the apparent direction from which each branch seemed to arise in relation to the Mountains in the distance gave credence to their mutual belief. **Captain Lewis.** "…I endeavored to impress on the minds of the party all of whom, except Captain Clark, being still firm in the belief that the North Fork was the Missouri and that which we ought to take. They said very cheerfully that they were ready to follow us anywhere we thought proper to direct…the men passed the evening in dancing, singing and were extremely cheerful."

June 10, 1805. Captain Lewis. "The day being very fair…we dried all our baggage…Shields renewed the main-spring of my air-gun…our Indian woman is very sick…Captain Clark bled her."

June 11, 1805. Captain Clark. "…we…complete our deposit, which took us all day…the Indian woman very sick."

June 12, 1805. Captain Clark. "The interpreters wife is very sick...I move her into the back part of our covered part of the Pirogue..."

The following Journal entries refer to map 15.
June 13, 1805. Discovering the Great Falls of the Missouri. **Captain Lewis.** "...we again ascended the hills of the river...overlooked a most beautiful and level plain...at least 50 or 60 miles. In this there were infinitely more Buffalo than I had ever before witnessed at a view... I altered my course nearly to the south...had proceeded on this course about two miles...when my ears were saluted with the agreeable sound of a fall of water...saw the spray arise above the plain like a column of smoke...a roaring too tremendous to be mistaken for any cause short of the great falls of the Missouri...the grandest sight I ever beheld...perfect white foam...a thousand forms...flying up in jets of sparkling...large roiling bodies...the rocks seem to be most happily fixed...I stand and seem to reverberate...a beautiful rainbow...majestically grand...I wished for the pencil of Salvator Rosa or the pen of Thompson that I might be enabled to give to the enlightened world some just idea of this truly magnificent and sublimely grand object, which has from the commencement of time been concealed from the view of civilized man..." **NOTE:** Salvator Rosa was an Italian Baroque painter remembered for his romantic landscapes, marine paintings, and battle pictures. James Thompson was a Scottish Poet. His most famous poem was *The Seasons.* In *The Seasons,* Thomson's descriptions of external nature influenced the forerunners of romanticism.
June 14, 1805. Captain Clark. "At 4 o'clock this evening Joe Fields returned from Captain Lewis with a letter for me. Captain Lewis dates his letter from the Great Falls of the Missouri, which Fields informs me is about 20 miles in advance...he (Captain Lewis) is convinced of this being the river the Indians call the Missouri." **Captain Lewis.** "I selected a fat Buffalo and shot him very well...while I was gazing attentively on the poor animal...and having entirely forgotten to reload my rifle, a large...(Grizzly) Bear had perceived and crept on me within 20 steps before I discovered him...at the same instant...he was then briskly advancing on me. I was in an open level plain, not a bush within miles nor a tree less than three hundred yards of me...I ran about 80 yards...into the water...about waist deep, and face about and presented the point of my Espontoon. At this instant, he arrived at the edge of the water within about 20 feet of me...he suddenly wheeled about as if frightened...and retreated...I returned to the shore and charged my gun, which I had still retained in my hand throughout this curious adventure...I saw him run...about 3 miles."
June 15 1805. Captain Clark. "...we can hear the falls this morning very distinctly. Our Indian woman sick and low spirited."

The following Journal entries refer to map 16.
June 16, 1805. Captain Lewis. "...found the Indian woman extremely ill...gave me some concern...her being our only dependence for a friendly negotiation with the Snake Indians on whom we depend for Horses to assist us in our portage from the Missouri to the Columbia River...Captain Clark determined to set out in the morning and survey the portage, and discover the best route." **NOTE:** Captain Lewis gave Sacajawea two doses of barks and opium when she arrived.
June 17, 1805. Captain Lewis. "The Indian woman much better today." **Captain Clark.** "I set out with 5 men...and proceeded up the river passing a succession of rapids and cascades to the falls...I beheld those cataracts with astonishment."
June 18, 1805. NOTE: As Captain Clark surveys the portage around the falls, Captain Lewis has his men prepare a Cache for storage, work on building wagon wheels and axles for the transport across the portage, and overhauling, airing, and repacking provisions.
June 19, 1805. Captain Lewis. "The Cache completed today...had the frame of my Iron Boat cleaned of rust and well greased."

June 20, 1805. Captain Lewis. "This morning we had but little to do; waiting the return of Captain Clark, I am apprehensive from his stay that the portage is longer than we had calculated on…Captain Clark and party returned late this evening." **Captain Clark.** "I direct stakes to be cut to stick up in the prairie to show the way…on the portage…all appear perfectly to have made up their minds to succeed in the expedition or perish in the attempt. We all believe that we are about to enter on the most perilous and difficult part of our voyage, yet I see no one repining. All appear ready to meet those difficulties which await us with resolution and becoming fortitude."

Portaging the Great Falls. June 21 – July 14, 1805.
NOTE: Hard. Hard. Hard. Everything about this portage was hard. It was long; it had hills and ravines, Grizzly Bears would bother the men; Prickly Pear Cactus pierced through moccasins; mosquitoes, heat, cold, wind, rain, hail, floods, heavy baggage and equipment broke. The days never seemed to end. On June 23, *only two days* after the process had begun, Captain Lewis wrote this passage that sums up the entire effort. **June 23, 1805. Captain Lewis.** "This evening the men repair their moccasins and put on double soles to protect their feet from the Prickly Pears. During the late rains, the Buffalo have trodden up the prairie very much which having now become dry, the sharp points of earth as hard as frozen ground stand up in such abundance that there is no avoiding them. This is particularly severe on the feet of the men who have not only their own weight to bear in treading on those hackle-like points, but have also the addition of the burden which they draw and which in fact is as much as they can possibly move with. They are obliged to halt and rest frequently for a few minutes. At every halt these poor fellows are asleep in an instant. In short their fatigues are incredible. Some limping from the soreness of their feet, others faint and unable to stand for a few minutes with heat and fatigue, yet no one complains. All go with cheerfulness."

June 28, 1805. Captain Lewis. "The White Bear (Grizzly) have become so troublesome to us that I do not think it prudent to send one man alone on an errand of any kind, particularly where he has to pass through the brush…they come close around our camp every night…I have made the men sleep with their arms by them as usual for fear of accidents." **NOTE: Grizzly Bears.** From The Grizzly, Enos A. Mills, Comstock Editions, Inc. 1919. From the Introduction; "Observing them without interfering, he (Mills) caught unusual glimpses of their way of life. These were animals who slid down snow banks or played hide-and-seek with their shadows for the sheer joy of it, gazed at sunsets and shooting stars for the wonder of it, and followed their all-consuming curiosity, often with hair-raising results." From page 105; "In 1826 Drummond, the botanist, collected plants in the Rocky Mountains. In stopping to examine, to gather, and to press them he was doing the unusual. He thus attracted the attention of numerous grizzlies, who even came close to watch him. They showed no inclination to attack. Bears are 'chock-full of curiosity' and will sometimes forget to eat in trying to understand at once the new or the unusual." From pages 114-115; "The novel outfit of Lewis and Clark, which appears to have attracted unusual attention even from frontier people, must naturally have aroused the highest pitch of interest in the numbers of bears congregated in places along the river. There were boats of odd type-some with sails-strange cargoes, men in picturesque accoutrements, and even a colored man. The frequent close approaches which the bears made in trying to satisfy their curiosity caused Lewis and Clark to think them ferocious. But is the grizzly bear ferocious? All the first-hand evidence I can find says he is not. Speaking from years of experience with him my answer is emphatically, 'No!' Nearly every one whom a grizzly has killed went out with the special intention of killing a grizzly. The majority of people who hold the opinion that he is not ferocious are those who have studied them without attempting to kill him; while the majority who say that he is ferocious are those who have killed or attempted to kill him."

June 29, 1805. Captain Lewis. "He (Clark) determined himself to pass by the way of the river to camp in order to supply…some notes and remarks which he had made as he first ascended the river but which he had unfortunately lost…(he) took with him his black man York, Charbonneau and his Indian woman...at the falls he perceived a very black cloud rising in the West which threatened immediate rain. He looked about for a shelter...he discovered a deep ravine where there were some shelving rocks under which he took shelter near the river...laying their guns, compass, etc. under shelving rock on the upper side of the ravine where they were perfectly secure from the rain. The first shower was moderate accompanied by a violent rain of which they did but little feel. Soon after a most violent torrent of rain descended accompanied with hail. The rain appeared to descend in a body and instantly collected in the ravine and came down in a roiling torrent with irresistible force driving rocks, mud and everything before it which opposed its passage. Captain Clark fortunately discovered it a moment before it reached them and seizing his gun and shot pouch with his left hand with the right he assisted himself up the steep bluff shoving the Indian woman before him who had her child in her arms...one moment longer and it would have swept them into the river just above the great cataract of 87 feet where they must have inevitably perished. Charbonneau lost his gun, shot pouch, horn, tomahawk, and my wiping rod, Captain Clark his umbrella and compass." **NOTE:** The following morning, two men were sent to see if they could recover any of the lost items. They only found Clark's compass.

NOTE: The Iron Boat. Captain Lewis had brought a collapsible boat made of iron. He had it made in Harpers Ferry with the intent of using it above the Great Falls of the Missouri. It was to have been covered with skins sown together with the seams sealed with pine tar. It was a great idea...Lightweight, strong, and able to carry 8,000 pounds of supplies. The problem was not with the idea, nor the design. The problem was the lack of pine trees in the area from which they had hoped to make the pine tar to seal leaks. They tried a sealant made with a combination of beeswax and charcoal with bad results. It was a sad day for **Captain Lewis** when he wrote, "I therefore relinquished all further hope of my favorite boat and ordered her to be sunk in the water...as it could probably be of no further service to us." Consequently, the Expedition, which could have departed the falls on July 9th, left on July 15th because they had to build extra canoes.

July 15, 1805. Captain Lewis. "At 10 A.M. we once more saw ourselves fairly under way much to my joy...the Prickly Pear is now in full bloom and forms one of the beauties as well as the greatest pests of the plains."
July 16, 1805. Captain Lewis. "...here for the first time I ate of the small guts of the Buffalo cooked over a blazing fire...found them very good."
July 17, 1805. Captain Lewis. "The sunflower is in bloom...the Indians...make use of the seed...for bread...first parch...then pound...to a fine meal...add marrow grease...and eat...I think a palatable dish."
July 18, 1805. Captain Lewis. "As we were anxious now to meet the Shoshone Indians...we thought it better for one of us...to take a small party and proceed on up the river some distance before the canoes, in order to discover them...before...our guns...should alarm and cause them to retreat to the mountains and conceal themselves, supposing us to be their enemies..." **NOTE:** Captain Clark began starting out ahead of the party each morning.
July 19, 1805. Captain Lewis. "...towering and projecting rocks in many places seem ready to tumble on us. The river appears to have forced it's way through this immense body of solid rock...I called it *the gates of the rocky mountains*...not being able to obtain much fire wood...substituted the dung of the buffalo..."
July 20, 1805. Captain Lewis. "This morning Captain Clark proceeded on...he fell in with (followed) an old Indian road...18 miles...much fatigued...feet cut with the flint and pierced with the Prickly Pears until they became so painful that he proceeded but little further and waited my arrival." **Captain Clark.** "I left signs to show the Indians, if they come on our trail, that we were not their enemy."
July 21, 1805. Captain Lewis. "the river...assumes a different ...character. It spread to a mile and upwards in width, crowded with Islands..." **NOTE:** They were so careful to not alarm the

Indians by gunfire that Clark went up the river three miles to see if there were any Indians, then returned to camp and went four miles down river to hunt.

July 22, 1805. Captain Lewis. "The Indian woman recognizes the country and assures us that this is the river on which her relations live, and that the three forks are at no great distance. This piece of information has cheered the spirits of the party who now begin to console themselves with the anticipation of shortly seeing the head of the Missouri yet unknown to the civilized world."

The following Journal entries refer to map 17.

July 23, 1805. NOTE: Captain Clark and four men left the main party to proceed ahead to locate the Indians. **Captain Lewis.** "I ordered the canoes to hoist their small flags in order that should the Indians see us they might discover that we were not Indians, nor their enemies."

July 24, 1805. Captain Clark. "...discovered a Horse...fat and very wild...could not get near him..."

July 25, 1805. Captain Clark. "We proceeded on a few miles to the three forks of the Missouri...I wrote a note informing Captain Lewis the route I intended to take and proceeded on up the main North fork through a valley."

July 26, 1805. Captain Clark. "I could see the course of the North fork about 10 miles meandering through a valley but could discover not Indians or sign which was fresh...We came to a spring of excessively cold water."

July 27-28-29, 1805. NOTE: Captain Lewis arrived at the Three Forks of the Missouri. **Captain Lewis.** "proceeded on but slowly the current still so rapid that the men are in a continual state of their utmost exertion...and they begin to weaken fast from this continual state of violent exertion...we arrived at 9 A.M. at the junction of the S.E. fork of the Missouri and the country opens suddenly to extensive and beautiful plains and meadows...supposing this to be the three forks of the Missouri, I halted the party...at the junction of the S.W. and Middle forks I found a note which had been left by Captain Clark informing me of his intended route...believing this to be an essential point in the geography of this Western part of the Continent, I determined to remain at all events until I obtained the necessary data for fixing it's latitude and longitude...At 3 P.M. Captain Clark arrived very sick with a high fever on him and much fatigued and exhausted...Captain Clark's indisposition was a further inducement for my remaining here a couple of days...We begin to feel considerable anxiety with respect to the Snake (Shoshone) Indians. If we do not find them or some other nation who have Horses I fear the successful issue of our voyage will be very doubtful." **Captain Clark.** " I take 5 Rushes Pills and bath my feet and legs in hot water." **NOTE:** Lewis procured Rushes Pills from Dr. Rush back east before the Expedition began. At that time they were considered the "cure-all" medicine of their day. While nobody knew what they contained, they caused the men to sweat profusely and become "unbound." **July 28. Captain Lewis.** "My friend, Captain Clark was very sick all last night but feels himself somewhat better this morning...we called the S.W. fork, that which we meant to ascend, Jefferson's River in honor of that illustrious personage Thomas Jefferson. The middle fork we called Madison's River in honor of James Madison, and the S.E. fork we called Gallatin's River in honor of Albert Gallatin...Our present camp is precisely on the spot that the Snake Indians were encamped at the time the Minitari of the Knife River...made our Indian woman...prisoner..." **July 29. Captain Clark.** "I feel myself something better today...men all dressing skins."

July 30, 1805. Captain Lewis. "...having completed my observations we reloaded our canoes and set out ascending Jefferson's River. Charbonneau, his woman and myself walked through a bottom...when we struck the place the woman informed us that she had been taken prisoner. Here we halted until Captain Clark arrived. I continued...Captain Clark had proceeded on after I separated from him and encamped about 2 miles below me..." **Captain Clark.** "We camped...Captain Lewis, who walked on shore, did not join me this evening."

July 31, 1805. Captain Lewis. "I now learned that the canoes were behind, they arrived shortly…They halted and breakfasted after which we all set out again and I continued my walk…Nothing killed today and our fresh meat is out. When we have a plenty of fresh meat, I find it impossible to make the men take any care of it, or use it with the least frugality. Though I expect that necessity will shortly teach them this art." **Captain Clark.** "The mountains on either side are high and rough. We have two men with tumors and unable to work. Captain Lewis determined to proceed on with three men in search of the Snake Indians, tomorrow."

The following Journal entries refer to map 18.
August 1-11, 1805. NOTE: The Expedition struggled up the Jefferson River looking for the Shoshone Indians. Captain Clark in charge of the canoes and baggage, Captain Lewis out front looking for the Indians and their much sought-after Horses.
August 1, 1805. Captain Lewis. "The men I took were the two Interpreters, Drewyer and Charbonneau and Sergeant Gass…The route we took lay over a rough high range of mountains…The mountains are extremely bare of timber, and our route lay through the steep and narrow hollows of the mountains exposed to the intense heat of the midday sun without shade or scarcely a breath of air. Add to my fatigue…I had taken a dose of Glibber salts in the morning in consequence of a slight dysentery with which I had been afflicted for several days. Being weakened by the disorder and the operation of the medicine, I found myself almost exhausted before we reach the river. I felt my spirits much revived on our near approach to the river at the sight of a herd of Elk…killed a couple. We then hurried to the river and allayed our thirst…We made a comfortable meal on the Elk, and left the balance…for Captain Clark and party."
August 2, 1805. Captain Lewis. "We resumed our march…The valley…beautiful level plain…little timber…fertile…covered with grass…the tips of these mountains are yet covered partially with snow, while we in the valley are nearly suffocated with the intense heat of the mid-day sun; the nights are so cold that two blankets are not more than sufficient covering…lost my tomahawk…unable to find it…saw many tracks of the Elk and Bear. No appearance of Indians…Clark continued…the rapidity of the current was such that his progress was slow, in short it required the utmost exertion of the men to get on…Captain Clark discovers a tumor rising on the inner side of his ankle…was painful."
August 3, 1805. Captain Lewis. We passed through a high plain for about 8 miles covered with prickley pear and bearded grass, though we found this even better walking than the wide bottoms of the river…although level, from some cause which I know not, were formed into myriads of deep holes as if rooted up by hogs; these the grass covered so thick that it was impossible to walk without the risk of falling down at every step…Captain Clark saw a track which he supposed to be that of an Indian…found that the person had ascended a point of a hill from which his camp of the last evening was visible….Rubin Fields killed a Panther. We called the creek…Panther Creek." NOTE: This creek is now called Pipestone Creek. The Panther was measured at 7.5 feet long.
August 4, 1805. NOTE: Captain Lewis explores a gentle flowing river that is safe to navigate. Its water is much warmer and more turbid indicating to Lewis that it's source is from a greater distance in the mountains and passes through a more open country. Under this impression he leaves a note for Clark telling him what route to take provided Clark gets the note before Lewis returns to the spot on the 6th. **Captain Lewis.** "Charbonneau complains much of his leg, and is the cause of considerable detention to us." **Captain Clark.** "I could not walk on shore today as my ankle was sore from a tumor on that part. The method we are compelled to take to get on is fatiguing and laborious in the extreme, haul the canoes over the rapids, which succeed each other every two or three hundred yards and between the water rapid oblige to tow and walk on stones the whole day except when we have poling. Men wet all day, sore feet."
August 5, 1805. Captain Lewis. "As Charbonneau complained of being unable to march far today, I ordered him and Sergeant Gass to pass the rapid river near our camp and proceed at their

leisure through the level bottom to a point of high timber about seven miles distant on the middle fork…I took Drewyer with me and continued my route…I took the advantage of a high projecting spur of the mountain which with some difficulty we ascended to it's summit…from this eminence I had a pleasing view of the valley…I did not hesitate in believing the middle fork the most proper for us to ascend…I resolved to return to Gass and Charbonneau…Drewyer missed his step and had a very dangerous fall…hurt his leg much…regained the bottom and struck the river…by this time is was perfectly dark and we hooped but could hear no tiding of them…they having mistaken a point of woods lower down, had halted short of the place…we continued our route after dark down the bottom through thick brush…about 2 hours when we arrived at their camp…(Earlier that day) at 4 P.M. (Captain Clark) arrived at the confluence of the two rivers where I had left the note. This note had unfortunately been placed on a green pole, which the beaver had cut and carried off together with the note; the possibility of such an occurrence never once occurred to me when I placed it on the green pole. This accident deprived Captain Clark of any information with respect to the country and supposing the rapid fork was most in the direction which it was proper we should pursue, or West, he took that stream and ascended it with much difficulty about a mile and encamped on an island that had been lately over-flowed and was yet damp; they were therefore compelled to make beds of brush to keep themselves out of the mud…Captain Clark's ankle is extremely painful…the tumor has not yet matured, he has a slight fever. The men were so much fatigued today that they wished much that navigation was at an end that they might go by land."

August 6, 1805. NOTE: Shannon gets lost again! **Captain Lewis.** "Shannon had been dispatched up the rapid fork this morning to hunt, by Captain Clark before he met with Drewyer or learned his mistake in the rivers. When he (Captain Clark) returned he sent Drewyer in search of him, but he (Drewyer) rejoined us this evening and reported that he had been several miles up the river and could find nothing of him…I am fearful that he is lost again. This is the same man (Shannon) who was separated from us 15 days as we came up the Missouri and subsisted 9 days…on grapes only." **Captain Clark.** "We proceeded on with much difficulty and fatigue over rapids and stones…where I met with Captain Lewis and party…one man Shannon did not return tonight."

August 7, 1805. Captain Lewis. "Dispatched Reubin Fields in search of Shannon. Our stores were now so much exhausted that we found we could proceed with one canoe less…" **Captain Clark.** "A fine morning, put out our stores to dry and took equal altitudes with the Sextant…all streams contain immense number of Beaver, Otter, Muskrats, etc."

August 8, 1805. Captain Lewis. "The Indian woman recognized the point of a high plain to our right which she informed us was not very distant from the summer retreat of her nation on a river beyond the mountains which runs to the west. This hill she says her nation calls the Beaver's Head from a conceived resemblance…She assures us that we shall either find her people on this river or on the river immediately west of it's source…I determined to proceed tomorrow with a small party to the source of the principal stream of this river and pass the mountains to the Columbia and down the river until I found the Indians. In short it is my resolution to find them or some others, who have Horses if it should cause me a trip of one month. For without Horses, we shall be obliged to leave a great part of our stores." **Captain Clark.** "R. Fields joined us this evening and informed (us) that he could not find Shannon."

August 9, 1805. Captain Lewis. "The morning was fair and fine; we set out…halted and we breakfasted…while we halted here <u>Shannon arrived</u>, and informed us that having missed the party the day on which he set out he had returned the next morning to the place from whence he had set out or first left them and not finding them that he had supposed that they were above him. That he then set out and marched one day up the Wisdom River, by which time he was convinced that they were not above him, as the river could not be navigated. He then returned to the forks and had pursued us up this river…I slung my pack and set out accompanied by Drewyer, Shields and

McNeil." **Captain Clark.** "Captain Lewis and 3 men set out after breakfast to examine the river above, find a portage if possible, also the Snake Indians."

August 10, 1805. Captain Lewis. "The mountains do not appear very high in any direction though the tops of some of them are partially covered with snow. This convinces me that we have ascended to a great height since we have entered the Rocky Mountains, yet the ascent has been so gradual along the valleys that it was scarcely perceptible by land…If the Columbia furnishes us such another example, a communication across the continent by water will be practicable and safe. But this I can scarcely hope from a knowledge of its having in it's comparatively short course to the ocean the same number of feet to descend which the Missouri and Mississippi have from this point to the Gulf of Mexico." **Captain Clark.** "…passed a remarkable cliff…the Indians call the Beaver's Head."

August 11, 1805. "I was overjoyed…" **Captain Lewis.** "…I discovered an Indian on Horseback about two miles distance coming down the plain towards us. With my glass I discovered from his dress that he was of a different nation from any that we had yet seen. And was satisfied of he being a Shoshone. (In) His arms were a bow and quiver of arrows and (he) was mounted on an elegant Horse…I proceeded towards him at my usual pace. When I had arrived within about a mile he made a halt which I did also and unloosing my blanket from my pack, I made him the signal of friendship…throwing (the blanket) up in the air higher than the head bringing it to the earth as if in the act of spreading it, thus repeating three times…this signal had not the desired effect…I now called to him in a loud a voice as I could command repeating the word *tab-ba-bone*, which in their language signifies *white-man*…Drewyer and Shields …were still advancing…I now made a signal to these men to halt, Drewyer obeyed but Shields who after words told me that he did not observe the signal still kept on…when I arrived within about 150 paces, I again repeated the word *tab-ba-bone* and…stripped up my shirt sleeve to give him an opportunity of seeing the color of my skin and advanced leisurely towards him…he suddenly turned his Horse about , gave him the whip, leaped the creek and disappeared in the willow brush…I now felt quite as much mortification and disappointment as I had pleasure and expectation at the first sight of this Indian." **Captain Clark.** "Passed a large Island which I call the 3000 Mile Island as it is situated that distance from the mouth of the Missouri by water."

August 12, 1805. The Headwaters of the Missouri and Columbia. **Captain Lewis.** "I now determined to…finding some Indian road which lead over the mountains…we fell in with a large…Indian road…the road took us to the most distant fountain of the waters of the Mighty Missouri in search of which we have spent so many toilsome days…I had accomplished one of those great objects on which my mind has been unalterable fixed for many years, judge then of the pleasure I felt in allaying my thirst with this pure and ice-cold water which issues from the base of a low mountain or hill of a gentle ascent for ½ a mile….I now descended the mountain on the opposite side to a handsome bold running creek of cold clear water. Here I first tasted the water of the great Columbia River." **Captain Clark.** "…men much fatigued and weakened…complain very much of the immense labor they are obliged to undergo…eat nothing but venison…"

August 13, 1805. The Shoshone Indians, at last. **Captain Lewis.** "We set out very early on the Indian road…we had proceeded through a wavy plain parallel to the valley…when at the distance of about a mile we saw two women, a man and some Dogs on an eminence immediately before us…when we had arrived within half a mile of them I directed the party to halt…took the flag…and advanced singly towards them…(all three soon disappeared)…we hastened to the top of the hill where they had stood but could see nothing…we had not continued our route more than a mile when we were so fortunate to meet with three female savages…a young woman immediately (set) to flight. An elderly woman and a girl of about 12 years remained…they…seated themselves on the ground holding down their heads as if reconciled to die…I gave these women some beads, a few moccasin awls, some pewter looking-glasses and a little paint….I informed them by signs that I wished them to conduct us to their camp…we marched about 2 miles when we met a party of about 60 warriors mounted on excellent Horses who came in nearly full speed...I advanced towards them with the flag, leaving my gun...the Chief...spoke to the women...these men advanced and embraced me very affectionately in their way which is by putting their left arm over your right shoulder, clasping your back, while they apply their left cheek to yours and frequently (speak) the word *ah-hi-e, ah-hi-e* that is, 'I am much please, I am much rejoiced'." **Captain Clark.** "The river obliges the men to undergo great fatigue and labor in hauling the canoes over the shoals in the cold water naked."

August 14, 1805. Captain Lewis. "As we had nothing but a little flour and parched meal to eat except the berries...Indians furnished us, I directed Drewyer and Shields to hunt...Indians furnished them with horses and most of their young men also turned out to hunt...Antelope, which they pursue on horseback...a single horse has no possible chance to over take them...the...stratagem...pursue the herd at full speed...six or seven miles...fresh horses...drive them back...wearing the poor animal down...lasted about 2 hours...my hunters returned soon after...unsuccessful. I now directed McNeal to make me a little paste with the flour and added some berries...found (it) very palatable...The means I had of communicating with these people was by way of Drewyer...signs which seems to be universally understood by all the Nations we have yet seen...told Cameahwait that I wished...to...engage them to go with me tomorrow to the forks of Jefferson's River where our baggage was by this time arrived with another Chief and a large party of white men...wish them to take...30 spare horses to transport our baggage to this place...he...informed me that they would be ready...in the morning...Drewyer...had a good view of their horses, estimated them at 400...several with Spanish brands..." **Captain Clark.** "...river very crooked and rapid...requires great labor to push and haul the canoes up...I checked our interpreter (Charbonneau) for striking his women at their dinner."

August 15, 1805. Captain Lewis. "I arose...as hungry as a Wolf...I hurried the departure of the Indians. The Chief addressed them several times before they would move. They seemed reluctant to accompany me...he told me that some foolish persons among them had suggested the idea that we were in league with the Pawnee and had come on in order to decoy them into an ambush where their enemies were waiting...but that for his part he did not believe it...told Cameahwait that I was sorry to find that they had put so little confidence in us, that I knew they were not acquainted with white men and therefore could forgive them...still hoped that...some among them...would go with me and convince themselves of the truth of what I had asserted...He now mounted his horse...he was joined by six or eight only...we had not proceeded far before our party was augmented by ten or twelve more, and before we reached the creek...we had all the men of the village and a number of women with us...I had sent Drewyer...to kill some meat but he was unsuccessful and did not return until after dark. I now cooked and divided among six of us...the remaining pound of flour stirred in a little boiling water." **Captain Clark.** "I have no accounts of Captain Lewis since he set out."

August 16, 1805. Captain Lewis. "I sent Drewyer and Shields...to kill some meat as neither the Indians nor ourselves had anything to eat...informed us that one of the white men had killed a deer. In an instant they (the Indians) all gave their horses the whip...when they arrived where the Deer was...they dismounted and ran in tumbling over each other like a parcel of famished Dogs each seizing and tearing away a part of the intestines which had been previously thrown out by Drewyer...some were eating the kidneys, paunch and guts...one...had provided himself with about nine feet of the small guts and one end of which he was chewing on while with his hands he was squeezing the contents out at the other...I viewed these poor starved devils with pity and compassion...Drewyer killed a second Deer; here nearly the same scene was enacted...Drewyer joined us after breakfast with a third Deer. Of this I reserved a quarter and gave the balance to the Indians...We now set out and rode briskly within sight of the forks...when we arrived...I discovered to my mortification that the party had not arrived and the Indians slackened their pace. I now scarcely knew what to do and feared every moment when they would halt altogether...determined to restore their confidence...gave the Chief my gun and told him that if his enemies were in those bushes before him that he could defend himself with that gun...and if I deceived him he might...shoot me. The men also gave their guns to other Indians, which seemed to inspire them...I wrote a note to Captain Clark...and directed Drewyer to set out early...the Chief...slept about my fire and others hid themselves in various parts of the willow brush to avoid the enemy whom they were fearful would attack them in the night." **Captain Clark.** "...men fatigued, stiff and chilled."

August 17, 1805. Note: Sacajawea meets her brother Cameahwait, the Shoshone Chief. **Captain Lewis.** "I arose very early and dispatched Drewyer and the Indian down the river...about 2 hours...an Indian reported that the white men were coming...shortly after Captain Clark arrived with Charbonneau and the Indian women who proved to be a sister of the Chief Cameahwait. The meeting of those people was really affecting, particularly between Sacajawea and an Indian woman, who had been taken prisoner at the same time with her and who had afterwards escaped...We now formed our camp...unloaded our canoes...formed a canopy of one of our large sails...for the Indians to set under while we spoke to them...we communicated to them...that they should render us such aids as they had it in their power to furnish in order to hasten our voyage and of course our return home. That such, were their Horses to transport our baggage...and a pilot to conduct us through the mountains...we did not ask either...without giving a satisfactory compensation in return...I am confident we shall not find game here to subsist us many days...I conceive it necessary to get underway as soon as possible." **Captain Clark.** "I had not proceeded on one mile before I saw at a distance several Indians on horseback coming towards me. The interpreter and squaw who were before me at some distance danced for the joyful sight, and she made signs to me that they were her nation. As I approached nearer them discovered one of Captain Lewis' party with them dressed in their dress."

August 18, 1805. Captain Lewis "This day I completed my thirty-first year, (his Birthday) and conceived that I had in all human probability now existed about half the period which I am to remain in this sublunary world. I reflected that I had as yet done but little, very little, indeed, to further the happiness of the human race, or to advance the information of the succeeding generations. I viewed with regret the many hours I have spent in indolence, and now sorely feel the want of that information which those hours would have given me had they been judiciously expended. But since they are past and cannot be recalled, I dash from me the gloomy thought, and resolved in future, to redouble my exertions and at least endeavor to promote those two primary objects of human existence, by giving them the aid of that portion of talents which nature and fortune have bestowed on me; or in future, to live for mankind, as I have heretofore lived for myself."

August 19, 1805. Captain Lewis describes the Shoshone Indians. "...the Shoshones...live in a wretched state of poverty. Yet...they are...cheerful...even gay, fond of gaudy dress and amusements...they are frank, communicative, fair in dealing, generous with the little they possess, extremely honest, and by no means beggarly. Each individual is his own sovereign master, and acts from the dictates of his own mind."

August 20, 1805. Captain Lewis. "Pack saddles and harness is not yet complete...we find ourselves at a loss for nails and boards...we substitute thongs of raw hide...and...cut off the blades of our oars and use the plank of some boxes...by this means I have obtained as many boards as will make 20 saddles...the hunters returned unsuccessful...I now prevailed on the Chief to instruct me with respect to the geography of his country. This he undertook very cheerfully...the Chief further informed me that he had understood from the Nez Perce Indians who inhabit this river below the Rocky Mountains that it ran a great way toward the setting sun and finally lost itself in a great lake of water (the Pacific Ocean) which was illy tasted, and where white men lived." **NOTE:** In addition to talking to Cameahwait, Lewis talked to an old Indian who told him of the hardships to come. *"Twenty days over the mountains and through a desert and the only food would be the Horses who died from exhaustion."* Captain Clark had set out this day in advance. His mission was to locate the easiest route possible for Lewis and the main party.

Captain Clark. "…proceeded on…to the camp of the Indians on a branch of the Columbia River…at 3 o'clock after giving a few small articles as presents…I set out accompanied by an old man as a guide (**NOTE:** They named him Old Toby.)…I left our interpreter and his woman (Charbonneau and Sacajawea) to accompany the Indians to Captain Lewis…"

August 21, 1805. Captain Clark. "The S.W. fork…was a handsome river…I shall in justice to Captain Lewis who was the first white man ever on this fork of the Columbia call this Lewis's River. **Captain Lewis.** "By evening I had all the baggage, saddles, and harness completely ready for a march."

August 22, 1805. Captain Clark. "We set out early…the assent was so steep that it is incredible to describe the rocks in many places loose and slipped from those mountains and is a solid bed of rugged, loose white and dark brown loose rock for miles…the Indian Horses…do not detain me any on account of those difficulties." **Captain Lewis.** "…Drewyer returned with…a considerable quantity of Indian plunder." **NOTE:** Drewyer was out hunting and came across several Pawnee Indians. One stole his rifle and after a chase of 10 miles wrestled the gun from the grip of the Indian. Upon returning to their camp, he picked their baggage up and brought it back to Captain Lewis.

August 23, 1805. Captain Clark. "…great difficulty as the rocks were so sharp, large and unsettled and the hillsides steep that the Horses could, with the greatest of risk and difficulty get on…no provisions…we came to a place the Horses could not pass without going into the river…as we have no path further…I determined to delay the party here and with my guide and three men proceed on down to examine if the river continued bad or was practicable…I proceeded on…climbing over the rocks for 12 miles…The river from the place I left my party to this creek is almost one continued rapid…the passage of either with canoes is entirely impossible." **Captain Lewis** writes later, "Captain Clark being now perfectly satisfied as to the impracticability of this route either by land or water, informed the old man, (Toby) that he was convinced of the veracity of his assertions and would now return to the village from whence they had set out where he expected to meet myself and party."

August 24, 1805. Captain Clark. "…descended to the place I left my party…wrote a letter to Captain Lewis informing him of prospects before us…stating two plans…dispatched one man and Horse and directed the party to get ready to march back…The plan I stated to Captain Lewis if he agrees with me…is…to procure as many Horses (one for each man)…proceed on by land to some navigable part of the Columbia River, or to the Ocean…a second plan to divide the party. One part to attempt this difficult river with what provision we had, and the remainder to pass by land on Horse back…"

August 25, 1805. NOTE: Captain Lewis, in casual conversation with Charbonneau discovers that he knows of a plan the Indians have to not assist the Expedition in taking their baggage to the water of the Columbia as was previously promised. Lewis severely reprimands Charbonneau for his "not sufficient sagacity to see the consequences" and immediately called a meeting with the three Chiefs. In his conversation with them, they admit to a plan to take their people, the next morning, to the Missouri to hunt leaving the Expedition to fend for themselves. As it turned out, it was Cameahwait's idea and he admitted that he had been induced to that measure from seeing all his people hungry. Lewis demanded that this order be immediately countermanded and that they depart for the river with the baggage immediately that day. While on the march to the Columbia, Lewis is almost shot when a bullet rebounded from the water when Frazier was shooting at a duck. Meanwhile, Clark was struggling to locate a trail and his hunters shot nothing for food.

August 26, 1805. Captain Lewis. "One of the women who had been assisting in the transportation of the baggage halted…I inquired of Cameahwait the cause of her detention…was informed by him in an unconcerned manner that she had halted to bring forth a child and would soon overtake us. About an hour the woman arrived with her newborn babe and passed us on her way to the camp apparently as well as she ever was….I found Colter here who had just arrived with a letter from Captain Clark (describing the two plans for continuing)...I found it a folly to think of attempting to descend this river in canoes and therefore determined to commence the purchase of Horses in the morning from the Indians." **Captain Clark.** "...not one mouthful to eat until night...one of my men shot a salmon...gave us supper."

August 27, 1805. Captain Clark. "...Captain Lewis would join me about 12 o'clock today...my party hourly complaining of their wretched situation...no game of any kind except a few fish."

August 28, 1805. Captain Clark. "...Captain Lewis...had procured 22 Horses for our route through by land...my hunters killed nothing."

August 29, 1805. Captain Clark. "...I...join Captain Lewis...found him much engaged in...attempting to purchase a few more Horses...our wish is to get a Horse for each man to carry our baggage...I purchased a Horse for which I gave my Pistol, 100 balls, powder and a knife. Our hunters killed 2 Deer...this meat was a great treat to me as I had eaten none for 8 days past."

August 30, 1805. Captain Clark. "...29 total Horses...set out on our route down the river by land guided by my old guide...Proceeded on 12 miles today." **NOTE:** They are following the Lemhi River.

The following Journal entries refer to maps 18 and 19.

August 31 – September 8, 1805. NOTE: Captain Clark's phrases and words edited from his entries describe the toil and hardship the Expedition endured during these nine days. **Captain Clark.** "proceeded on...let our Horses graze...proceeded on...high rugged hills...rain today...continued (to travel) all night...shot two Bear...could get neither of them...through thickets...cut a road...rocky hill sides...Horses were in perpetual danger...Horses fell, some turned over, and others slipped down steep hillsides...crippled and 2 gave out...Horses very stiff...steep sides...slipping down...injured...great difficultly...covered with snow...immense hills...worst roads...snow...sleet...very cold...wet...ascended...descended...nothing but berries to eat...crossed a mountain...struck a river...shallow...stony...rained...nothing to eat...rainy day...snow top mountains...did not make camp until dark for the want of a good place...Prickly Pear..."

September 9, 1805. Captain Lewis. "The guide informed us that a man might pass to the Missouri (from this point) in four days." **NOTE:** Lewis calculated the point of intersect on the Missouri would be about 30 miles above the *gates of the Rocky Mountains* where the Expedition was in mid July!

September 10, 1805. Captain Lewis. "...one of our hunters returned accompanied by three men of the Flathead Nation...the Indians were mounted on very fine Horses...they told us they were in great haste. We gave them some boiled venison...two...departed...the third remained, having agreed to continue with us as a guide, and to introduce us to his relations whom he informed us were numerous and resided in the plain below the mountains on the Columbia River. From whence he said the water was good and capable of being navigated to the sea...he said it would require five sleeps (days)."

September 11, 1805. Captain Clark. "...our Flathead Indian, being restless, thought proper to leave us and proceed on alone."

September 12, 1805. Captain Clark. "The road...is very bad passing over hills and through steep hollows...party and Horses much fatigued."

September 13. 1805. Captain Clark. "...passed several springs...found this water nearly boiling hot...spouted from the rocks." **NOTE:** From the Original Journals of Lewis and Clark, Thwaites, 1904, vol. 3, part 1, p. 64, footnote by O.D. Wheeler; "There is now (1903) a good road up Lolo Creek to both springs, and a daily stage-coach to and from Missoula."

September 14, 1805. Captain Clark. "...we were compelled to kill a Colt for our men and selves to eat for the want of meat and we named the South fork Colt-Killed Creek, and this river we call Flathead River…The mountains which we passed today much worse than yesterday…our men and Horses much fatigued…"

September 15, 1805. Captain Clark. "Several Horses slipped and rolled down steep hills…the one which carried my desk and small trunk turned over and rolled down a mountain for 40 yards and lodged against a tree, broke the desk…From this mountain, I could observe high rugged mountains in every direction as far as I could see…could only make 12 miles…"

September 16, 1805. Captain Clark. "…began to snow…continued all day…by night we found it from 6 to 8 inches deep…I have been wet and as cold in every part as I ever was in my life, indeed I was at one time fearful my feet would freeze in the thin moccasins which I wore…"

September 17, 1805. Captain Clark. "Snow falling from the trees which kept us wet…Killed a few pheasants which was not sufficient for our supper which compelled us to kill something, a Colt being the most useless part of our stock, he fell a prey to our appetites…made only 10 miles today."

September 18, 1805. Captain Clark. "I proceeded on in advance with six hunters to try and find…something to kill…Creek passing to the left which I call Hungry Creek as at that place we had nothing to eat."

September 19, 1805. Captain Lewis. "…several of the men are unwell of the dysentery. Breaking out, or eruptions of the skin have also been common." **Captain Clark.** "…we found a Horse…him killed and hung up for the party after taking-off a breakfast for ourselves which we thought fine…proceed on…"

September 20, 1805. Captain Clark. "I set out early…descended…to a small plain in which I found many Indian lodges…met 3 boys…sent them forward to the village…a man…told me…his great Chief, who had set out 3 days previous with all the warriors of the nation to war…would return in 15 or 18 days…They call themselves *Cho pun-nish or Pierced noses* (Chopunnish, or Nez Perce)… I find myself very unwell all the evening from eating the fish and roots too freely."

Captain Lewis. "We had proceeded about 2 miles when we found the greater part of a Horse which Captain Clark had met with and killed for us. He informed me by note that he should proceed as fast as possible to the level country which lay to the S.W. of us."

The following Journal entries refer to map 20.

September 21, 1805. Captain Clark. "Sent out all the hunters…I myself delayed with the Chief to prevent suspicion and to collect…information…about the river and country in advance…I am very sick today and puke which relieves me." **Captain Lewis.** "…continued down…and encamped in a small open bottom where there was tolerable food for our Horses. I directed the Horses to be hobbled to prevent delay in the morning being determined to make a forced march tomorrow in order to reach, if possible, the open country. We killed a few pheasants, and I killed a prairie Wolf which together with the balance of our Horse beef and some crawfish which we obtain in the creek, enabled us to make one more hearty meal, not knowing where the next was to be found."

September 22, 1805. Captain Lewis. "Notwithstanding my positive directions to hobble the Horses last evening, one of the men neglected to comply…this…detained us…we arrived at 5 o'clock in the afternoon…the pleasure I now felt in having triumphed over the Rocky Mountains and descending once more to a level and fertile country where there was every rational hope of finding a comfortable subsistence for myself and party can be more readily conceived than expressed, nor was the flattering prospect of the final success of the expedition less pleasing."

NOTE: There was a story told by the Nez Perce Indians that when Lewis and Clark visited them they had plotted to kill all in the Expedition. They were spared by the influence of a Nez Perce woman who had received help from white men in escaping from her capture by hostile Indians.

September 23, 1805. The men spent this day recuperating and trading small items for food. In the evening they moved to a second Indian camp.

September 24-25, 1805. Captain Clark. "Set out for the River...formed a camp on a large island." **NOTE:** Still recuperating. Clark gave some of the men Rushes Pills. Captain Lewis was very sick and did not write.

September 26, 1805. Captain Clark. "...proceeded on...formed camp...ready to commence building canoes...tomorrow...Captain Lewis still very unwell."

September 27, 1805. Captain Clark. "...commenced building 5 canoes...hunters returned sick without meat...Captain Lewis very sick."

September 26 - October 6, 1805. NOTE: The Expedition did not move. They spent all their time reconditioning themselves and their equipment. They built their canoes in the Indian manor, burning out the inside rather than chopping it out with axes. They branded their Horses and gave them to some Indians to take care of, having bartered a knife and other trinkets for the service. The last evening before they departed they dug a hole and buried their saddles, a canister of powder, and a bag of balls. During this entire period, the Expedition subsisted on nothing more than fish, roots, three Deer, one Horse, one small prairie Wolf and some berries. Now the Expedition was going down river for the first time in a year and a half. Think of the joy to not be pushing, pulling, and paddling against the current.

October 7, 1805. Captain Clark. "I continued very unwell but obliged to attend everything. All the canoes put into the water and loaded...proceeded on past 10 rapids which were dangerous...mended a small leak."

October 8-9, 1805. Captain Clark. "Passed 15 rapids...one canoe...split open...filled with water and sunk...everything wet. All day drying goods and articles...our old guide (Old Toby)...left us and had been seen running up the river...without receiving his pay...or letting us know anything of his intentions...Captain Lewis recovering fast." **NOTE:** It is speculated that Old Toby was simply terrified of "shooting the rapids" with these "crazy" white men.

October 10, 1805. Captain Clark. "...we landed near 8 lodges of Indians...having passed...rapids, several of them very bad...we purchased fish and Dogs...dined and proceeded on...The Indians came down all courses of this river on each side on Horses to view us as we were descending...not one stick of timber on the river...flies extremely bad."

October 11, 1805. Captain Clark. "I saw a curious sweat house underground with a small hole at top to pass in or throw in the hot stones...to create the temperature of heat they wish...passed today nine rapids."

October 12, 1805. Captain Clark. "...rapids...very bad...long and dangerous about 2 miles in length, and many turns necessary to steer clear of the rocks which appeared to be in every direction."

The following Journal entries refer to map 21.

October 13, 1805. Captain Clark. "We should make more portages (around rapids) if the season was not so far advanced and time precious with us."

October 14, 1805. Captain Clark. "We found some split timber the parts of a house which the Indians had very securely covered with stone. We also observed a place where the Indians had buried their fish. We have made it a point at all times not to take anything belonging to the Indians even their wood. But at this time we are compelled to violate that rule and take a part of the split timber we find here buried for firewood, as no other is to be found in any direction."

October 15, 1805. Captain Clark. "...only made 29 miles today, owing to the detention in passing rapids."

October 16-17, 1805. The Columbia River. Captain Clark. "After getting safely over the rapid and having taken dinner, set out and proceeded on seven miles to the junction of this river and the Columbia which joins from the N.W...In every direction from the junction of those rivers the country is one continued plain, low and rises from the water gradually...We halted...smoke with the Indians who had collected there in great numbers to view us...spoke to their Chief...informing them of our friendly disposition...gave the principal Chief a large Medal, Shirt and handkerchief. A 2nd Chief a Medal of small size...Indians were drying Salmon...for the purpose of food and fuel...The number of dead Salmon on the shores and floating in the river is incredible to say...and at this season they have only to collect the fish, split them open and dry them on their scaffolds...how far they have to raft their timber they make their scaffolds of I could not learn, but there is no timber of any sort...in any direction...The waters of this river is clear, and a Salmon may be seen at the depth of 15 or 20 feet...one man set about preparing me something to eat. First he brought in a piece of a drift log of pine and with a wedge of the Elks horn, and a mallet of stone...he split the log into small pieces and laid it open on the fire on which he put round stones. A woman handed him a basket of water and a large Salmon about half dried. When the stones were hot, he put them into the basket of water with the fish, which was soon sufficiently boiled for use. It was then taken out put on a platter of rushes neatly made and set before me...the boiled fish...was delicious."

October 18, 1805. Captain Clark. "We thought it necessary to lay in a store of provision for our voyage...we purchased 40 Dogs...Took our leave of the Chiefs and all those about us and proceeded on down the great Columbia River."

October 19, 1805. NOTE: While Captain Clark was waiting for Lewis, he noticed some Indians on the opposite side of the river who seemed to be very afraid of them. Thinking that they had not heard of their friendly intentions, Clark went to meet them. When he arrived, they had hidden from him in a large house. Upon entering, he discovered 32 people "crying and ringing their hands, others hanging their heads. Clark tried to befriend these people but they were not completely pacified until Captain Lewis showed up with Sacajawea. **Captain Clark.** "As soon as they saw the squaw wife of the interpreter (Charbonneau) they pointed to her and...they immediately came out and appeared to assume new life. The sight of this Indian woman...confirmed those people of our friendly intentions, as no woman ever accompanies a war party of Indians in this quarter."

October 20, 1805. Captain Clark. "We made 42 miles today!"

October 21, 1805. Captain Clark. "We could not cook...for the want of wood or something to burn...One of our party, J. Collins, presented us with some very good beer made of the *Pa-shi-co-quar-mash* bread...by frequently wet, molded, and soured."

The following Journal entries refer to map 22.

October 22-23, 1805. Captain Clark. "We landed and walked down accompanied by an old man to view the falls, and the best route for to make a portage...the distance, 1200 yards...we returned...to the head of the rapids and took every article except the canoes across the portage where I had formed a camp...We dispatched two men to examine the river on the opposite side and they reported that the canoes could be taken down a narrow channel...which place the Indians take over their canoes...we purchased a Dog for supper." **October 23.** "Took the canoes over the portage...with much difficulty...one of the old Chiefs who had accompanied us from the head of the river, informed us that he heard the Indians say that the nation below intended to kill us. We examined all the arms...complete the ammunition to 100 rounds. The natives leave us earlier this evening than usual...we are at all times and places on our guard...our two old Chiefs appeared very uneasy this evening."

October 24, 1805. Captain Clark. "...the natives approached us this morning with great caution. Our two old Chiefs expressed a desire to return to their band...We requested them to stay with us two nights longer...they replied they were anxious to return...we insisted...they agreed. Our views were to detain those Chiefs with us...that they might inform us of any designs of the natives, and if possible, to bring about a peace between them and the tribes below...I set out with the party and proceeded on down...a tremendous black rock presented itself high and steep appearing to choke up the river. Nor could I see where the water passed further...I heard a great roaring. I landed...went...to the top of this rock...from...which I could see the difficulties we had to pass for several miles below. At this place the water of this great river is compressed into a channel between two rocks not exceeding 45 yards wide and continues for a ¼ of a mile when it again widens…as the portage of our canoes…would be impossible…I thought…by good steering we could pass down safe. Accordingly I determined to pass through this place notwithstanding the horrid appearance of this agitated gut swelling, boiling and whirling in every direction, (which from the top of the rock did not appear as bad as when I was in it). However we passed safe to the astonishment of all the Indians…I dispatched a sufficient number of the good swimmers back for the 2 canoes above…the party and canoes…all arrived safe…We formed a camp near the village. The principal Chief from the nation below…visited us, and afforded a favorable opportunity of bringing about a peace and good understanding between this Chief and his people and the two Chiefs who accompany us which we have the satisfaction to say we have accomplished, as we have every reason to believe and that those two bands or nations are, and will be, on the most friendly terms…Peter Cruzatte played on the violin and the men danced."

October 25-26-27, 1805. Captain Clark. "…we determined to attempt the channel after breakfast…the Indians pointed out as the worst place in passing through the gut…we concluded…portage our most valuable articles…run the canoes through…a great number of Indians viewing us…the first three canoes passed through very well, the 4th nearly filled with water, the last passed by taking in a little water. Thus safely below what I conceive to be the worst part of this channel felt myself extremely gratified and pleased…had not proceeded more than 2 miles before than the canoe, which filled with water…was in great danger of being lost…our situation well calculated to defend ourselves from any designs of the natives…fleas which the party got on them at the upper and great falls, are very troublesome and difficult to get rid of, particularly as the men have not a change of clothes to put on. They strip off their clothes and kill the fleas during which time they remain naked."

October 28, 1805. Captain Clark. "…we were about to set out…observed an Indian with round hat, jacket, and wore his hair cued…we proceeded on…we landed at a village…I saw a British musket, a cutlass and several brass tea kettles…The wind, which is our delay, does not retard…their (Indian) canoes…they are built of White Cedar or Pine, very light, wide in the middle and tapers at each end, with heads of animals carved on the bow…we encamped on the sand, wet and disagreeable…"

October 29, 1805. Captain Clark. "Came to…a village of 7 houses…I observed in the lodge of the Chief…a scarlet and blue cloth, sword, jacket and hat…he…took out his bow and quiver to show me…then directed his wife to hand him his medicine bag which he opened and showed us 14 fingers…of his enemies which he had taken in war…I concluded they were Snake Indians…we purchased three Dogs…we smoked…all much pleased with the violin."

October 30-31, 1805. Captain Clark. "Day dark and disagreeable…I took two men…to examine the Chute…this great Chute or falls is about ½ mile, with the water of this great river compressed within the space of 150 paces…with great velocity, foaming, and boiling in a most horrible manner …I found by examination that we must make a portage of the greater proportion of our stores 2 ½ miles, and the canoes we could haul over the rocks."

November 1, 1805. Captain Clark. "The Indians who arrived last evening took their canoes on their shoulders and carried them below the great Chute…we got the 4 large canoes over by slipping them over the rocks on poles placed across from one rock to another, and at some places along partial stream of river. In passing those canoes over the rocks, three of them received injuries which obliged us to delay to have them repaired." **NOTE:** Clark describes the Indians having flat heads and notes seeing young children "in the press for the purpose of compressing their heads in their infancy into a certain form, between two boards."

November 2, 1805. Captain Clark. "Examined the rapid below us…the danger appearing too great to hazard our canoes loaded. Dispatched all the men who could not swim with loads to the end of the portage below…canoes arrived safe. Here we breakfast…Passed a rapid at 2 miles and one at 4 miles…passed three islands covered with tall timber…here the river widens to near a mile, and the bottoms are more extensive and thickly timbered…we encamped under a high projecting rock…here the mountains leave the river on each side…we made 29 miles today from the Great Chute."

November 3, 1805. Captain Clark. "The fog so thick this morning that we could not see a man 50 steps off. This fog detained us until 10 o'clock at which time we set out…arrived at the entrance of a river…and did not appear to be 4 inches deep in any part. I attempted to wade this stream and to my astonishment found the bottom a quick sand and impassable. I call to the canoes to put to shore. I got into the canoe and landed below the mouth…A mountain which we supposed to be Mount Hood is…about 47 miles distant…and is of a conical form but rugged…proceeded on to the center of a large island in the middle of the river which we call Diamond Island from its appearance." **NOTE:** This Island is now Government Island near Portland, Oregon.

November 4, 1805. Captain Clark. "We landed at a village of 25 houses…This village contained 200 Men…counted 25 canoes…gave us a roundish root about the size of a small Irish potato which they roasted in the ember until they became soft. This root they call *Wap-pa-to*…has an agreeable taste and answers very well in place of bread…joined Captain Lewis at a place he had landed with the party for dinner. Soon after several canoes of Indians from the village above came down dressed for the purpose, as I supposed of paying us a friendly visit. They had scarlet and blue blankets, sailor jackets, overalls, shirts and hats independent of their usual dress. The most of them had either muskets or pistols and tin flasks to hold their powder. Those fellows we found assuming and disagreeable. However, we smoked with them and treated them with every attention and friendship. During the time we were at dinner those fellows stole my pipe tomahawk, which they were smoking with. (**NOTE:** Remember this on the return trip.) I immediately search each man and the canoes but could find nothing of my tomahawk. While searching for the tomahawk, one of those scoundrels stole a coat…which was found stuffed under the root of a tree near the place they sat. We became much displeased with those fellows which they discovered and moved off on their return home to their village…The Indians which we have passed today…are thievishly inclined as we have experienced."

November 5, 1805. Captain Clark. "I slept but very little last night for the noises kept up during the whole of the night by the Swans, Geese, White and Grey Brant Ducks, etc. on a small sand Island close under the Larboard Side. They were immensely numerous and their noise horrid…The day proved cloudy with rain the greater part of it, we are all wet, cold and disagreeable…This is the first night which we have been entirely clear of Indians since our arrival on the water of the Columbia River."

The following Journal entries refer to map 23.
November 6, 1805. Captain Clark. "…set out early…we came too to dine…found the woods so thick with under growth…could not get any distance into the island…killed nothing today…cloudy with rain all day. We are all wet and disagreeable. Had large fires made…dried our bedding and kill fleas."

November 7, 1805. The Pacific Ocean at last. Captain Clark. "A cloudy, foggy morning…set out early…fog so thick we could not see across the river. Two canoes of Indians met and returned with us to their village…after delaying at this village…we set out piloted by an Indian dressed in a sailor's dress, to the main channel of the river…We proceeded on…under a high mountainous country…and encamped under a high hill…our small canoe, which got separated in the fog this morning joined us this evening…Great joy in camp! We are in view of the Ocean. This great Pacific Ocean which we have been so long anxious to see. And the roaring, or noise, made by the waves breaking on the rocky shores may be heard distinctly." **NOTE:** Actually what the Expedition thought was the Pacific Ocean was the estuary where the Columbia River and the Pacific Ocean meet. The mouth of the Columbia River expands to a width of over 15 miles and acts, smells, sounds, and looks like the Ocean.

November 8-9, 1805. Captain Clark. "...we took the advantage of a returning tide and proceeded on...we found the swells or waves so high that we thought it imprudent to proceed...we are all wet and disagreeable, as we have been for several days past...we have not level land sufficient for an encampment and for our baggage to lie clear of the tide. The high hill jutting so close and steep that we cannot retreat back, and the water of the river too salt to be used...the seas rolled and tossed the canoes in such a manner this evening that several of our party were sea sick." **November 9. Captain Clark.** "Wind hard...at 2 o'clock P.M. the flood tide came in accompanied with immense waves and heavy winds...with every exertion and the strictest attention by every individual of the party was scarcely sufficient to save our canoes from being crushed by those monstrous trees many of them nearly 200 feet long and from 4 to 7 feet through. Our camp entirely under water during the height of the tide. Every man as wet as water could make them...the rain continued all day. At 4 o'clock P.M. the wind shifted...and blew with great violence immediately from the Ocean for about two hours...At this dismal point we must spend another night as the wind and waves are too high to proceed."

November 10-14, 1805. Captain Clark. "The wind has lulled and the waves are not high...we proceed on...10 miles...the waves became so high that we were compelled to return about 2 miles to a place we could unload our canoes...when the river appeared calm, we loaded and set out, but was obliged to return finding the waves too high...we again unloaded...stowed the loading on a rock above the tide water and formed a camp on the drift logs which appeared to be the only situation we could find...we are all wet, the rain having continued all day...nothing to eat but dried fish pounded which we brought from the falls." **November 11. Captain Clark.** "During the last tide the logs on which we lay was all on float...5 Indians came down in a canoe...tremendous waves breaking with great violence against the shores, rain falling in torrents...we purchase of the Indians, 13 Red Char which we found to be an excellent fish...those people left us and crossed the river...through the highest waves I ever saw a small vessel ride. Those Indians are certainly the best canoe navigators I ever saw. Rained all day." **November 12. Captain Clark.** "...the waves tremendous, breaking with great fury against the rocks and trees on which we were encamped. Our situation is dangerous. We took the advantage of a low tide and moved our camp around a point to a small wet bottom, at the mouth of a brook...It would be distress to see our situation, all wet and cold...half the bedding is rotten...in a wet bottom scarcely large enough to contain us, our baggage half a mile from us, and canoes at the mercy of the waves...Fortunately for us our men are healthy." **November 13. Captain Clark.** "...we dispatched 3 men, Colter, Willard and Shannon...in the Indian canoe to get around the point if possible and examine the river, and the bay below for a good harbor for our canoes to lie in safety...nothing to eat but pounded fish." **November 14. Captain Clark.** "...Colter returned by land and informed us...that it was but a short distance from where we lay around the point to a beautiful sand beach, which continued for a long ways. That he had found a good harbor in the mouth of a creek near 2 Indian lodges...Willard and Shannon had proceeded on...Captain Lewis concluded to proceed on land and find, if possible, the white people the Indians say is below and examine if a bay is situated near the mouth of this river...if there is white traders, to find them."

November 15-24, 1805. Captain Clark. "Fortunately the wind lay about 3 o'clock... we loaded in great haste and set out past the blustering point below which is a sand beach...on which is a large village of 36 houses deserted...and in full possession of the fleas...Shannon and 5 Indians met me here, Shannon informed me...the Indians with him were rogues. They had the night before, stole both his and Willard's guns from under their heads. Captain Lewis and party arrived at the camp of those Indians at so timely a period that the Indians were alarmed and delivered up the guns...I concluded to form a camp on the highest spot I could find...and proceed no further...the Ocean is immediately in front and gives us an extensive view of it from Cape Disappointment to Point Adams...Evening fare and pleasant, our men all comfortable in the camps they have made of the boards they found at the town above." **November 16-23. NOTE:** The Expedition rested, repaired their equipment and explored Cape Disappointment, the bay and the seacoast to the North. Lewis and Clark noted in their Journals that a great many of the Indians had guns, powder, ball, items for cooking, and clothes from the trading ships that frequented the area. These Indians knew how to barter. In fact, one of the biggest problems that faced the Expedition was that their supply of trade goods was almost exhausted. **November 24. Captain Clark.** "Being now determined to go into winter quarters as soon as possible...induces every individual of the party to make diligent inquiries of the natives for the part of the country in which the wild animals are most plenty. They generally agree that the most Elk is to the opposite shore. (The South side of the bay) The Elk being an animal much larger than Deer, (was) easier to kill and meat and skins better for the clothes of our party. Added to this a convenient situation to the sea coast where we could make salt, and probability of vessels coming into the mouth of the Columbia...conclude to cross the river and examine the opposite side, and if a sufficient quantity of Elk...added to the...advantages of being near the sea coast, (versus inland)...the climate which must be from every appearance much milder than that above the 1st range of Mountains...The Indians...give an account of but little snow, and the weather which we have experienced since we arrived in the neighborhood of the sea coast has been very warm...if this should be the case it will most certainly be the best situation of our naked party dressed as they are altogether in leather."

November 25. Captain Clark. "The wind being high rendered it impossible for us to cross the river from our camp...determined to proceed on up where it was narrow...near our encampment of the 7th..."

November 26, 1805. Captain Clark. "We set out early and crossed...to the South side of the Columbia..."

November 27 - December 6, 1805. NOTE: The Expedition was desperately in need of a permanent winter camp. The winter storms of the Pacific Ocean, with their torrential rains and violent winds, kept the party land-bound. They found it nearly impossible to go through the forests in quest of anything. The density of the pine forests and undergrowth including the tremendous number of deadfalls and debris made them impenetrable without extraordinary effort. They lacked a good diet of meat and were in need of new clothes. **November 27. Captain Clark.** "...Indians came...to sell, they asked such high prices that we were unable to purchase anything...we proceeded on between many small islands...the waves became so high we were compelled to land, unload and draw up the canoes...we are all wet and disagreeable...The water at our camp salt, that above on the isthmus, fresh and fine." **November 29. NOTE:** Captain Lewis and five men got in the only canoe that could ride the waves and took off to locate game and a place to winter. **December 2. NOTE:** Joseph Fields killed an Elk six miles from camp. This was the first Elk killed on the western side of the Rocky Mountains. **December 3. NOTE:** Pryor and Gibson shot six Elk. Again at great distance from the camp. Things started to look up. **December 5. NOTE:** Captain Lewis returned and informed Clark that he had found their wintering location and that it had "sufficient number of Elk." **December 6. Captain Clark.** "We accordingly determined to proceed...as soon as the wind and weather should permit and commence building huts..."

December 7, 1805. Captain Clark. "This morning fair. Have everything put on board the canoes and set out to the place Captain Lewis had viewed and thought well situated for winter quarters."

5. Wintering at Fort Clatsop. December 8, 1805 – March 22, 1806.

NOTE: If there were a word to describe the living conditions at Fort Clatsop it would have to be **"wet."** It rained 85 out of the 105 days they were encamped. **Captain Clark described a typical day of weather on January 1, 1806.** "Sun visible for a few minutes about 11 A.M. The changes of the weather are exceedingly sudden. Sometimes, though seldom, the sun is visible for a few moments, the next it hails and rains. Then it ceases and remains cloudy. The wind blows and it again rains. The wind blows by squalls most generally, and is almost invariably from the S.W. These vicissitudes of the weather happen two, three or more times a day."

The shelter was built in a scant 15 days. It was very small. Only 50 feet square and consisted of a contiguous outer wall to enclose everything, and keep the Indians out. It had seven rooms and a parade ground through the center. Captains Lewis and Clark shared the larger of the rooms. Charbonneau, Sacajawea and "Little Pomp" were together, and each of the three squads of men had a room. There was a common orderly room and a meat storage locker. (See web site: http://www.lewis-clark.org/FTCLVIRTUAL/fc_sitem.htm) A latrine was located outside the Fort. Thirty-three people shared this small home from December 24, 1805 through March 22, 1806.

During the occupation of Fort Clatsop, the Expedition kept very busy. Everyday was spent gathering food. Elk was the primary item on the menu. The men preferred Elk above other offerings and it was their only source of good leather for clothes and moccasins. They supplemented their diet with waterfowl, seafood, Beaver, Deer and vegetable items. Beaver and Otter were trapped for their fur to keep the men warm. Salt was the first item the Expedition had exhausted so a number of men spent time working at a salt cairn located on the beach 15 miles from the main camp. Their objective was to make a gallon of salt per day by boiling seawater. Everybody but Captain Clark loved salt on food. This was also the time for the men to make themselves new clothing. What they had, had literally rotted-away due to the incessant wetness of the Pacific Northwest winter. Most in demand were tuff moccasins, and lots of them. The Captains spent their time rewriting and editing their Journals, making maps, and visiting and writing about the Indians, plants, and animals of the region. If it moved, either by its own power or the power of the wind, Lewis wrote about it.

Captain Lewis writes about Indian Culture:

Women. "They (the Indians) do not hold the virtue of their women in high estimation, and will prostitute…for a fishing hook…(However) not withstanding the servile manner in which they treat their women, they pay much more respect to their judgment and opinions in many respects than most Indian nations. Their women are permitted to speak freely before them, and sometimes appear to command with a tone of authority. They (the Men) generally consult them in their traffic and act in conformity to their opinions."

Hunting. "In hunting are the gun, the bow and arrow, deadfalls, pits, snares, and spears or gigs. Their guns are usually of an inferior quality being old American and British muskets…they appear not to have been long accustomed to firearms…they have no rifles (versus smoothbore). Their guns and ammunition they reserve for the Elk, Deer and Bear…they keep their powder in small tin flasks which they obtain with their ammunition from the traders. When they happen to have no ball or shot, they substitute gravel or pieces of pot metal, and are insensible of the damage done thereby to their guns. The bow and arrow is the most common instrument among them…every man being furnished with them…employed…in hunting every species of animal…(Lewis continues on describing how they make their bow and arrow.) many of the Elk we have killed…have been wounded with these arrows…the barb remaining in the animal and grown up in the flesh…deadfalls and snares are used in taking Wolf, the Raccoon and Fox…the spear or gig is used to take the Sea Otter, the common Otter…and Beaver…their pits are employed in taking the Elk, and of course are large and deep. Some of them a cube of 12 or 14 feet. These are usually placed by the side of a large fallen tree which as well as the pit lie across the roads frequented by the Elk. These pits are disguised with slender boughs of trees and moss. The unwary Elk in passing the tree precipitates himself into the pit which is sufficiently deep to prevent his escape, and thus taken."

Fishing. "In fishing (they) employ the common straight net, the scooping or dipping net with a long handle, the gig and the hook and line…their nets and fishing lines are made of the silk-grass or white cedar bark, and their hooks are generally of European manufacture, though before whites visited them they made hooks of bone…"

Culinary articles. "…consist of wooden bowls or troths, baskets, wooden spoons and wooden squires or spits. Their wooden bowls and troths…are generally dug out of a solid piece. These are extremely well executed and many of them neatly carved. The larger vessels with hand-holes…In these vessels they boil their fish or flesh by means of hot stones which they immerse in the water with the article to be boiled. They also render the oil of fish or other animals in the same manner. Their baskets are formed of Cedar bark and Beargrass so closely interwoven with the fingers that they are watertight without the aid of gum or rosin. Some of these are highly ornamented with strands of Beargrass, which they dye of several colors and interweave in a great variety of figures. This serves a double purpose of holding their water or wearing on their heads…it is for the construction of these baskets that the Beargrass becomes an article of traffic among the natives. This grass grows only on their high mountains near the snowy region…Their meat is roasted with sharp squires the end of which is inserted in the meal with the other set erect in the ground. The spit for roasting fish has its upper extremity split, and between…the fish is inserted…head down,…and secured with a string. The sides of the fish…are expanded by means of small splinters of wood, which extend crosswise the fish. A small mat of rushes…is the usual plate or dish on which their fish, flesh, roots or berries are served. They make a number of bags and baskets…of Cedar bark…in these they (store) dried fish, roots, berries…"

House Construction. "…they are from 14 to 20 feet wide and from 20 to 60 feet in length and accommodate one or more families…posts of split timber…are secured with strings of the cedar bark…smaller sticks of timber are now provided and placed by pairs in the form of rafters…the ends, sides and partition are formed with…boards of about two inches thick, which are sunk in the ground…secured to the rafters by chords of Cedar bark…the roof is then covered with a double range of thin boards, and an aperture of 2 by 3 feet is left in the center of the roof to permit the smoke to pass. These houses are sometimes sunk to the depth of 4 or 5 feet in which case the eve of the house comes nearly to the surface of the earth….mats are spread around the fire on all sides."

Canoes. "The natives inhabiting the lower portion of the Columbia River make their canoes remarkably neat, light and well adapted for riding high waves…They are built of White Cedar or Arborvitae generally, but sometimes of the Fir. They are cut out of a solid stick of timber. The gunwales at the upper edge fold over outwards…forming a kind of rim to the canoe to prevent the water beating into it. They all (were) furnished with…crossbars…these serve to lift and manage the canoe on land…some of the large canoes are upwards of 50 feet long and will carry from 8 to 10 thousand lbs. or from 20 to 30 persons…some of them…are waxed, painted and ornamented with curious images at bow and stern."

Excerpts from the Journals while encamped at Fort Clatsop.
December 25, 1805. Captain Clark. "At day light this morning we awoke by the discharge of fire arms of all our party and a salute, shouts and a song which the whole party joined in…"

December 26, 1805. Captain Clark. "We dry our wet articles...and have our blankets (de) flea-ed...so abundant that we have to have them killed out of our blankets everyday or get no sleep..."

January 1, 1806. Captain Lewis. "Our repast of this day...consisted principally in the anticipation of the 1st day of January 1807, when in the bosom of our friends we hope to participate..."

January 6, 1806. NOTE: Sacajawea got very upset. She was told she was not going to be permitted to see both the ocean and the large whale that had washed up on the shore. She was permitted to go!

On the Indians practice of seeming to swallow tobacco smoke: "...they frequently give us sounding proofs of it's creating a dismorality of order in the abdomen."

Proof that other white men visit the Indians: "The Indians inform us that they (the sailors) speak the same language with ourselves, and give us proofs...'damned rascal'...'son of a bitch', etc."

January 30, 1806. Captain Lewis. "Nothing transpired today worthy of notice."

February 2, 1806. Captain Lewis. "...all are pleased that one month of the time which binds us to Fort Clatsop and which separates us from our friends has now elapsed."

February 7, 1806. Captain Clark. "This evening we had what I call an excellent supper. It consisted of a marrowbone, a piece of brisket of boiled Elk that had the appearance of a little fat on it. This for Fort Clatsop is living in high style, and in fact feasting."

February 22, 1806. Captain Lewis. "We were visited today by two Clatsop women...two brought a parcel of excellent hats made of Cedar bark and ornamented with Beargrass. Two of these hats had been made by measures which Captain Clark and myself had given one of the women some time since with a request to make each of us a hat. They fit us very well and are in the form we desired them. We purchased all their hats and distributed them among the party."

February 24, 1806. NOTE: Captain Lewis describes eating a small fish that is running the Columbia River and provided to him by *Comowool* the Clatsop Chief. **Captain Lewis.** "I find them best when cooked in Indian style, which is by roasting a number of them together on a wooden spit without any previous preparation whatever. They are so fat they require no additional sauce, and I think them superior to any fish I ever tasted, even more delicate and luscious than the Whitefish of the (Great) lakes...the bones are so soft and fine that they form no obstruction in eating this fish."

March 17, 1806. Captain Lewis. "We have had our pirogues prepared for our departure and shall set out as soon as the weather will permit."

March 18, 1806. Captain Lewis. "...rain and hail...nothing further could be done to the canoes."

March 19, 1806. Captain Lewis. "...rain and hail...nothing further could be done to the canoes."

March 20, 1806. Captain Lewis. "...rain and blow so violently..."

March 21, 1806. Captain Lewis. "...could not set out."

March 22, 1806. Captain Lewis. "...it continues to rain in such a manner that there is no possibility of getting our canoes completed."

March 23, 1806. Captain Lewis. "The wind is pretty high but it seems to be the common opinion that we can pass point William. We accordingly distributed the baggage and directed the canoes to be launched and loaded for our departure. At 1 P.M. we bid a final adieu to Fort Clatsop."

6. Homeward Bound. March 24 to September 26, 1806.

March 24, 1806. Captain Lewis. "We arrived at the *Cathlahmah* village...purchased some Wappato...a Dog...and a hat...set out...we mistook our route, which an Indian perceiving, pursued, overtook us and put us in the right channel."

March 25, 1806. Captain Lewis. "...halted and dined...Clatsops came to us in a canoe loaded with dried Anchovies...and Sturgeon."

The following Journal entries refer to map 22.

March 26, 1806. Captain Lewis. "...tobacco...our stock is now reduced...our men who have been accustomed to the use...suffer much for the want of it. They substitute the bark of the wild crab which they chew...the smokers substitute the inner bark of the red willow..."

March 27, 1806. Captain Lewis. "...the Skillutes who came along side in a small canoe...gave us dried Anchovies, Sturgeon, Wappato, Quamash...most of the party were served...with as much as they could eat...resumed our voyage."

March 28, 1806. Captain Lewis. "...set out very early and at 9 A.M. arrived at...Deer Island where we found our hunters...they had arrived last evening...they killed seven Deer...and brought in the remnant which the Vultures and Eagles had left us. These birds had devoured 4 Deer in the course of a few hours...Drewyer also killed a Tiger Cat."

March 29, 1806. Captain Lewis. "The Garter Snakes are innumerable and are seen entwined around each other in large bundles of forty or fifty...Frogs are croaking...heard a...Hooting Owl hollowing this evening." **Captain Clark.** "...the natives...collect great quantities of Wappato which the women collect by getting into the water, sometimes to their neck holding by a small canoe and with their feet loosen the Wappato or bulb of the root from the bottom...those deep roots are the largest and best..."

March 30, 1806. Captain Lewis. "...we were joined by several...canoes of natives...their principal object I believe was merely to indulge their curiosity in looking at us...The natives who inhabit this valley...have also a very singular custom among them of bathing themselves all over with urine every morning."

March 31, 1806. Captain Lewis. "...we continued our route...opposite to the upper entrance of the Quicksand River. Here we encamped having traveled 25 miles today."

April 1-6, 1806. Captain Lewis. "We were visited by...natives...whom were descending the river...they informed us...that they did not expect the Salmon to arrive until the full of the next moon which happens on the 2nd of May...This information gave us much uneasiness with respect to our future means of subsistence. Above the falls or through the plains from thence to the Chopunnish there are not Deer, Antelope nor Elk on which we can depend for subsistence ...there seems to be but a gloomy prospect for subsistence on any terms. We therefore took it into serious consideration what measures we were to pursue on this occasion." **April 2.** "This morning we came to a resolution to remain at our present encampment...until we had obtained as much dried meat as would be necessary for our voyage as far as the Chopunnish. To exchange our pirogues for canoes...these canoes...exchanging for Horses...a large stock of Horses...shall...secure...transporting our baggage...also...provide...our only certain resource for food...We now informed the party of our intention of laying in a store of meat at this place." **April 3.** "The Indians ...descending the river...appeared to be almost starved...they confirm the report of the scarcity of provision above." **April 4.** "...dispatched (men)...up the Columbia...to hunt until our arrival." **April 5.** "...meat...so illy dried that we feared it would not keep...directed it to be cut thinner and re-dried...proposed setting out early..." **April 6.** "...dried meat secured...canoes loaded...continued up...met our hunters...set...all hands...to prepare the meat...continued their operations until late at night."

April 7-8, 1806. Captain Lewis. "I hope we have now a sufficient stock of dried meat to serve us as far as the Chopunnish provided we can obtain a few Dogs, Horses, and roots by the way." **April 8.** "The wind blew so violently this morning that we were…compelled to remain during the day."

April 9, 1806. Captain Lewis. "…continued our route to the *Wah-clel-lah* village…John Colter…observed the tomahawk in one of the lodges which had been stolen from us on the 4th of November last as we descended this river. The natives attempted to wrest the tomahawk from him but he retained it…purchased two Dogs…the evening being far spent and the wind high, raining and very cold, we thought best not to attempt the rapids this evening."

April 10-11, 1806. Captain Lewis. "…we drew them (canoes) up the rapid by a cord about a quarter of a mile which we soon performed…we set out and continued our route…by evening we arrived at the portage…and conveyed our baggage to the top of the hill about 200 paces distance where we formed a camp." **April 11.** "…we concluded to take our canoes first to the head of the rapids…this portage is two thousand eight hundred yards along a narrow, rough and slippery road…a few men…guard our baggage from the *Wah-clel-lars*…the greatest thieves and scoundrels we have met…by the evening Captain Clark took 4 of our canoes above the rapids though with much difficulty and labor…the canoes were much damaged…the men complained of being…fatigued…we postponed taking up our 5th canoe until tomorrow…the water appears to be…20 feet higher than when we descended…three of this…tribe of villains stole my Dog this evening…sent three men in pursuit…with orders if they made the least resistance…in surrendering my Dog, to fire on them…the Indians…left the Dog and fled…informed them by sign that …any further attempts to steal…we should put them to instant death…The Chief…informed us…a trader visited him last winter over land…as a further proof…he gave us a well baked sailors biscuit…I have no doubt…"

April 12, 1806. Captain Lewis. "…determined to take up the remaining pirogue this morning…in hauling…the bow unfortunately took the current at too great a distance…she turned her side to the stream…all the party were unable to resist the force…were compelled to let loose the cord…the loss…will compel us to purchase…canoes…at an extravagant price…after breakfast, all hands were employed in taking our baggage over the portage."

April 13, 1806. Captain Lewis. "We found the additional loading which we had been compelled to put on board, rendered our vessels…unsafe…passed over the river above the rapids to the *Y-eh-hih* village in order to purchase one or more canoes…obtained two (canoes)…four paddles and three Dogs…the Dog…has become a favorite food…I prefer it to lean venison or Elk, and it is very far superior to the Horse.

April 14, 1806. Captain Lewis. "At 1 P.M. we arrived at a large village…they have some good Horses…these are the first Horses we have met with since…last fall."

April 15-17, 1806. Captain Lewis. "We delayed this morning…in order to purchase some Horses…we exposed some articles in exchange…natives were unwilling to barter…we set out…continued…four miles to another village…would not take articles which we had in exchange for (Horses)…wanted…Eye-dag (Northwest traders called a sort of war hatchet an "Eye-dag") which we had not…departed…halted at another village…were equally unsuccessful…halted at two villages…no better success…landed and formed our camp." **April 16. Captain Clark.** "…I passed the river…in order to trade…for…Horses…took with me a good part of our stock of merchandise…formed a camp…Great numbers of Indians came…some Horses were offered for sale, but they asked nearly half the merchandise…for one Horse…this price I could not think of giving. The Chief informed me if I would go to his town…his people would sell me Horses." **April 17. Captain Clark.** "I rose early…divided the articles of merchandise into parcels…I thought best calculated to please the Indians…informing the Indians that each parcel was intended for a Horse. They tantalized me the greater part of the day…made a bargain with the Chief for 2 Horses. About an hour after, he cancelled the bargain. We again bargained for 3 Horses…only one could possibly be used…I refused to take two of them which displeased him and he refused to part with the 3rd...I then packed up the articles and was about setting out...when a man came and sold me two...and another man one...this induced me to continue...another day.

April 18, 1806. Captain Lewis. "I walked up to the *Skillute* Village and joined Captain Clark. He had procured four Horses...they have a great abundance of Horses but will not dispose of them. We determined to make the portage to the head of the long narrows with our baggage and five small canoes. The 2 pirogues we could take no further and therefore cut them up for fuel."

April 19-20, 1806. Captain Lewis. "...employed all hands in transporting our baggage...by means of the four pack-Horses, over the portage...there was great joy with the natives last night...of the arrival of the salmon. One...was caught...This fish was dressed and being divided into small pieces was given to each child...this custom...will hasten the arrival of the salmon...with much difficulty we obtained four other Horses...I directed the Horses to be hobbled...one of the men...was negligent in his attention to his Horse...it rambled off...not found...This, in addition to the other difficulties under which I labored was truly provoking. I reprimanded him more severely for this piece of negligence than had been usual with me." **April 20.** "This morning I was informed that the natives had pilfered six tomahawks and a knife...one Horse which I had purchased ...yesterday...could not be found...I was now informed (it) had been gambled away by the rascal who had sold it to me...I obtained two...Horses...I found that I should get no more Horses and therefore resolved to proceed tomorrow...ordered the Indians from our camp this evening and informed them that if I caught them attempting to purloin any article from us I would beat them severely. They went off in rather a bad humor."

April 21, 1806. Captain Lewis. "Notwithstanding all the precautions...they stole another tomahawk...I detected a fellow in stealing an iron socket of a canoe pole and gave him several severe blows and made the men kick him out of camp. I now informed the Indians that I would shoot the first of them that attempted to steal an article from us. That we were not afraid to fight them, that I had it in my power at that moment to kill them all and set fire to their houses, but it was not my wish to treat them with severity provided they would let my property alone...We took breakfast and departed...having nine Horses loaded and one which Bratton rode." (**Note:** The Captains divided their Corp into two groups. Water by canoe, and land by Horse. Bratton was still suffering from his crippling ailment.) **Captain Clark.** "I found it useless to make any further attempts to trade Horses."

The following Journal entries refer to map 21.

April 22, 1806. Captain Lewis. "Charbonneau's Horse threw his load...ran at full speed down the hill. Near the village he (the Horse) disengaged himself from the saddle and robe. An Indian hid the robe...I...request Captain Clark to...send back some of the men to my assistance being determined either to make the Indians deliver the robe or burn their houses...I returned to their village...just as Labiche met me with the robe...observed our two canoes passing up on the opposite side...Charbonneau purchased a Horse this evening...can only afford...one fire, and are obliged to lie without shelter."

April 23, 1806. Captain Lewis. "At 8 A.M. Fields and Sergeant Gass proceeded in the canoe...at eleven we loaded our Horses and set out...Passed five lodges...people...were waiting the arrival of the salmon...we caused all the old and brave men to set around and smoke with us. We had the violin played...natives promised to barter their Horses with us in the morning we therefore entertained a hope that we shall be enabled to proceed by land from hence with the whole of our party and baggage...sands made the march fatiguing."

April 24, 1806. Captain Lewis. "...purchased three Horses...hired three others...sold our canoes for a few strands of beads. Loaded up and departed...most of the party complain of the soreness of their feet and legs this evening..."

April 25, 1806. Captain Lewis. "We traded for two Horses...having now a sufficiency to transport with ease all our baggage and the packs of the men."

April 26, 1806. Captain Lewis. "…willows…afforded us a sufficient quantity of fuel to cook our dinner which consisted of the balance of the Dogs…"

April 27-28, 1806. Captain Lewis. "…marched through a high plain…thought it best to halt…Horses and men much fatigued…the principal Chief of the Walla Walla joined us…this Chief by name *Yel-lept!*…we continued our march accompanied by…his party to the village…This Chief is a man of much influence not only of his own nation but also among the neighboring tribes and nations…his village…furnish us with fuel and provision…wood and roasted Mullets…we purchase four Dogs…supped heartily…The Indians informed us that there was a good road…it would shorten our route at least 80 miles…the country was level…we did not hesitate in pursuing the route recommended by our guide whose information was collaborated by *Yellept*." **April 28, Captain Clark.** "…Chief *Yellept* brought a very elegant white Horse to our camp and presented him to me…I gave him my sword, 100 balls and powder…he appeared perfectly satisfied…it was necessary before we entered on our route through the plains where we were to meet with no lodges…that we should lay in a stock of provisions…Frazer…we…entrusted…to lay in as many fat Dogs as he could procure. He soon obtained 10, being anxious to depart, we requested the Chief to furnish us canoes to pass the river, but he insisted on our remaining with him this day at least…he had sent for the *Chim-na-pums*…to come and join and dance…the *Chim-na-pums* arrived…the fiddle was played…the men amused themselves with dancing…then requested the Indians to dance…350…sung and danced at the same time."

April 29, 1806. Captain Lewis. "…were detained…in not being able to collect our Horses. Our guide informed us that it was too late…to reach an eligible place to encamp. That we could not reach any water before night…thought it best to remain on the Walla Walla River until the morning"

April 30, 1806. Captain Lewis. "We purchased two…Horses…several Dogs…and…proceed on…accordingly took leave of these friendly, honest people…"

The following Journal entries refer to map 20.

May 1, 1806. Captain Lewis. "…pursued the Indian road…26 miles and encamped…sometime after…three young men from the Walla Walla village bringing with them a steel trap belonging to one of our party…this is an act of integrity rarely witnessed among Indians…they are the most hospitable, honest, and sincere people that we have met with in our voyage."

May 2, 1806. Captain Lewis. "We had much difficulty in collecting our Horses."

May 3, 1806. Captain Lewis. "…proceeded…met *We-ark-koomt* whom we have usually distinguished by the name of the Bighorn Chief…his always wearing a horn of that animal suspended by a cord to the left arm…this man went…last fall…to the Columbia and I believe was very instrumental in procuring us a hospitable and friendly reception among the natives. He had now come a considerable distance to meet us…divided the last of our dried meat…the balance of our Dogs…had not anything for tomorrow."

May 4, 1806. Captain Lewis. "The hills…are high and…one of our packhorses slipped from one of those heights and fell into the creek with its load consisting…of ammunition…neither…suffered."

May 5, 1806. Captain Lewis. "Not able to obtain any provision…continued our march…an Indian man gave Captain Clark a very elegant Grey Mare for a phial of eye-water…last fall…Captain Lewis gave an Indian …liniment to rub his knee…he…has never ceased to extol the virtues of our medicines…we arrived here extremely hungry…we had several applications to assist their sick which we refused unless they would let us have some Dogs or Horses to eat…They produced us several Dogs."

May 6, 1806. Captain Lewis. "We received a…Horse for medicine…Captain Clark…administering eye-water to a crowd…once more obtained a plentiful meal…The river here called Clark's River…I have thus named it in honor of my worthy friend and fellow traveler Captain Clark."

May 7, 1806. Captain Lewis. "We saw several Deer…we determined to remain here…in order to obtain some venison…The Indians inform us that the snow is yet so deep on the mountains that we shall not be able to pass them until the next full moon, or about the first of June."

May 8, 1806. Captain Clark. "…Collins wounded one (Deer) which our Dog caught near our camp…our stock of provisions, 4 Deer and some Horse…The great Chief of the bands below who has a *Cut Nose* joined us this morning…We loaded up and set on the road leading…to the lodge of *The Twisted Hair*, the Chief in whose care we had left our Horses…we were very coolly received by *The Twisted Hair*. He spoke aloud and was answered by *The Cut Nose*…plainly…a misunderstanding had taken place between them…we encamped…The parties of those two Chiefs took…position at some distance from each other…it appears that the cause of the quarrel…is about our Horses…*Cut Nose* said that *Twisted Hair* was a bad man…that he had not taken care of our Horses…that he himself…caused our Horses to be watered in the winter…*The Twisted Hair* told us that he wished to smoke with us at his lodge…if we would delay at his lodge tomorrow he would go after our saddles and Horses…" **Captain Lewis.** "We informed *The Cut Nose* of our intentions of spending tomorrow at *The Twisted Hair's* lodge…and that we should proceed the next day to *The Broken Arm's* lodge. He…said he would continue with us, and give any assistance."

May 9, 1806. Captain Clark. "…we halted at the lodge of *The Twisted Hair*…for our saddles…powder…lead…they returned with 21 of our Horses and about half our saddles…" **Captain Lewis.** "*The Cut Nose* lodged with *The Twisted Hair*…they have become good friends again."

May 10-12, 1806. Captain Lewis. "This morning…snow…8 inches deep…road was slippery…in the afternoon we…arrived at the village of *The Broken Arm*, the Chief at whose lodge we had left the flag last fall…now displayed on a staff…stated our situation with respect to provision…we proposed exchanging a Horse in rather low order for a young Horse in tolerable order with a view to kill…the Chief revolted at the idea of an exchange…they soon produced us two fat young Horses…This is a much greater act of hospitality than we have witnessed from any nation or tribe since we have passed the Rocky Mountains. In short be it spoken to their immortal honor…a principal Chief by name *Ho-hast-ill-pilp* arrived…we spoke…and gave…each a medal…The Indians seem well pleased, and I am confident that they are not more so than our men who have their stomachs once more well filled with Horse beef and mush of the bread of cows. The house of Coventry is also seen here." **May 11. Captain Clark.** " The last evening we were much crowded with the Indians in our lodge, the whole floor…covered with their sleeping carcasses…a Chief of great note…arrived…his name is *Yoom-park-kar-tim*…we gave him a medal (**NOTE:** All the large peace medals have now been disposed of except one)…the principle Chiefs of the Chopunnish nation…were present in our lodge we thought it a favorable time to repeat…the views of our government with respect to the inhabitants…establishing trading…restore peace and harmony…they appeared highly pleased. After…we amused…with showing them the power of magnetism, the spyglass, compass, watch, air gun and sundry other articles…many of the natives apply to us for medical aid which we gave them cheerfully…The Chopunnish…are much more clean…than any nation…since we left the Oto on the river Platte."

May 12. Captain Lewis. "Captain Clark…administer eye-water to…at least 50…Indians held a council among themselves…resolved to pursue our advice…gave each a flag…gave *The Twisted Hair* one gun…hundred balls…2 lbs. of powder…for his attention to our Horses and promised the other gun…when we received the balance of our Horses…" **Captain Clark.** "*The Twisted Hair* who has several sons…who are well acquainted, as well as himself, with the various roads through the Rocky Mountains and will answer very well as guides to us through those mountains." (**NOTE:** Captain Lewis invites *The Twisted Hair* and his family to move and stay with the Corp while they remain camped in the area. Lewis obviously wants them as guides and to provide information for the trek ahead.)

May 13, 1806. Captain Lewis. "…Captain Clark…engaged with his patients…set out…halted on the bank of the river…to meet the canoe…as the canoe did not arrive until after sunset, we remained here all night…the Chopunnish…stout, well formed, active men…cheerful but not gay…fond of gambling…I observe a tippet…formed of human scalps and ornamented with the thumbs and fingers of several men…slain in battle."

May 14 - June 9, 1806. NOTE: The Expedition waits for the snow pack to melt. **Captain Clark.** "A fine day…Horses collected…all our baggage crossed over the Flathead River…and formed a camp…I feel perfectly satisfied with our position…killed two Bear…gave Indians…two shoulders and a ham of the Bear…This nation esteem the killing of (the Bear) equally great with that of an enemy in the field of action." **May 15. Captain Lewis.** "…a party…passed our camp on a hunting excursion…had decoys for the Deer…these are the skins of the heads and upper portions of the necks…extended in their natural shape…the hunter…conceals himself and with his hand give to the decoy the action of a Deer at feed. And thus induces the Deer within arrowshot…" **May 16. Captain Lewis.** "Sacajawea gathered…roots of fennel which we found very agreeable…they dispel the wind which the roots called Cows and Quamash are apt to create…the mush of roots we find adds much to the comfort of our diet." **May 17. Captain Lewis.** "…rain…last night…chronometer got wet…found it nearly filled with water…wiped…with dry feathers…hope she has sustained no material injury…visited by no Indians today…am pleased at finding the river rise so rapidly…attributable to the melting snows of the mountains. That icy barrier which separates me from my friends and country, from all which makes life esteem-able.—patience, patience." **May 18. Captain Lewis.** "…no Deer or Bear…cold…we lay in water…" **May 19. Captain Lewis.** "Purchase roots to eat." **May 20, Captain Lewis.** "Men at work to build a canoe for the purpose of taking fish and passing the river." **May 21. Captain Lewis.** "The Indians have given us another horse to kill for provision which we keep as a reserved store. Our dependence for subsistence is on our guns, the fish we may perhaps take, roots we can purchase from the natives, and as the last alternative our horses. We eat the last morsel of meat which we had for dinner this evening, yet nobody seems much concerned about the state of provision." **May 22. Captain Clark.** "Charbonneau's son…is dangerously ill. His jaw and throat is much swelled. We apply a poultice of onions…" **May 24. Captain Lewis.** "…child…more swollen…though fever has abated…Bratton still…unwell…Shields observed…men in a similar situation restored by violent sweats. Bratton requested that he might be sweated (**NOTE:** A hole is dug and heated with a large fire. Bratton is lowered in and the hole covered with blankets. Bratton sprinkles water on the bottom and sides of the hole to create steam. After 20 minutes he is plunged into cold water and returned to the hole for a second sweat. He is taken out and covered with blankets and allowed to cool gradually. He drank strong tea of Horsemint.) "Bratton feels himself better and is walking about…nearly free from pain." **May 25. Captain Lewis.** "The child is more unwell…gave it a Clyster (enema)." **May 26. Captain Lewis.** "The Clyster given…operated very well…clear of fever…much better…saw a salmon in the river today…the river still rising fast and snows of the mountains visibly diminished." **May 27. Captain Clark.** "Sergeant Ordway…ordered to…Lewis's River and procure some salmon." **May 28. Captain Lewis.** "…obtained four bags of the dried roots…eight Deer." **May 29. Captain Lewis.** "We have once more a good stock of meat and roots. Bratton is recovering his strength very fast." **Captain Clark.** "Our Horses…have become so wild that we cannot take them without the assistance of the Indians who are extremely dexterous in throwing a rope… we had a strong pound (coral) formed today in order to take them at pleasure." **May 30. Captain Lewis.** "…in landing…the canoe was…sunk…lost three blankets and a blanket coat…merchandise…this was a serious loss…also lost our canoe." **May 31. Captain Lewis.** "The Indians brought us another of our original stock of Horses. There are only two absent now…those…the Indians inform us our Shoshone guide

(Old Toby) rode back when he returned. We have sixty-five Horses…fine, strong…" **June 1. Captain Lewis.** "…we begin to feel some anxiety with respect to Sergeant Ordway and party who were sent to Lewis's River for salmon." **June 2. Captain Lewis.** "Having exhausted all our merchandise we are obliged to have recourse to every subterfuge in order to prepare in the most ample manner in our power to meet that wretched portion of our journey, the Rocky Mountains…not any of us have yet forgotten our suffering in those mountains in September last…Sergeant Ordway returned with 17 Salmon…most…spoiled…those which were sound were extremely delicious…their flesh is of a fine rose color." **June 3. Captain Lewis.** "Today the Indians dispatched an express over the mountains to Travellers Rest…to learn…the occurrences that have taken place on the East side of the mountains…we thought it probable that we could also pass…they inform us that we may pass conveniently in twelve or fourteen days." **June 4. Captain Lewis.** "The three chiefs left us and returned to their villages…they gave us no positive answer to a request which we made, that two or three of their young men should accompany me to the falls of the Missouri." **June 5. Captain Clark.** "The child is recovering fast. I applied a plaster of salve made of the rosin of the long leafed pine, Bees Wax and Bears oil…" **June 6. Captain Clark.** "I visited *The Broken Arm* today…with respect to the young men who we had requested to accompany us to the falls of Missouri…not yet selected…we therefore do not calculate any assistance from them as guides, but depend more upon engaging some…in the neighborhood of Travellers Rest…I met The Twisted Hair…he informed me he could not accompany us across the mountains as his brother was sick." **June 7. Captain Lewis.** "Our party are much engaged in preparing their saddles…loads, provisions, etc. for our departure." **June 8, Captain Lewis.** "Bratton has…recovered…several foot races were run this evening between the Indians and our men…one of them proved as fleet as Drewyer and R. Fields, our swiftest runners…violin played and danced…" **June 9. Captain Clark.** "…we eat the last of our meat…our party seem much elated with the idea of moving on towards their friends and country…everything is readiness…river has been falling…we view as a strong evidence that the great body of snow has left the mountains."

June 10-14, 1806. Captain Lewis. "At 11 A.M. we set out with the party each man being well mounted and a light load on a second Horse…we therefore feel ourselves perfectly equipped for the mountains. We ascended the river hills which are very high…The country through which we pass is extremely fertile and generally free of stone, is well timbered." **Captain Clark.** "…we intend to delay a few days for the laying in some meat…" **June 11.** NOTE: The party killed a Bear and two Deer. **June 12. Captain Lewis.** "The days are now very warm and the Mosquitoes, our old companions, have become very troublesome…nothing interesting occurred …this day." **June 13. Captain Lewis.** "We made a digest of the Indian Nations West of the Rocky Mountains…they amount by our estimate to 69,000 souls." **June 14. Captain Lewis.** "We had all our articles packed up and made ready for an early departure…from hence to Travellers Rest, we shall make a forced march…we have now been detained near five weeks in consequence of the snows. A serious loss of time at this delightful season for traveling…everybody seems anxious to be in motion, convinced that we have not now any time to delay if the calculation is to reach the United States this season…" **Captain Clark.** "…I shudder with the expectation with great difficulties in passing those mountains, from the depth of snow and the want of grass."

The following Journal entries refer to map 19.
June 15, 1806. Captain Clark. "We took our final departure from the Quamash fields and proceeded on with much difficulty…passed through bad fallen timber…a high mountain…an extensive view of the Rocky Mountains…the Columbia plains…also the waters of Lewis' and Clarks' Rivers."
June 16, 1806. Captain Clark. "…proceeded on through most intolerable bad fallen timber over a high Mountain on which great quantity of snow is yet lying…in may places…4 feet

deep...dined on a small creek in a small open valley...found grass for our Horses...after taking a hasty meal...our route through a thick wood...fallen timber...steep ravines and hills...the snow...sufficiently firm to bear our Horses...lay in immense masses...8 or ten feet deep...much difficulty in finding the road...we arrived...remain here all night...the air...becomes very cold."

June 17, 1806. Captain Lewis. "We proceeded...found it difficult and dangerous...snow from 12 to 15 feet deep...here was winter with all its rigors. The air was cold, my hands and feet were numbed. We knew it would require five days...provided we were so fortunate...to lead us to that place (Travellers Rest)...under these circumstances we conceived it madness in this stage of the expedition to proceed...as our Horses could not...sustain...5 days without food. We therefore came to the resolution to return with our Horses while they were yet strong...and...procure an Indian to conduct us over the snowy mountains...we ordered a deposit for all the baggage which we had not immediate use...and well covered we began our retrograde march...This is the first time...we have ever been compelled to retreat."

June 18-20, 1806. Captain Lewis. "We set out...dispatched Drewyer and Shannon to the Chopunnish Indians...in order to hasten the arrival of the Indians who had promised to accompany us or procure a guide...We sent...a rifle which we offered as a reward to any of them who would engage to conduct us to Travellers Rest. We also directed them if they found difficulty in inducing any of them to offer a reward of two other guns...and ten Horses at the Falls of the Missouri...Potts cut his leg very badly...one of the large veins on the inner side of the leg...much difficulty in stopping the blood...after dinner we proceeded on to Collin's Creek...hope...to subsist until our guide arrives...good food here to sustain our Horses." **June 19.** "Cruzatte brought me several large morels (mushrooms) which I roast...our stock of salt is now exhausted." **June 20.** "we determined to return...Quamash flats and...lay in another stock of meat...(**NOTE:** Lewis and Clark conceive this plan if they fail to procure a guide.)...Captain Clark or myself shall take four of our most expert woodsmen with...best Horses and proceed two days in advance...this party to follow the road by the marks which the baggage of the Indians has made in many places on the sides of the trees by rubbing against them, and to blaze the trees with a tomahawk as they proceeded...after...two days...two of those men would be sent back...to inform the main party of the probable success of...finding the road and...progress...should it be necessary, the main party ...delay of a day or two...should give the advance time to mark the road through...the route where no food is to be obtained for our Horses should...the advance...not find the road...after attempting it for two days, the whole...would return to the main party. In which case we would...attempt a passage...through the country of the Shoshones further to the South...where...not obstructed by snow, though...very distant and would require...a month...the snow bears the Horses perfectly...the only difficulty is finding the road, and I think the plan we have devised will succeed..."

The following Journal entries refer to map 20.
June 21-23, 1806. Captain Lewis. "...set out...to the flats. We all felt mortification...to retrace our steps through this tedious and difficult part of our route...we met two Indians who were on their way over the mountain...they had seen Drewyer and Shannon...we pressed these Indians to remain with us and to conduct us over the mountain on the return of Drewyer and Shannnon. They consented to remain two nights..." **June 22.** "...all hands who could hunt were sent out. The result of this day...was...eight Deer and three Bear...Potts's leg is inflamed and very painful..." **June 23.** "...the two Indians who had promised to wait...would set out today...directed...Sergeant Gass and Wiser...accompany the Indians by whatever route they might take to Travellers Rest and blaze the trees...and wait...until our arrival...At 3 P.M. Drewyer and Shannon returned...with three Indians who had consented to accompany us to the Falls of the Missouri...all young men of good character and much respected by their nation...determined to make an early start."
The following Journal entries refer to map 19.

June 24, 1806. Captain Lewis. "...set out...we found Sergeant Gass and Wiser and the two Indians..."

June 25, 1806. Captain Lewis. "Last night the Indians entertained us with setting the Fir trees on fire...reminded me of a display of fireworks...their object...was to bring fair weather for our journey..."

June 26, 1806. Captain Lewis. "We passed...our deposit...halted...arranged our baggage and prepared our loads...the Indians hastened to be off, and informed us that it was a considerable distance to the place which they wished to reach this evening where there was grass for our Horses...we ascended and descended...but keeping on the ridge...we arrived at the desired spot and encamped."

June 27, 1806. Captain Lewis. "...without the assistance of our guides I doubt much whether we...could find our way to Travellers Rest...for the marked trees on which we had placed considerable reliance are much fewer and more difficult to find than we had apprehended. These fellows are most admirable pilots. We find the road wherever the snow has disappeared though it be only for a few hundred paces...we encamped...Our meat being exhausted, we issued a pint of Bears oil to each mess, which with their boiled roots made an agreeable dish. Potts' leg...is much better."

June 28, 1806. Captain Lewis. "...We continued our route along the dividing ridge...we found an abundance of grass for our Horses as the Indians had informed us...we determined to remain at this place..."

June 29, 1806. Captain Lewis. "...dispatched Drewyer and R. Fields...to hunt...when we descended from the ridge we bid adieu to the snow...found a Deer which the hunters had killed...halted to graze our Horses and dine...continued our march...to the warm springs...the principal spring...I bathed and remained in 19 minutes...men and Indians...use...bath this evening."

June 30, 1806. Travellers Rest. Captain Lewis. "...just as we had prepared to set out...a Deer came in to lick at these springs and one of our hunters killed it. This secured us our dinners...my Horse slipped...almost fell off backwards...Horse was near falling on me...we both escaped unhurt...Deer are abundant in the neighborhood of Travellers Rest...we arrived...we encamped with a view to remain two days in order to rest ourselves and Horses and make our final arrangements for separation."

July 1, 1805. The plan to divide the Expedition. **Captain Lewis.** "...from this place I determined to go with a small party by the most direct route to the Falls of the Missouri, there to leave Thompson, McNeal and Goodrich to prepare carriages and gear for the purpose of transporting the canoes and baggage over the portage, and myself and six volunteers to ascend Maria's River with a view to explore the country and ascertain whether any branch of that river lies as far north as Latitude 50. And again return and join the party who are to descend the Missouri, at the entrance of Maria's River...The other part of the men are to proceed with Captain Clark to the head of Jefferson's River where we deposited sundry articles and left our canoes. From hence Sergeant Ordway with a party of 9 men are to descend the river with the canoes. Captain Clark with the remaining ten including Charbonneau and York will proceed to the Yellowstone River at its nearest approach to the Three Forks of the Missouri, here he will build a canoe and descend the Yellowstone River with Charbonneau, the Indian woman, his servant York and five others to the Missouri where should he arrive first he will wait my arrival. Sergeant Pryor with two other men are to proceed...by land to the Mandans and thence to the British posts...with a letter...to engage to prevail on the Sioux Chiefs to join us on the Missouri, and accompany...us to the seat of the general government."

July 2, 1806. Captain Lewis. "All arrangements being now complete we determined to set out in the morning...we had much conversation with the Indians...prevailed on them to go with me as far as the East branch of Clark's River and put me on the road to the Missouri."

Lewis's Expedition

July 3, 1806. "Saddled our Horses and set out. I took leave of my worthy friend and companion, Captain Clark, and the party that accompany him. I could not avoid feeling much concern…although I hoped this separation was only momentary. Indians…afraid of meeting with their enemies, the Minitari…they wish now to proceed down Clark's River in search of their friends, the Shalees…they informed us…the best route…to the Falls of the Missouri."

July 4, 1806. "…entered the mountains…encamped in a handsome bottom on the river where there was an abundance of excellent grass for our Horses."

July 5, 1806. "…we encamped on the lower side of the last creek just above it's entrance. Here a war party had encamped…and concealed their fires."

The following Journal entries refer to map 16.

July 6, 1806. "…we expect to meet with the Minitari and are therefore much on our guard both day and night."

July 7, 1806. "…saw some sign of Buffalo…"

July 8, 1806. "…saw two Buffalo below us at some distance…the first that have been seen."

July 9, 1806. "…had not proceeded far before it began to rain…wet us to the skin…killed a very fat Buffalo…feasted."

July 10, 1806. "…no timber in the river bottom…great quantities of Prickly Pear…the ground is rendered so miry because of the rain…that it is excessively fatiguing to the Horses…a very large Bear…had pursued Sergeant Gass and Thompson some distance but their Horses enabled them to keep out of its reach. They were afraid to fire on the Bear lest their Horses should throw them as they were unaccustomed to the gun."

July 11, 1806. NOTE: Lewis arrives at the Great Falls of the Missouri. "…the plains looked beautiful…the air was pleasant…proceeded with the party across the plain to the White Bear Islands…it is now the season at which the Buffalo begin to copulate and the bulls keep a tremendous roaring...our Horses had not been acquainted with the Buffalo, they appeared much alarmed at their appearance and bellowing…set all hands to prepare two canoes…after the Mandan fashion, with a single skin…I intend giving my Horses a couple of days rest at this place and deposit all my baggage which is not necessary to my voyage up (Maria's) River."

July 12-15, 1806. "…our canoes…we completed by 10 A.M….two men whom I had dispatched…in quest of the Horses, returned with seven…ten…could not be found. I fear that they are stolen…I now dispatched Joseph Fields and Drewyer in quest of them, the former returned at dark, unsuccessful and the later continued absent all night." **July 13.** "Moved to the upper point of White Bear Island…had the Cache opened found my Bearskins…destroyed…specimens of plants also lost. The chart of the Missouri fortunately escaped…found my papers damp…destroyed a great part of my medicine…Drewyer did not arrive." **July 14.** "Had the carriage wheels dug up. Found them in good order. I find the fat Buffalo meat a great improvement to the mush of roots…Drewyer did not return this evening." **July 15.** "Sent McNeal down this morning to the lower part of the portage to see whether the large pirogue and Cache were safe. Drewyer returned without the Horses…I had already settled it in my mind that a White-Bear had killed him and should have set out tomorrow in search of him…I (shall) take the two Fields' and Drewyer…McNeal returned with his musket broken…and informed me…he had approached a White Bear within ten feet without discovering him…the Horse…threw him…under the Bear. This animal raised himself…for battle…he (McNeal) struck the Bear over the head…and broke off the breech. The Bear…fell to the ground and began to scratch his head…McNeal…climb(ed) a willow tree. There seems to be a certain fatality attached to the neighborhood of these falls, for there is always a chapter of accidents prepared for us during our residence at them."

July 16, 1806. "…we proceeded to the Grand Falls where we arrived at sunset."

The following Journal entries refer to map 15.

July 17, 1806. "...departed. It being my design to strike Maria's River about the place at which I left it on my return to it's mouth...we passed through the plains...on our arrival at Rose River...saw a wounded...Buffalo...probable that the Indians were near at hand...as they are vicious, lawless...I am determined to take every precaution to avoid them..."

July 18, 1806. "After dinner we proceeded...across the plain to Maria's River...we were above the point to which I had formerly ascended this river...I keep a strict lookout every night, I take my tour of watch..."

July 19, 1806. "...ascended the river."

July 20, 1806. "A great quantity of small gravel...renders traveling extremely painful to our barefoot Horses...there is scarcely any water...our provision is nearly out, we wounded a Buffalo...could not get him."

July 21, 1806. "We struck a northern branch of Maria's River...the water of this stream is nearly clear...being convinced that this stream came from the mountains, I determined to pursue it...which I now fear will not be as far north as I wished."

July 22-25, 1806. "...the ravines were steep...Horses feet...sore...continued up river...make fire with the Buffalo dung...as I could see from hence very distinctly where the river entered the mountains...I thought it unnecessary to proceed...encamped...resolving to rest...take the necessary observations...I have now lost all hope of the waters of this river ever extending to N. Latitude 50 degrees...game of every description is extremely wild which induces me to believe that the Indians are now, or have been lately, in this neighborhood." **July 23.** "Drewyer...reported...no game...in this quarter. We now rendered the grease from our tainted meat and made some mush of cows with a part of it, reserving as much meal of cows and grease as would afford us one more meal tomorrow." **July 24.** "...clouded up...rain the balance of the day...unable to complete observations...I determined to remain another day...Wolves visited our camp today..." **July 25.** "...weather still continues cold, cloudy and rainy...determine that if tomorrow continued cloudy, to set out as I now begin to be apprehensive that I shall not reach the United States within this season unless I make every exertion in my power."

July 26, 1806. "The morning was cloudy and continued to rain...set out, bidding a lasting adieu to this place which I now call Camp Disappointment...after dinner I continued my route down the river...Drewyer passed the river and kept down the valley...I had scarcely ascended the hills before I discovered to my left...an assemblage of about 30 Horses. I halted and used my spy glass...discovered several Indians on top of an eminence...who appeared to be looking down...at Drewyer...This was a most unpleasant sight, however I resolved to make the best...and to approached them in a friendly manner. I directed Fields to display the flag...advanced slowly toward them. About this time they discovered us and appeared to run about...confused...much alarmed...I calculated their number being nearly...that of their Horses, and our running would invite pursuit. Added to this, Drewyer...not being appraised of the Indians...would most probably fall a sacrifice...one of them...rode full speed towards us...came within a hundred paces, halted, looked at us...and returned briskly to his party...they all...advanced toward us leaving their Horses behind...I expected that we were to have some difficulty with them...in which case...I should resist to the last extremity preferring death to that of being deprived of my papers, instruments and gun...I shook hands...the Indians soon asked to smoke...I told them that the man whom they had seen pass down the river had my pipe...a young man set out with R. Fields in search of Drewyer...they appeared to be much agitated...I believe they were more alarmed at this first interview than we were...concluded they were only eight in number and became much better satisfied with our situation...that we could manage that number should they attempt any hostile measures...the Indians...invited us to partake of their shelter, which Drewyer and myself accepted and the Fields' lay near the fire in front...I found them extremely fond of smoking...I told them...I wished...their Chief and warriors to...council with me at the entrance of Maria's River...where I was anxious to meet my men...that if they would go with me I would give them 10 Horses and some tobacco. To this proposition, they made no reply. I took the first watch...the Indians were all asleep."

July 27, 1806. "...the Indians got up and crowded around the fire, J. Fields, who was on post, had carelessly laid his gun down behind him near where his brother was sleeping. One of the Indians...took his gun and that of his brother... At the same instant, two others advanced and seized the guns of Drewyer and myself. J. Fields seeing this...called to his brother who instantly jumped up and pursued the Indian with him whom they overtook...seized their guns and wrestled them...R. Fields as he seized his gun, stabbed the Indian to the heart with his knife. The fellow ran about 15 steps and fell dead. Drewyer, who was awake, saw the Indian take his gun and instantly jumped up and seized her and wrestled her from him...his crying, 'damn you let go my gun' awakened me...I reached to seize my gun but found her gone. I drew a pistol from my holster and turning myself about saw the Indian making off with my gun. I ran at him...and bid him lay down my gun...he dropped the gun and walked slowly off...they (the Indians) ran and endeavored to drive off all the Horses. I now hollered to the men and told them to fire on them if they attempted to drive off our Horses...I pursued them so closely that they could not take twelve of their own Horses, but continued to drive one of mine...I called to them...that I would shoot them if they did not give me my Horse and raised my gun. One of them jumped behind a rock...the other...stopped at a distance of 30 steps from me and I shot him through the belly. He fell to his knees and...fired at me...he overshot me, being bareheaded, I felt the wind of his bullet very distinctly...I did not think it prudent to rush on them...I therefore returned leisurely towards camp...we...began to catch the Horses and saddle them and put on the packs...set out...having no doubt but that they would pursue us with a large party...no time was to be lost and we pushed our Horses...our whole route...was as level as a bowling green...we traveled until 2 o'clock in the morning..."

The following Journal entries refer to map 14.

July 28, 1806. "I was so sore from my ride yesterday that I could scarcely stand...we had proceeded about 12 miles...when we found ourselves near the Missouri...we heard the report of several rifles...on arriving at the bank of the river, had the unspeakable satisfaction to see our canoes coming down. We hurried...joined them, stripped our Horses...embarking without loss of time with our baggage...we descended the river...to our principal Cache...found...most articles...were injured...having no time to air these...we dropped down to...several small Caches. These we found in good order...as good fortune would have it Sergeant Gass and Willard...joined us at 1 P.M....Having now nothing to detain us, we...now re-embarked on board the white pirogues and five small canoes."

July 29, 1806. "...a violent storm...I lay in the water all night...I placed the two Fields' and Colter and Collins in the two smallest canoes with orders to hunt, and kill meat for the party and obtain as many Elk skins as are necessary to cover our canoes...the current being strong we proceeded with great rapidity...killed 9 Big Horns of which I preserved the skins and skeletons of 2 females and one male. The flesh of this animal is extremely delicate, tender and well flavored."

July 30, 1806. "...rain still continued...the men anxious to get on, they plied their oars faithfully and we went at the rate of about seven miles an hour."

July 31, 1806. "The rain still continuing..."

The following Journal entries refer to map 13.

August 1-2, 1806. "...we passed the entrance of Mussel Shell River...rain continued...I determined to halt...to dry my skins of the Big Horn which had every appearance of spoiling, an event which I would not should happen on any consideration as we have now passed the country in which they are found and I therefore could not supply the deficiency were I to loose these I have...A White Bear came within 50 paces of our camp...stood erect...with much apparent unconcern. We seized our guns...killed it...we fleeced it and extracted several gallons of oil..."

August 2. "The morning proved fair and I determined to remain all day...We are all extremely anxious to reach the entrance of the Yellowstone River where we expect to join Captain Clark and party."

August 3, 1806. "…set out…We soon passed the canoe of Colter and Collins who were on shore hunting…directed that in future the party should cook as much meat in the evening after encamping as would be sufficient to serve them the next day. By this means we forward our journey at least 12 or 15 miles per day…"

August 4, 1806. "We arrived at the entrance of Milk River…halted a few minutes…Colter and Collins have not yet overtaken us."

August 5, 1806. "Colter and Collins not having arrived…I remained until noon…and set out concluding that…they had passed us after dark."

The following Journal entries refer to map 12.

August 6, 1806. "…game is so abundant and gentle that we kill it when we please."

August 7, 1806. "At 4 P.M. we arrived at the entrance of the Yellowstone River…and found that Captain Clark had been encamped at this place and from appearances, had left it about 7 or 8 days. I found a paper on a pole…learned that he intended halting a few miles below where he intended waiting my arrival…I…descended the river in the hope of reaching Captain Clark's camp before night. About 7 miles below the point…I saw some meat that had been lately fleeced and hung on a pole. I directed Sergeant Ordway to go on shore and examine the place. On his return, he reported that he saw the tracks of two men, which appeared so recent, that he believed they had been there today. The fire he found at the place was blazing and appeared to have been mended up afresh or within the course of an hour past…pursued our route until dark with the hope of reaching his camp. In this…we were disappointed…encamped."

August 8, 1806. "Believing from the recent appearances about the fire…I set out early…not finding Captain Clark, I knew not what calculation to make with respect to his halting and therefore determined to proceed as though he was not before me and leave the rest to the chapter of accidents…I therefore determine to halt…the pirogue and canoe could be repaired and the men dress skins and make themselves the necessary clothing…"

August 9, 1806. "…the men were all engaged dressing skins and making themselves clothes…Colter and Collins have not yet overtaken us. I fear some misfortune has happened them for their previous fidelity and orderly deportment induces me to believe that they would not thus intentionally delay. The pirogue is not yet sufficiently dry for repairing. We have not pitch and will therefore be compelled to use coal and tallow."

August 10, 1806. "…at 5 P.M. got underway."

The following Journal entries refer to map 11.

August 11, 1806. "It being my wish to arrive at the burned hills by noon in order to take the latitude of that place as it is the most northern point of the Missouri…When I arrived here it was about 20 minutes after noon and of course the observation for the meridian altitude was lost. Just opposite to the burned hills there happened to be a herd of Elk…I determined to land and kill some…I went out with Cruzatte…I was in the act of firing on the Elk…when a ball struck my left thigh about an inch below my hip joint. Missing the bone it passed through the left thigh and cut the thickness of the bullet across the hinder part of the right thigh. The stroke was very severe. I instantly supposed that Cruzatte had shot me in mistake for an Elk as I was dressed in brown leather and he cannot see very well…I called out to him 'damn you, you have shot me' but received no answer. I was now persuaded that it was an Indian that had shot me…I thought best to make good my retreat…calling out…to Cruzatte to retreat, that there were Indians…I called the men to their arms…told them that I was wounded…by an Indian…and directed them to follow me…and relieve Cruzatte…I returned about a hundred paces when my wounds became so painful and my thigh so stiff that I could scarcely get on…and ordered the men to proceed and if they found themselves overpowered by numbers to retreat in order, keeping up a fire. I now go back to the pirogue...when the party return with Cruzatte and reported that there were not Indians. Cruzatte seemed much alarmed and declared if he had shot me it was not his intention...I have no doubt in my own mind of his having shot me...I took off my clothes and dressed my wounds myself...proceeded on...we passed an encampment which had been evacuated this morning by Captain Clark. Here I found a note from Captain Clark informing me that he had left a letter for me at the entrance of the Yellowstone River, but that Sergeant Pryor, who had passed that place since he left it, had taken the letter. That Sergeant Pryor, having been robbed of all his Horses had descended the Yellowstone River in skin canoes and had overtaken him at this encampment. This I fear puts an end to our prospects of obtaining the Sioux Chiefs to accompany us..."

August 12, 1806. "At 1 P.M. I overtook Captain Clark and party and had the pleasure of finding them all well. As writing in my present situation is extremely painful to me I shall desist until I recover and leave to my friend Captain Clark the continuation of our Journal." **NOTE:** This is the last Journal entry of Captain Lewis during the active Expedition."

Clark's Expedition

The following Journal entry refer to map 19.
July 3, 1806. "I took my leave of Captain Lewis and...at 8 A.M. set out with (20) men, interpreter Charbonneau and his wife and child...with 50 Horses. We proceeded on through the valley of Clark's River...making a total of 36 miles today."

The following Journal entries refer to map 18.
July 4, 1806. "This being the day of the Declaration of Independence of the United States and a day commonly celebrated by my country, I had every disposition to celebrate this day and therefore halted early and partook of a sumptuous dinner of a fat saddle of Venison and mush of Cows. After dinner we proceeded...I sent out 2 men to hunt, and 3 in search of a ford to pass the river."

July 5, 1806. "I found a practical ford...and passed over tolerably well. The water running over the back of the 2 smaller Horses only...Shields...informed me that the best road...appeared to be a plain beaten path. As this route of the *Oat-lash-shoots* can be followed it will evidently shorten our route at least 2 days...I am determined to make the attempt and follow their trail if possible."

July 6, 1806. "I observe the appearance of old Buffalo roads...the Indian woman...informed me that she had been in this plain frequently and knew it well...and when we ascended the higher part of the plain we would discover a gap in the mountains...we proceeded on. The squaw pointed to the gap through which she said we must pass."

July 7, 1806. "This morning our Horses were very much scattered. I sent out men in every direction in search of them. They...informed me that they could not find...9. They had reasons to believe that the Indians had stolen them...I determined to leave a small party and hunt for them...and proceed on with the main party and all the baggage to the canoes, raise them out of the water and expose them to the sun to dry...We arrived at a boiling spring...too hot for a man to endure his hand in it 3 seconds...put ...a piece of meat in the water of different sizes. The one about the size of my 3 fingers cooked done in 25 minutes, the other much thicker was 32 minutes...we proceeded on...through a gap of a mountain."

July 8, 1806. "...proceeded on...to our encampment of 17 August at which place we sunk our canoes and buried some articles...most of the party with me being chewers of tobacco become so impatient to be chewing it that they scarcely gave themselves time to take their saddles off their Horses before they were off to the deposit. I found every article safe...I gave each man who used tobacco about two feet."

July 9, 1806. "…I had the canoes raised, washed, brought down, and drawn up on shore to dry and repair…Sergeant Ordway and party arrived with the Horses we had lost…The wind dried our canoes."

July 10, 1806. "I had all the canoes put into the water and every article which was intended to be sent down, put on board and the Horses collected and packed with what few articles I intend taking with me…we set out…I halted to let the Horses graze, having come 15 miles. I ordered the canoes to land. Sergeant Ordway informed me…he thought the canoes could go as fast as the Horses…I determined to put all the baggage…in the canoes and proceed on…saw several large Rattle Snakes…they were fierce."

July 11, 1806. "I arrived at the entrance of Wisdom River and encamped at the camp of August 6th last…here we found a bayonet which had been left and the canoe quite safe. I directed that all the nails be taken out of this canoe and paddles to be made of her sides…"

The following Journal entries refer to map 17.

July 12, 1806. "…was detained until 7 A.M. making paddles and drawing nails…the current I find much stronger…very difficult to keep the canoes from running against the shore."

July 13, 1806. "…proceeded on…to the entrance of Madison's River…had all the baggage of the land party taken out of the canoes and after dinner, the 6 canoes and the party of 10 men under the direction of Sergeant Ordway, set out…At 5 P.M. I set out from the head of Missouri at the 3 forks, and proceeded on nearly east 4 miles and encamped on the bank of Gallatin's River…The Indian woman who has been of great service to me as a pilot through this country recommends a gap in the mountain more south which I shall cross."

July 14, 1806. "…crossed Gallatin's River…through an open, level plain…struck the river…and attempted to proceed on through the river bottoms…I proceeded on…different channels all of which was dammed with Beaver in such a manner as to render the passage impracticable…here the squaw informed me that there was a large road passing through the upper part of this low plain from Madison's River through the gap…I…camped on a small branch of the middle fork on the N.E. side at the commencement of the gap of the mountain…"

July 15, 1806. NOTE: Clark reached the Yellowstone River. "…proceeded up the branch to the head, thence over a low gap in the mountain, thence across the heads of the N.E. branch of the fork of Gallatin's River…to the Yellowstone River, at which place I arrive at 2 P.M.…the Horses feet are very sore…the Roche passes out of a high rugged mountain covered with snow…I can see no timber sufficiently large for a canoe which will carry more than 3 men and…would be too small to answer my purpose."

July 16, 1806. "We had not proceeded far before I saw a Buffalo and sent Shannon to kill it…had most of the flesh brought on and a part of the skin to make moccasins for some of our lame Horses…to relieve them very much in passing over the stony plains…no other alternative for me but to proceed on down until I can find a tree…to make a canoe."

July 17, 1806. "I proceed down the Yellowstone…encamp opposite a small island…saw…an old Indian fort which appears to have been built last summer…The logs…put up very closely lapping on each other about 5 feet and closely chinked…This work is about 50 feet diameter and nearly round. The squaw informs me that when the war parties find themselves pursued, they make those forts to defend themselves in…"

The following Journal entries refer to map 24.

July 18, 1806. "…great quantities of…currents, ripe…excellent flavor…I observe a smoke rise…in the plains…this smoke must be raised by the Crow Indians…I think it most probably that they have discovered our trail and taking us to be their enemy, made this signal for other bands to be on their guard."

July 19-23, 1806. "…saw a low mountain in…the high lands, is partially covered with pine…after dinner I proceeded on the high lands…the timber which is cotton wood…would make very small canoes…Charbonneau informed me that he saw an Indian on the high lands on the opposite side of the river…I saw a smoke in the same direction…it appeared to be in the mountains." **July 20.** "I determined to have two canoes made out of the largest of those trees and lash them together which will cause them to be sturdy and fully sufficient to take my small party and self with what little baggage we have down this river." **July 21.** "This morning I was informed that half of our Horses were absent…I am apprehensive that the Indians have stolen our Horses, and probably those who had made the smoke a few days past…I determined to have the balance of the Horses guarded and for that purpose sent out 3 men. On their approach near, the Horses were so alarmed that they ran away and entered the woods and the men returned…we appear to be in the beginning of the Buffalo country…The wolves which are the constant attendants of the Buffalo are in great numbers…" **July 22.** "The plains…so dry and hard that the track of a Horse cannot be seen…I begin to suspect that they are taken by the Indians and taken over the hard plains to prevent our following them. My suspicion is grounded on the improbability of the Horses leaving the grass and rushes of the river bottoms of which they are very fond…if they had continued in the bottoms…their tracks could be followed very well. I directed Labiche, who understands tracking very well, to set out early in the morning and find what route the Horses had taken if possible." **July 23.** "Last night the wolves…came into our camp and eat…our dried meat…found an Indian moccasin and a small piece of a robe…those Indian signs are conclusive…they have taken the 24 Horses… Labiche returned having taken a great circle and informed me that he saw the tracks of the Horses making off into the open plains…going very fast…the men finished both canoes…I gave Sergeant Pryor his instruction and a letter to Mr. Haney and directed that he, G. Shannon and Windsor take the remaining Horses to the Mandans…I directed Sergeant Pryor to set out.

July 24, 1806. "Had all our baggage put on board of the two small canoes which, when lashed together, is very sturdy…proceeded on very well to a riffle…at the riffle, the small canoes took in a good deal of water which obliged us to land a little above the entrance of the (Clarks Fork) River to dry our articles and bail the canoes…I proceeded on the river much better than above the entrance of the Clarks Fork. Deep and the current regular and rapid, from 200 to 300 yards in width…the different species of wild animals on this river…incredible…we have a great abundance of the best of meat." **NOTE:** 69 miles traveled.

July 25, 1806. "…at 4 P.M. arrived at a remarkable rock situated in an extensive bottom on the Starboard Side of the river and 250 paces from it. This rock I ascended and from it's top had a most extensive view…This rock which I shall call Pompey's Tower is 200 feet high and 400 paces in circumference and only accessible on one side…The Indians have made 2 piles of stone on the top of this tower…The natives have engraved on the face of this rock the figures of animals and near which I marked my name and the day of the month and year." **NOTE:** 58 miles traveled.

July 26, 1806. "…proceeded on very well…This river is said to be…without falls." **NOTE:** 62 miles traveled.

The following Journal entries refer to map 25.

July 27, 1806. "I marked my name with red paint on a Cotton tree near my camp." **NOTE:** 80.5 miles traveled.

July 28, 1806. They passed by the confluence of the Rosebud River and noted that Beaver were very plentiful. **NOTE:** 73 miles traveled.

July 29, 1806. "…I arrived at the entrance of the Tongue River…it is shallow and throws out great quantities of mud…caught 3 catfish." **NOTE:** From The Original Journals of Lewis and Clark, Thwaites, vol. 5, page 307. The Tongue is one of the largest affluents of the Yellowstone; its chief southeastern tributary is the Pumpkin, but the valley of Powder River lies between that and the sources of the Cheyenne. The western sources of the Tongue mingle with those of the

Little Big Horn. At the mouth of the former was an unnamed cantonment, from which Custer's forces set out in June, 1876.

July 30, 1806. "...arrived at the commencement of shoals...for 6 miles...here we were compelled to let the canoes down by hand for fear of there striking a rock...I call the Buffalo Shoals from the circumstance of one of those animals being in them...at 20 miles below the Buffalo Shoals, passed a rapid...I call Bear Rapids from the circumstance of a Bear being on a rock in the middle of this rapids...no timber to be seen." **NOTE:** 48 miles traveled.

July 31, 1806. "I was much disturbed last night by the noise of the Buffalo which were about me. One gang swam the river near our camp, which alarmed me a little for fear of their crossing our canoes and splitting them to pieces...passed a rapid which I call Wolf Rapid from the circumstance of one of those animals being at the rapid...this evening saw a White Bear and the largest I ever saw! **NOTE:** 66 miles traveled.

The following Journal entry refer to map 12.

August 1, 1806. "...wind was high and ahead...we had showers of rain all day...my situation a very disagreeable one. In an open canoe, wet and without a possibility of keeping myself dry." **NOTE:** 45 miles traveled. Captain Clark's Birthday.

Note: Clark's campsite locations from August 2nd to August 12th are not recorded on the maps.

August 2, 1806. "...a Bear of the large vicious species...looked at us as we passed...he plunged into the water and swam toward us, either from a disposition to attack or from the scent of the meat...we shot him with three balls and he returned to shore badly wounded." **NOTE:** 86 miles traveled.

August 3, 1806. "At 8 A.M. I arrived at the junction of the Yellowstone with the Missouri, and formed my camp...had the canoes unloaded and every article exposed to dry...many of our things were wet, and nearly all the store of meat...spoiled...Several skins are also spoiled which is a loss, as they are our principal dependence for clothes to last us to our home." **NOTE:** 8 miles traveled.

August 4, 1806. "Mosquitoes excessively troublesome...the torments of those mosquitoes, and the want of a sufficiency of Buffalo meat to dry, those animals not to be found in this neighborhood, induce me to determine to proceed to a more eligible spot on the Missouri below...I ordered the canoes to be reloaded...wrote a note to Captain Lewis informing him of my intentions and tied it to a pole...at 5 P.M. set out and proceeded on down to the 2nd point which appeared to be an eligible situation for my purpose...the child of Charbonneau has been so much bitten by the mosquitoes that his face is much puffed up and swelled..."

August 5, 1806. "The mosquitoes was so troublesome...I set out...to proceed to a new situation...I saw a ram of the Big Horn...I ascended the hill with a view to kill the ram. The Mosquitoes was so numerous that I could not keep them off my gun long enough to take sight and by that means missed...landed on a sand bar...intending to form a camp...finding that there were no Buffalo...I determined to proceed on...our situation was exposed to a light breeze of wind which ...blew away the mosquitoes."

August 6, 1806. "I killed five Deer and the man with me killed two. Four others were killed in the course of the day by the party. Only two of those Deer were fat owing as I suppose to the Mosquitoes which are so numerous and troublesome...that they cannot feed except under the torments of millions of those mosquitoes."

August 7, 1806. "Soon after we landed the wind blew very hard for about 2 hours, when it lulled a little. The air was exceedingly clear and cold and not a mosquito to be seen...a joyful circumstance to the party."

August 8, 1806. "At 8 A.M. Sergeant Pryor, Shannon, Hall and Windsor came down the river in two canoes made of Buffalo skins. Sergeant Pryor informed me that the second night after he parted with me on the Yellowstone River...found...they (Indians) had caught and drove off all the Horses. They pursued on five miles, the Indians there divided into two parties…finding that there was not the smallest chance of overtaking them, they returned to their camp…made a canoe…The note I left on a pole at the mouth of the Yellowstone River, Sergeant Pryor, concluding that Captain Lewis had passed, took the note and brought it with him…Sergeant Pryor, being anxious to overtake me, set out…and forgot his saddlebags which contains his papers. I sent Bratton back with him in search of them…My purpose is to procure as many skins as possible for the purpose of purchasing corn and beans of the Mandans. As we have now no article of merchandise nor Horses to purchase with, our only resort is skins, which those people were very fond."

August 9, 1806. "…proceeded…about 6 miles and landed…I walked on shore…10 miles…on my arrival…found that the canoes had been waiting for me nearly two hours. The squaw brought me a large and well flavored Gooseberry."

August 10, 1806. "…finished a copy of my sketches of the Yellowstone River."

August 11, 1806. "I observed a canoe near the shore…I found two men from the Illinois. Jos. Dixon, and Handcock. Those men are on a trapping expedition up the Yellowstone River. They inform me that they left the Illinois in the summer 1804…The Tetons (Sioux) robbed them of the greater part of the goods and wounded Dixon in the leg…Those men further informed me that the Mandans and Minitari were at war with the Arikara…The Assinniboins were also at war with the Mandans and had prohibited the N.W. traders from coming to the Missouri to trade…those difficulties, if true will, I fear, be a bar to our expectations of having the Mandans, Minitari and Arikara accompany us to the U. States.

August 12, 1806. "…Captain Lewis hove in sight with the party…I was alarmed on landing…to be informed that Captain Lewis was wounded by an accident. I found him lying in the pirogue, he informed me that his wound was slight and would be well in 20 or 30 days. This information relieved me very much. I…found it a very bad flesh wound…at 3 P.M. we proceeded on all together…I washed Captain Lewis's wound which has become sore and somewhat painful to him."

NOTE: The Expedition is together again and they proceed down river as fast as they can paddle.

The following Journal entries refer to map 11.

August 13, 1806. "Passed the entrance of the Little Missouri River…Some Indians were seen in a skin canoe…two Indians on a high hill. Nothing very remarkable took place."

August 14-15-16, 1806. "When we were opposite the Minitari Grand Village…we directed the Blunderbusses fired several times…those people were extremely pleased to see us…I proceeded on *The Black Cats* (Mandan) Village…and smoked a pipe…dispatched Charbonneau to the Minitari, inviting the Chief to visit us, and Drewyer down to the lower Village of the Mandans to ask Mr. Jessome to come and interpret for us…we now repeated our invitation to the principal Chief…to accompany us to the U. States. *The Black Cat* Chief…wished to visit…but was afraid of the Sioux…I endeavored to do away his objections by informing him that we would not suffer those Indians to hurt any of our red children who would think proper to accompany us, and on their return they would be equally protected…The Chief promised us some corn tomorrow."

August 15. "After assembling the Chiefs and smoking one pipe, I informed them that I still spoke the same words which we had spoken to them when we first arrived in their country in the fall of 1804. We then invited them to visit their Great Father the President of the United States and to hear his own councils and receive his gifts from his own hands…the Great Chief of the Minitari spoke, he said he wished to go down and see his Great Father very much, but that the Sioux were in the road and would most certainly kill him or any other who should go down. They were bad people and would not listen to anything which was told them…as they were all afraid of the Sioux they should not go down…*Black Cat*…requested me to go over to his

81

village…he had a parcel of corn about 12 bushels in a pile…after taking a smoke he informed me that as the Sioux were very troublesome and the road to his Great Father dangerous, none of this village would go down with us…a young man offered to go down, and they all agreed for him to go down. The character of this young man I knew as a bad one and made an objection…at this time Gibson, who was with me, informed me that this young man had stole his knife and had it then in his possession. This I informed the Chief and directed him to give up the knife…I then reproached those people for wishing to send such a man to see and hear the words of so great a man as their great father. They hung their heads and said nothing for some time when the Chief spoke and said that they were afraid to send anyone for fear of their being killed by the Sioux…being informed by one of our interpreters that the 2nd Chief of the Mandans commonly called *The Little Crow* intended to accompany us down…he told me he had determined to go down, but wished to have a council first with his people…Colter, one of our men, expressed a desire to join some trappers…as we were disposed to be of service to anyone of our party who had performed their duty as well as Colter had done. We agreed to allow him the privilege…we gave Colter some small articles…and some powder and lead…" **August 16.** "As our swivel (gun) could no longer be serviceable to us as it could not be fired on board the largest pirogue, we concluded to make a present of it to the Great Chief of the Minitari (*The One Eye*) with a view to ingratiate him more strongly in our favor…appeared to be much pleased and conveyed it immediately to his village. We settled with the discharged Colter. In the evening I walked to the village to see *The Little Crow* and know when he would be ready…but to my astonishment he informed me he had declined going down…we sent for Mr. Jessome and told him to use his influence to prevail on one of the Chiefs to accompany us and we would employ him. He informed us soon after that *The Big White* Chief would go if we would take his wife and son and Jessome's wife and 2 children…were obliged to agree…"

August 17, 1806. "Settled with Charbonneau for his services as an interpreter, the price of a Horse, and lodge purchased of him for public service, in all amounting to $500 and 33 1/3 cents…at 2 o'clock we left our encampment…we also took our leave of Charbonneau, his Snake Indian wife and their child, who had accompanied us on our route to the Pacific Ocean…We offered to convey him down to the Illinois if he chose to go. He declined…observing that he had no acquaintance or prospect of making a living below…I offered to take his little son, a beautiful, promising child who is 19 months old to which they both himself and wife were willing, provided the child had been weaned. They observed that in one year the boy would be sufficiently old to leave his mother and he would then take him to me if I would be so friendly as to raise the child for him in such a manner as I thought proper, to which I agreed…As I was about to shake with the Grand Chiefs of all the villages there assembled, they requested me to set one minute longer with them…the Chiefs informed that when we first came to their country they did not believe all we said…But they were now convinced that everything we had told them were true, that they should keep in memory everything which we had said to them, and strictly attend to our advice, that their young men should stay at home and should not go again to war against any nation…they also requested me to tell the Arikara to come and see them, not to be afraid that no harm should be done them, that they were anxious to be in peace with them…informed them that we should inform the Arikara what they had requested…we then saluted them with a gun and set out and proceeded on to Fort Mandan where I landed and went to view the old works. The houses, except one in the rear bastion, was burned by accident…"

The following Journal entries refer to map 10.
August 18, 1806. "…saw an Indian running down the beach and appeared to be anxious to speak to us…this Indian proved to be the brother of the Chief we had on board and came down…to take his leave of his brother." **NOTE:** Captain Lewis' birthday.
August 19, 1806. "The wind rose and blew with great violence…we were very much distressed with the clouds of sand…rain…Jessome…let me have a piece of a lodge and the squaw pitched

or stretched it over some sticks. Under this piece of leather, I slept dry, it is the only covering which I have had...to keep off the rain since I left the Columbia...the Indians appear well satisfied with the party and mode of procedure."

The following Journal entries refer to map 9.
August 20, 1806. "I observe a great alteration in the current course and appearance of this part of the Missouri. In places where there were sand bars in the fall 1804, at this time the main current passes, and where the current then passed is now a sand bar. Sand bars which were then naked are now covered with willow several feet high."
August 21-22, 1806. "Men put all their arms in perfect order and we set out...met three Frenchmen...informed us...that 700 Sioux had passed the Arikara on their way to war with the Mandans and Minitari and that their encampment...was some place near the Big Bend of this river. No Arikara had accompanied them...they were informed that the Pawnee or Arikara Chief who went to the United States last spring...died on his return...we arrived in view of the upper Arikara villages...observed several very white lodges...the Arikara...informed me they were Cheyenne's who had just arrived...both of Arikara and Cheyenne...appeared anxious to hear what we had done...I informed them...and invited some of their Chiefs to accompany us down and see their great father...told them not to be afraid...requested they inform me as soon as possible of their intentions of going down with us...in the evening, the Great Chief requested that I would walk to his house...this Chief informed me that none of his Chiefs wished to go down with us they all wished to see the Chief who went down return first. That the Cheyenne were a wild people and were afraid to go...I inform the Arikara...that the Mandans had opened their ears...that this Chief was on his way to see their Great Father...and was under our protection...I told the Arikara that they had told us lies, they promised to be at peace with the Mandans and Minitari. That our back was scarcely turned before they went to war and killed them and stole their Horses...the 2nd Chief informed me...it was the Sioux who killed them and not the Arikara...that the Mandan Chief was as safe as if he was in his own village...A long conversation of explanations took place between the Arikara and Mandan Chief which appeared to be satisfactory on both sides...everything appeared to be made up. **August 22.** "The Cheyenne...men are large. Their dress in summer is simply a robe of Buffalo skin...a breach cloth, some leggings and moccasins...They wear Bears claws about their necks...they are rich in Horses and Dogs. The Dogs carry a great proportion of their light baggage. They confess to be at war with no nation except the Sioux...As I was about to leave, the Chief of the Cheyenne lodge requested me to send some traders to them, that their country was full of Beaver and they would then be encouraged to kill Beaver...my worthy friend, Captain Lewis is recovering fast, he walked a little today for the first time."
August 23, 1806. "...landed on a small sand bar...I had chosen to avoid the mosquitoes."

The following Journal entries refer to map 8.
August 24, 1806. "We saw only 6 Buffalo today. The Sioux have been lately encamped on the river and have secured the...game."
August 25, 1806. "This day proved a fine, still day and the men plied their oars and we made 48 miles...saw no game on the plains today."
August 26, 1806. "...passed the place the Tetons...attempted to stop us in September 1804...passed the entrance of the Teton River...a few miles below...I observed a Buffalo skin canoe and a raft, which induces me to suspect that the Tetons are not on the Missouri at the Big Bend as we were informed...but up the Teton River...we were much on our guard, determined to put up with no insults from those bands of Sioux. All the arms in perfect order."
August 27, 1806. "My friend, Captain Lewis, hurt himself very much by taking a longer walk on the sand bar...than he had strength to undergo, which caused him to remain very unwell all night."

August 28, 1806. "We are determined to delay one day for the purpose of procuring the skeletons of the Mule Deer and Antelope, and some Barking Squirrels...procured two of the Barking Squirrels."

The following Journal entries refer to map 7.

August 29, 1806. "...killed 2 common deer but no Mule Deer or Antelope...I have observed that in the country between the nations which are at war with each other the greatest numbers of wild animals are to be found..."

August 30, 1806. "I saw several men on Horseback which with the help of a spy glass, I found to be Indians on the high hills to the N.E. We landed on the S.W. side and I sent out two men to a village of Barking Squirrels...immediately after landing, about 20 Indians were discovered on an eminence a little above us on the opposite side...immediately after, 80 or 90 Indian men all armed with Fusses and bows and arrows came out of a wood on the opposite bank about ¼ mile below us. They fired off their guns as a salute. We returned the salute with 2 rounds...I determined to find out who they were without running any risk...therefore took three French men who could speak the Mahar, Pawnee and some Sioux...to a sand bar...near the opposite shore to converse...They informed me that they were Tetons and their Chief was *The Black Buffalo*. This Chief I knew very well to be the one we had seen with his band at Teton River which band had attempted to detain us in the fall of 1804 as we ascended this river and with whom we were near coming to blows. I told those Indians that they had been deaf to our councils and ill-treated us as we ascended this river two years since. I believed them to be bad people and should not suffer them to cross to the side on which the party lay, and directed them to return with their band to their camp, that if any of them come near our camp, we should kill them certainly. I left them on the bar and returned to the party and examined the arms. Those Indians seeing some corn in the canoe requested some of it, which I refused being determined to have nothing to do with those people...I also told them that I was informed that a part of all their bands were going to war against the Mandans and that they would be well whipped as the Mandans had a plenty of guns, powder and ball, and we had given them a cannon to defend themselves....all this time were extremely anxious for the arrival of the 2 Fields' and Shannon whom we had left behind...to our joy those men hove into sight at 6 P.M. Jo. Fields had killed 3 Black Tail or Mule deer."

August 31, 1806. "Saw several Indians on the hills."

The following Journal entries refer to map 6.

September 1, 1806. "9 Indians ran down the bank and beckoned to us to land. They appeared to be a war party and I took them to be Teton and paid no kind of attention...those Indians informed me they were Yankton...I invited them down to the boats to smoke...they all eagerly saluted the Mandan Chief...proceeded on down...to the place where we met the Yankton in council at the Calumet Bluffs and which place we left on the 1st of September 1804. (**NOTE:** Exactly two years to the date. It took the Expedition 109 days to reach this point going up river in 1804. I took them only 23 days to reach St. Louis from this point going down river in 1806.) I observed our old flag staff or pole standing as we left it."

September 2, 1806. "Passed the James River...I observed the remains of a house which had been built since we passed up. This most probably was McClellan's trading house with the Yankton in the winter of 1804 and 5. The wind was hard a head...did not set out until near sunset." **NOTE:** Both Lewis and Clark had known Robert McClellan while he served as a scout in Wayne's army. Upon moving to St. Louis, he entered upon the fur trade.

NOTE: September 3, 1806 campsite location is the last Eastbound Campsite recorded on the United States Department of the Interior's "A Proposal for Development" 1965 study.

September 3, 1806. "Wind...blew the sand over us...part of the night...we spied two boats and several men...met Mr. Airs from Mackinaw by way of Prairie du Chien and St. Louis. This gentleman is of the house of Dickson & Company who has a license to trade for one year with the

Sioux...Our first inquire was after the President of our country and then our friends and the state of politics of our country...this gentleman informed us of may changes and misfortunes which had taken place...that Mr. Burr and Hamilton fought a duel, the latter was killed...Captain Lewis is so well as to walk about with ease."

September 4, 1806. "As we were in want of some tobacco, I proposed to Mr. Airs to furnish us with 4 carrots for which we would pay the amount to any merchant of St. Louis. He very readily agreed...Mr. Airs also insisted on our accepting a barrel of flour. We gave this gentleman what corn we could spare amounting to about 6 bushels...set out...came to Floyds Bluff...ascended the hill...found the grave had been opened by the natives...we had this grave completely filled up, and returned to the canoes and proceeded on."

September 5, 1806. "Here the river...becomes...more rapid and crowded with snags...We saw no game on the shores today worth killing."

September 6, 1806. "...we met a trading boat...bound to the James River to trade...we purchased a gallon of whiskey...and gave each man...a dram which is the first spirituous liquor which had been tasted by any of them since the 4ᵗʰ of July 1805. Several of the party exchanged leather for linen shirts and Beaver for hats...the Chief and the squaws and children are weary of their journey. Children cry."

September 7, 1806. "I am obliged to replenish my ink stand every day with fresh ink. At least 9/10 of which must evaporate...sent out all hunters. They killed 3 Elk...after taking a sumptuous dinner we all set out."

September 8, 1806. "...all being anxious to get to the River Platte today, they plied their oars...we arrived at our old encampment at White Catfish camp 12 miles above the River Platte...The Missouri at this place does not appear to contain more water than it did 1000 miles above this, the evaporation must be immense. In the last 1000 miles this river receives the water of 20 rivers and may creeks...the quantity of water does not appear to increase."

September 9, 1806. "Passed the entrance of the great River Platte...our party appears extremely anxious to get on, and every day appears to produce new anxieties in them to get to their Country and friends. My worthy friend, Captain Lewis has entirely recovered his wounds are heeled up and he can ...even run."

September 10, 1806. "...we met a Mr. Alexander La Fass...informed us that...(Zebulon) Pike had set out on an expedition up the Arkansas River...met a large pirogue...bound to the Mahar...We find the river in this timbered country narrow and more moving sands and a much greater quantity of sawyers or snags than above. Great caution and much attention is required to steer clear of all those difficulties."

September 11, 1806. "The mosquitoes are no longer troublesome...Wolves were howling...Prairie Wolves...barking...the Paw Paws nearly ripe." **NOTE:** The Pawpaw is a tree of temperate humid zones, requiring warm to hot summers, mild winters, and minimum of 32 inches of rainfall. Pawpaws are native over a wide range of latitude, from the Gulf to southern Michigan. Ripe Pawpaws are best when they are just about ready to drop from the tree. Their flavor is like custard. Pawpaws have a quality compared to the best pears and peaches.

September 12, 1806. "...met 2 pirogues from St. Louis, one contained...the Frenchman who had accompanied us as high as the Mandans. He informed us that Mr. McClellan was a few miles below...met Mr. McClellan...here we found Mr. Gravelin the Arikara interpreter whom we had sent down with an Arikara Chief in the spring of 1805...we...found that Gravelin was ordered to the Arikara with a speech from the President of the United States to that nation and some presents which had been given the Arikara Chief who had visited the United States and unfortunately died at the City of Washington. He was instructed to teach the Arikara agriculture and make every inquiry after Captain Lewis, myself and party."

September 13, 1806. "The wind being too high...we concluded to lay by...I felt myself very unwell and directed a little Chocolate which Mr. McClellan gave us, prepared of which I drank about a pint and found great relief...5 p.m. ...proceeded on down...18 miles only today."

September 14, 1806. "This being the part of the Missouri the Kansas nation resort to at this season of the year for the purpose of robbing the pirogues…we have every reason to expect to meet with them and…are determined not to allow of and for the smallest insult we shall fire on them…we met three boats bound to the Yankton and Mahar…received us with great friendship and pressed on us some whisky for our men, biscuit, pork and onions…our party received a dram and sung songs until 11 o'clock at night in the greatest of harmony."

September 15, 1806. "We landed one time only to let the men gather Paw Paws or the custard apple of which this country abounds and the men are very fond of…"

September 16, 1806. "…we met a large trading pirogue bound for the Pawnee…an extraordinary license…without the Seal of the territory annexed…we were somewhat doubtful…we made some inquiries of this young man and cautioned him against pursuing the steps…to degrade the American character in the eyes of the Indians."

September 17, 1806. "Pass the island of the Little Osage Village which is considered by the navigators of this river to be the worst place in it…met a Captain McClellin, late a Captain of Artillery of the United States Army, ascending in a large boat. This gentleman, an acquaintance of my friend Captain Lewis, was somewhat astonished to see us return and appeared rejoiced to meet us…this gentleman informed us that we had been long since given up by the people of the U.S. generally, and almost forgotten. The President of the United States had yet hopes of us…Captain McClellin informed us that he was on rather a speculative expedition to the confines of New Spain…calculated to attract the Spanish government…to exchange his merchandise for silver and gold…if the Spanish government favors his plan, he proposes taking his merchandise on mules and Horses which can easily be procured from the Pawnee, to some point convenient to the Spanish settlements within the Louisiana Territory to which place the inhabitants of New Mexico may meet him for the purpose of trade. Captain McClellin's plan I think a very good one if strictly pursued."

September 18, 1806. "Our party entirely out of provisions. Subsisting on Paw Paws."

September 19, 1806. "The men plied their oars and we descended with great velocity…continue on without halting to hunt. We calculate on arriving at the first settlement on tomorrow."

September 20, 1806. "We saw some cows on the bank which was a joyful sight…and caused a shout to be raised for joy…we came in sight of the little French village called La Charette. The men raised a shout and sprung upon their oars and we soon landed…our party requested to be permitted to fire off their guns which was allowed and they discharged 3 rounds with a hearty cheer…we landed and were very politely received by two young Scotch men from Canada…furnished us with beef, flour and some pork for our men and gave us a very agreeable supper…we purchased…two gallons of whiskey…every person…seems to express great pleasure in seeing us return. They informed us that we were supposed to have been lost long since…the American inhabitants express great disgust for the government of this territory. From what I can learn it arises from a disappointment of getting all the Spanish grants confirmed." **NOTE:** The Spanish grant question was difficult to adjust. Land grants were given by Spain to settlers without surveys and with little or no written records. Because this land was now owned by the United States, Spain had little interest in helping to reconcile any of the records.

September 21, 1806. "At 4 P.M. we arrived in sight of St. Charles…we were met by great numbers of the inhabitants…"

September 22, 1806. "This morning being very wet…and our party being all sheltered in the houses of those hospitable people, we did not…proceed on until after the rain was over…I took this opportunity of writing to my friends in Kentucky…at 10 A.M…set out and proceeded on down to the containment at Coldwater Creek about 3 miles up the Missouri."

September 23, 1806. "We rose early took the Chief to the public store and furnished him with some clothes and took an early breakfast with Col. Hunt and set out. Descended to the Mississippi and down the river to St. Louis at which place we arrived about 12 o'clock. We suffered the party to fire off their pieces as a salute to the town. We were met by all the village and received a hearty welcome from its inhabitants…we accepted of the invitation of Mr. Peter Choteau and took a room in his house. We paid a friendly visit…some of our old friends this evening."

September 24, 1806. "Slept but little last night…Captain Lewis wrote…the President…after dinner went to a store and purchased some clothes. Captain Lewis in opening his trunk, found all his papers wet and some seeds spoiled."

September 25, 1806. "Had all of our skins, etc. sunned and stored away in a storeroom…paid some visits of form to the gentlemen of St. Louis. In the evening a dinner and ball."

September 26, 1806. "A fine morning. We commenced writing." **END.**

.

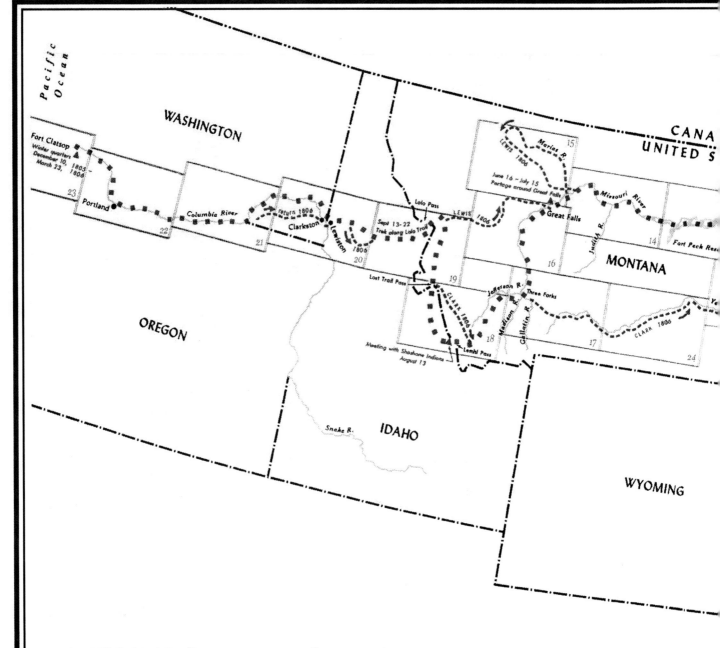

LEWIS and CLARK
Expedition Route
1804-06

SCALE IN MILES

CANADA
D STATES

Peck Reservoir

NORTH DAKOTA

13

12   Garrison Reservoir   11   ▲ Fort Mandan Winter Quarters
                                      November 20, 1804—April 7, 1805

Yellowstone

25   ● Bismarck

24

10

SOUTH 9 DAKOTA

● Pierre
▲ Council with Teton Sioux, September 25

8

Missouri River

7   ● Sioux City
     Death and burial
     of Sergeant Floyd
     August 20 6

First council with
Indians, August 3
● Omaha

IOWA

5

NEBRASKA

Mississippi River

ILLINOIS

4

Wood River
Preparation Camp for Expedition
▲ which began May 14, 1804.

● Kansas City ● Kansas
                  City

3

St. Louis ●
2   1

Expedition completed its journey
at St. Louis on September 23, 1806

KANSAS

MISSOURI

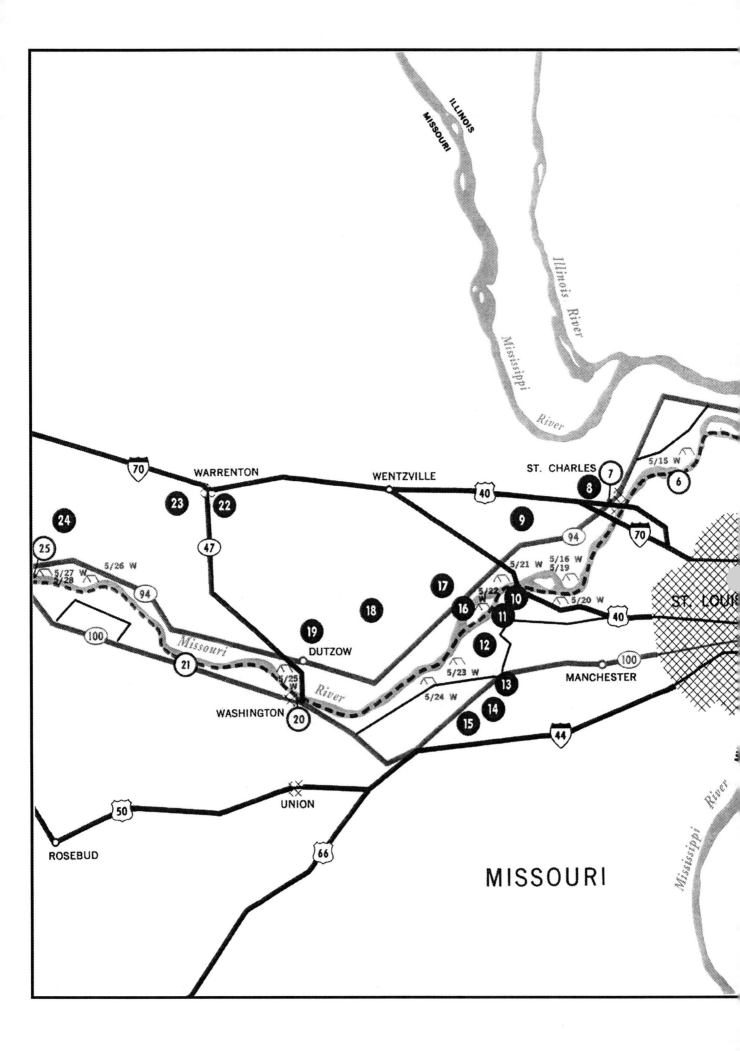

ILLINOIS

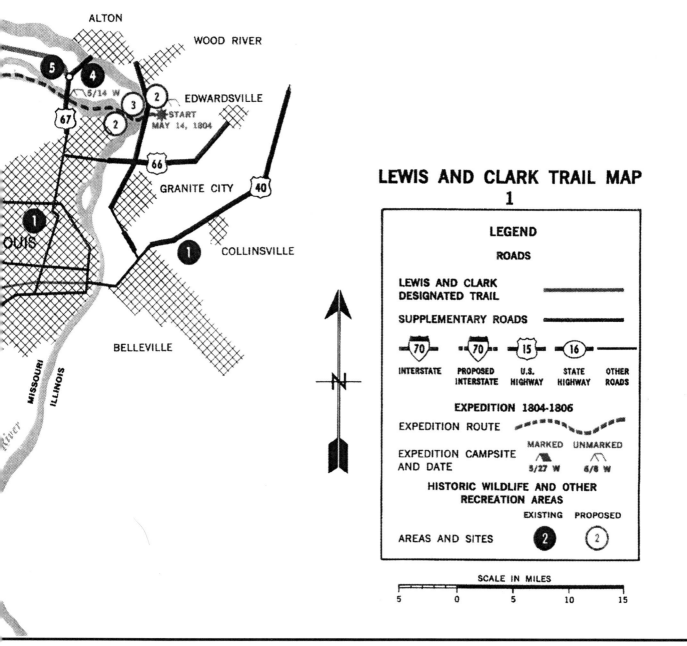

ALTON

WOOD RIVER

EDWARDSVILLE

START
MAY 14, 1804

5/14 W

GRANITE CITY

COLLINSVILLE

BELLEVILLE

OUIS

MISSOURI

ILLINOIS

River

LEWIS AND CLARK TRAIL MAP
1

LEGEND

ROADS

LEWIS AND CLARK
DESIGNATED TRAIL

SUPPLEMENTARY ROADS

70	70	15	16	
INTERSTATE	PROPOSED INTERSTATE	U.S. HIGHWAY	STATE HIGHWAY	OTHER ROADS

EXPEDITION 1804-1806

EXPEDITION ROUTE

EXPEDITION CAMPSITE
AND DATE

MARKED   UNMARKED

5/27 W   6/8 W

**HISTORIC WILDLIFE AND OTHER
RECREATION AREAS**

EXISTING   PROPOSED

AREAS AND SITES   2   2

SCALE IN MILES

5   0   5   10   15

HISTORIC, WILDLIFE and OTHER

AREA NUMBER		OWNERSHIP *	ADMINISTRATION *	RECREATION USE			RECREATION ACTIVITIES AND ATTRACTIONS															TOTAL LAND AND WATER ACREAGE
				Day	Overnight	Vacation	Camping	Picnicking	Boating	Water Skiing	Swimming	Hunting	Fishing	Hiking	Horse Trails	Sightseeing	Nature Study	Winter Sports	Historic	Archeologic	Geologic	
	ILLINOIS																					
1	Cahokia Mounds State Park & Museum	S	S	▲	▲			●	●										●	●		225
2	Lewis and Clark Memorial Park ~	SF	SF	▲					●										●			—
	MISSOURI																					
1	St. Louis Historic Sites & County Parks	C	C	▲				●							●	●	●		●			—
2	Coldwater Camp Park ~	C	C	▲	▲		●	●	●	●	●		●	●	●	●	●					6
3	Westward Ho! Park ~	C	C	▲	▲		●	●	●	●	●		●	●	●	●	●					12
4	West Alton Recreation Access	F	F	▲	▲		●	●	●			●	●		●							3
5	Dresser Island Recreation Access	F	S	▲	▲		●	●	●			●	●		●							2
6	Northwest Passage Park ~	C	C	▲	▲		●	●	●	●	●		●	●	●	●	●		●			7
7	First Capitol Park ~	M	M	▲	▲		●	●	●	●	●		●	●	●	●	●		●			—
8	First Missouri State Capitol Shrine	S	S	▲											●	●			●			—
9	Fort Zumwalt State Park	S	S	▲	▲	▲	●	●						●			●		●			48
10	Babler Park Recreation Area	S	S	▲	▲		●	●	●	●	●		●	●	●	●	●		●			—

* P - Private   C - County
   Q - Quasi-public   S - State
   M - Municipal   F - Federal

~Proposed Site

RECREATION AREAS (EXISTING and PROPOSED)

Area Number		Ownership	Administration	Day	Overnight	Vacation	Camping	Picnicking	Boating	Water Skiing	Swimming	Hunting	Fishing	Hiking	Horse Trails	Sightseeing	Nature Study	Winter Sports	Historic	Archeologic	Geologic	Total Land and Water Acreage
	MISSOURI (Continued)																					
11	Babler State Park	S	S	▲	▲		•	•						•	•	•	•		•			2,400
12	Rockwoods Reservation and Range (2 units)	S	S	▲												•	•					3,185
13	Rockwoods County Park	C	C	▲	▲	▲	•	•						•		•	•					1,700
14	Rockwoods Lookout Tower	P	S	▲				•								•						10
15	(See No. 12)																					
16	U. of Missouri Weldon Springs Exp. Sta.	S	S	▲										•								7,000
17	August A. Busch Wildlife Area	S	S	▲	▲		•	•				•	•	•		•	•					6,996
18	Daniel Boone Shrine	P	P	▲				•						•		•	•		•			509
19	Daniel Boone Burial Site	P	P	▲												•	•		•			—
20	*Devil's Race Park ~*	M	M	▲	▲		•	•	•	•	•		•	•		•	•		•			—
21	*La Charrette Park ~*	M	M	▲	▲		•	•	•	•	•		•	•		•	•		•			—
22	Reifsnider State Forest	S	S	▲	▲		•	•				•		•		•	•					1,345
23	Warrenton Tower	S	S	▲	▲									•		•	•					10
24	Daniel Boone State Forest	S	S	▲	▲		•	•				•		•		•	•		•			2,860
25	*Patrick Gass Park ~*	M	M	▲	▲		•	•	•	•	•		•	•		•	•		•			—

~Proposed Site

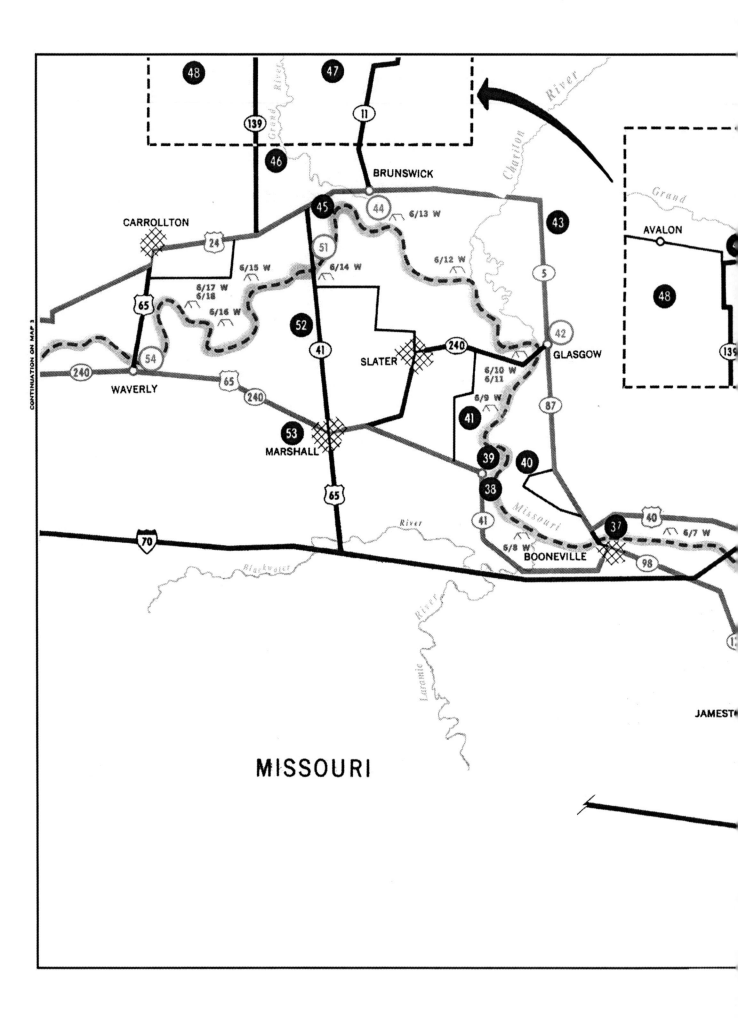

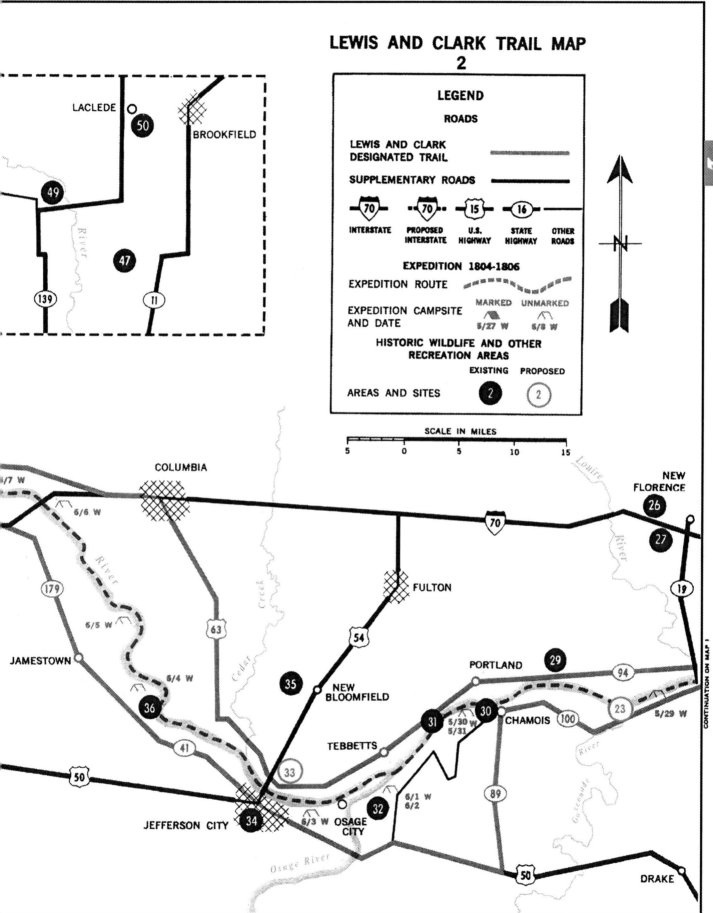

LEWIS AND CLARK TRAIL MAP
2

LEGEND
ROADS

LEWIS AND CLARK DESIGNATED TRAIL

SUPPLEMENTARY ROADS

70 INTERSTATE 70 PROPOSED INTERSTATE 15 U.S. HIGHWAY 16 STATE HIGHWAY OTHER ROADS

EXPEDITION 1804-1806

EXPEDITION ROUTE

EXPEDITION CAMPSITE AND DATE — MARKED 5/27 W UNMARKED 6/3 W

HISTORIC WILDLIFE AND OTHER RECREATION AREAS

AREAS AND SITES — EXISTING 2 PROPOSED 2

SCALE IN MILES
5 0 5 10 15

N

HISTORIC, WILDLIFE and OTHER RECREATION

Area Number		Ownership	Administration	Recreation Use			Recreation Activities and Attractions															Total Land and Water Acreage
				Day	Overnight	Vacation	Camping	Picnicking	Boating	Water Skiing	Swimming	Hunting	Fishing	Hiking	Horse Trails	Sightseeing	Nature Study	Winter Sports	Historic	Archeologic	Geologic	
	MISSOURI (Continued)																					
26	Graham Cave State Park	S	S	▲	▲											•			•			200
27	Mineola Fire Tower	S	S	▲				•								•						23
28	*Gasconade Park* ~	*F*	*F*	▲	▲		•	•	•	•	•		•	•		•	•		•			---
29	Reform Tower	S	S	▲												•		•				10
30	Chamois Access (Grindstone Park)	M	S	▲								•	•									9
31	Mokane Access (Ordway Park)	S	S	▲								•	•									10
32	Bonnots Mill Recreation Access	S	S	▲								•	•									6
33	*Broken Mast Park* ~	*M*	*M*	▲	▲		•	•	•	•	•		•	•		•			•			---
34	State Capitol & Historic Sites	S	S	▲												•			•			–
35	Cedar Creek Recreation Area	F	F	▲									•			•						12,000
36	Marion Access (Projecting Cliff Park)	S	S	▲					•			•	•									3
37	Historic City of Franklin	M	M	▲															•			–
38	Prairie of Arrows Public Use Area	S	S	▲							•	•	•									–
39	Arrow Rock State Park	S	S	▲	▲		•	•											•			38
40	Boonslick State Park	S	S	▲				•						•					•			17

* P - Private   C - County
   Q - Quasi-public   S - State
   M - Municipal   F - Federal

~Proposed site

AREAS (EXISTING and PROPOSED)

Area Number		Ownership*	Administration*	Recreation Use			Recreation Activities and Attractions															Total Land and Water Acreage
				Day	Overnight	Vacation	Camping	Picnicking	Boating	Water Skiing	Swimming	Hunting	Fishing	Hiking	Horse Trails	Sightseeing	Nature Study	Winter Sports	Historic	Archeologic	Geologic	
	MISSOURI (Continued)																					
41	William Ashley Grave	P	P	▲												•			•			–
42	*Stump Island Public Use Area* ~	M	M	▲	▲		•	•	•													–
43	Sterling Price Community Lake	S	S	▲					•		•		•									84
44	*Camp of the Missouris Public Use Area* ~	M	M	▲	▲						•	•	•									–
45	Fort Orleans	P	P	▲												•			•	•		–
46	Bosworth Access Area	S	S	▲					•				•	•								7
47	Swan Lake National Wildlife Refuge	F	F	▲								•	•				•					10,700
48	Fountain Grove Wildlife Mgt. Area	S	S	▲								•	•				•					4,146
49	Pershing Memorial State Park	S	S	▲	▲	▲	•	•				•	•				•					1,836
50	General John J. Pershing Home	S	S	▲															•			–
51	*Snake Bluff Recreation Area* ~	S	S	▲	▲		•	•	•		•		•									–
52	*Van Meter State Park*	S	S	▲	▲		•	•									•	•		•	•		727
53	Malta Bend Community Lake	S	S	▲				•					•									25
54	*Oar Markers Park* ~	S	S	▲	▲		•	•	•				•									–

~Proposed Site

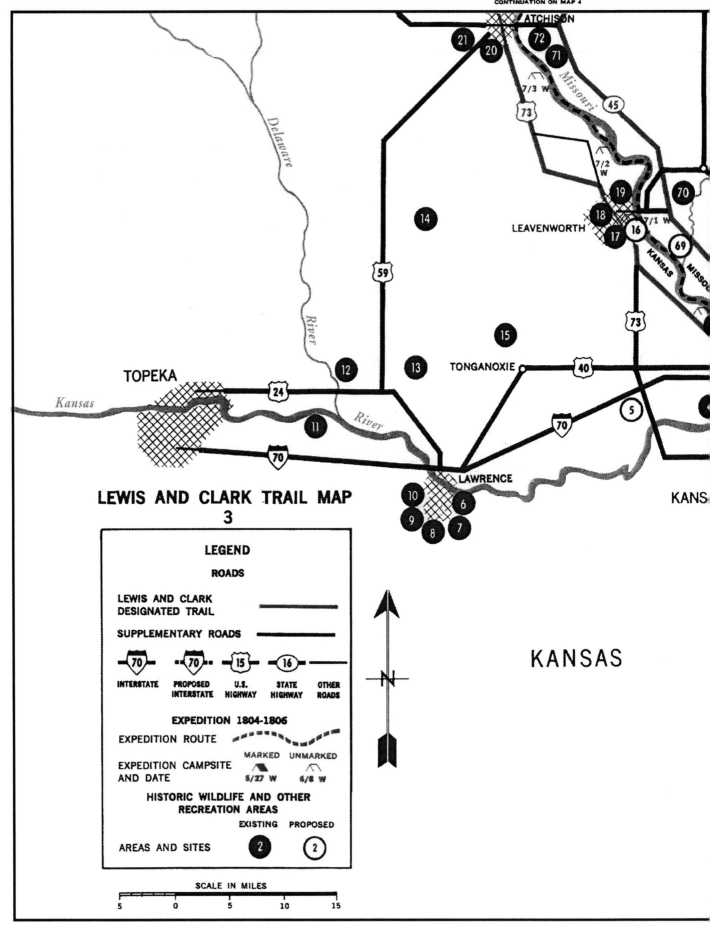

CONTINUATION ON MAP 4

ATCHISON

Missouri

LEAVENWORTH

TOPEKA

Kansas

Delaware River

River

TONGANOXIE

LAWRENCE

KANS

KANSAS

MISSOU

LEWIS AND CLARK TRAIL MAP 3

LEGEND

ROADS

LEWIS AND CLARK
DESIGNATED TRAIL

SUPPLEMENTARY ROADS

| INTERSTATE | PROPOSED INTERSTATE | U.S. HIGHWAY | STATE HIGHWAY | OTHER ROADS |

EXPEDITION 1804-1806

EXPEDITION ROUTE

EXPEDITION CAMPSITE AND DATE

MARKED 5/27 W   UNMARKED 6/8 W

HISTORIC WILDLIFE AND OTHER RECREATION AREAS

EXISTING   PROPOSED

AREAS AND SITES

SCALE IN MILES

5   0   5   10   15

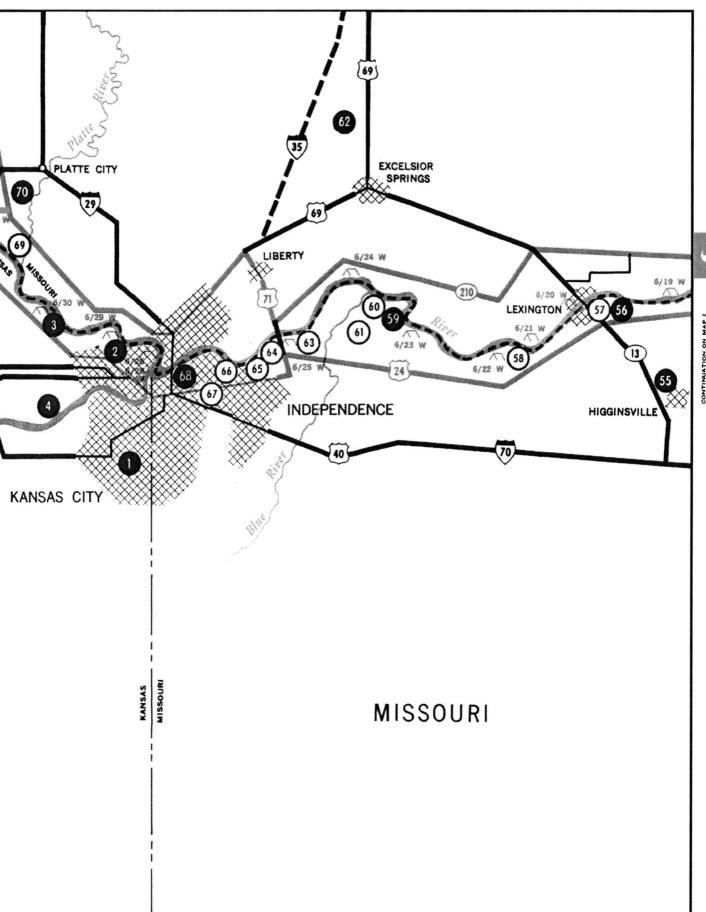

PLATTE CITY

EXCELSIOR
SPRINGS

LIBERTY

LEXINGTON

INDEPENDENCE

HIGGINSVILLE

KANSAS CITY

KANSAS

MISSOURI

MISSOURI

Area Number		Ownership *	Administration *	Recreation Use			Recreation Activities and Attractions															Total Land and Water Acreage
				Day	Overnight	Vacation	Camping	Picnicking	Boating	Water Skiing	Swimming	Hunting	Fishing	Hiking	Horse Trails	Sightseeing	Nature Study	Winter Sports	Historic	Archeologic	Geologic	
	MISSOURI (Continued)																					
55	Confederate Memorial State Park	S	S	▲				●					●						●			95
56	Civil War Battle of Lexington State Pk.	S	S	▲												●			●			77
57	Sauk Prairie ~	S	S	▲	▲		●	●	●		●		●	●					●			—
58	Matthews Tavern ~	C	C	▲	▲		●	●	●		●	●	●						●			165
59	Fort Osage County Park	C	C	▲				●								●			●			36
60	Hay Corbin ~	C	C	▲	▲		●	●	●		●	●	●									—
61	Jackson County Park (Unnamed) ~	C	C	▲	▲	▲	●	●	●		●	●	●									1,600
62	Watkins Mill State Park	S	S	▲												●			●			780
63	La Benite ~	C	C	▲	▲		●	●	●		●		●	●								—
64	Jackson County Park (Unnamed) ~	C	C	▲	▲		●	●	●		●		●	●								100
65	Jackson County Park (Unnamed) ~	C	C	▲	▲		●	●	●		●		●	●								125
66	Jackson County Park (Unnamed) ~	C	C	▲	▲	▲	●	●	●		●		●	●								1,100
67	Jackson County Park (Unnamed) ~	C	C	▲	▲		●	●	●		●		●	●								225
68	Kansas City Historic Sites and Parks	M	M	▲	▲		●	●	●	●	●		●	●		●	●		●			700
69	Platte Park ~	C	C	▲	▲		●	●	●	●	●		●	●		●	●		●			24
70	Humphrey Access Recreation Area	S	S	▲				●														5
71	Lewis and Clark Hatchery	S	S	▲													●	●				43
72	Lewis and Clark State Park	S	S	▲	▲		●	●	●				●	●			●	●				61

RECREATION AREAS (EXISTING and PROPOSED)

Area Number		Ownership *	Administration *	Day	Overnight	Vacation	Camping	Picnicking	Boating	Water Skiing	Swimming	Hunting	Fishing	Hiking	Horse Trails	Sightseeing	Nature Study	Winter Sports	Historic	Archeologic	Geologic	Total Land and Water Acreage
	KANSAS																					
1	Shawnee Methodist Mission	Q	Q	▲															●			12
2	Huron Cemetery	P	P	▲															●			2
3	Wyandotte County Lake	C	C	▲	▲	▲	●	●	●	●	●		●			●			●			1,195
4	Moses Grinter House	P	P	▲															●			1
5	*Agriculture Hall of Fame ~*	P	P	▲															●			–
6	Governor Charles Robinson House	Q	Q	▲															●			–
7	Pioneer Cemetery	M	M	▲												●			●			–
8	Historic City of Lawrence	M	M	▲												●	●		●			–
9	Dyche Natural History Museum	Q	Q	▲															●			–
10	Haskell Indian Institute	F	F	▲															●			–
11	Constitution Hall and Lane Univ. Bldg.	P	P	▲												●			●			–
12	Perry Reservoir	F	F	▲	▲	▲	●	●	●	●	●		●			●	●	●				–
13	Daniel M. Boone Farm	P	P	▲															●			–
14	Battle of Hickory Point	P	P	▲															●			–
15	Leavenworth County State Lake	S	S	▲	▲		●	●	●	●	●		●	●		●						506
16	*Leavenworth Park ~*	F	F	▲	▲	▲	●	●	●	●	●		●	●		●						•••
17	Fort Leavenworth	F	F	▲												●			●			–
18	Fred Harvey Home	Q	Q	▲												●			●			–
19	Historic Fort Cavagnal	P	P	▲															●	●		–
20	Amelia Earhart Birthplace	P	P	▲															●			–
21	Old Priory, St. Benidicts	P	P	▲															●			–

~Proposed Site

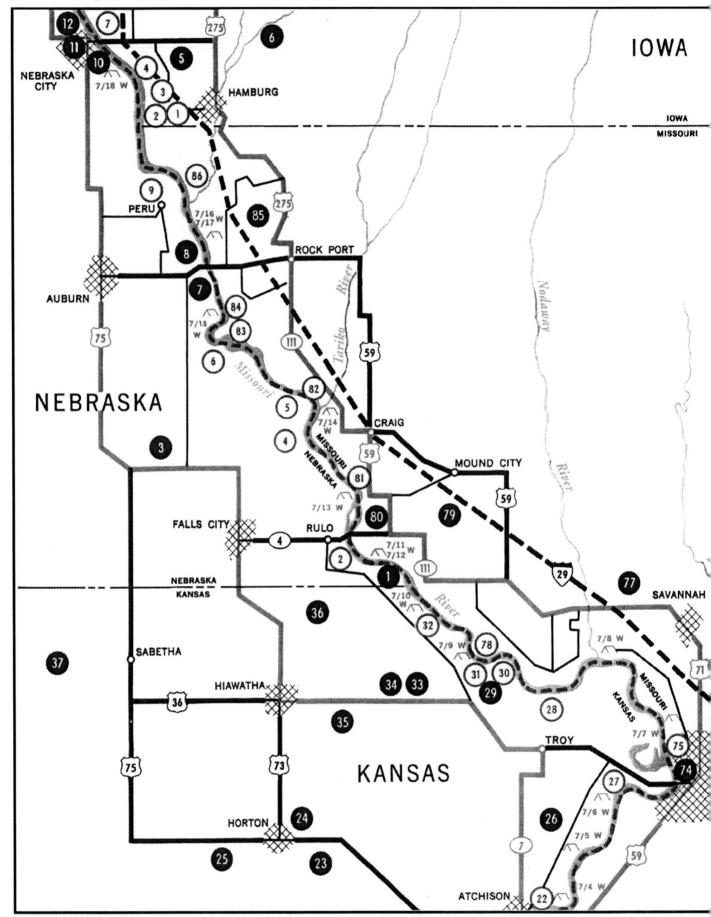

CONTINUATION ON MAP 5

IOWA

IOWA

MISSOURI

NEBRASKA CITY

HAMBURG

PERU

AUBURN

NEBRASKA

ROCK PORT

Turiko River

Nishnabotna River

Missouri River

CRAIG

MOUND CITY

MISSOURI
NEBRASKA

SAVANNAH

FALLS CITY

RULO

NEBRASKA
KANSAS

SABETHA

River

MISSOURI
KANSAS

HIAWATHA

TROY

KANSAS

HORTON

ATCHISON

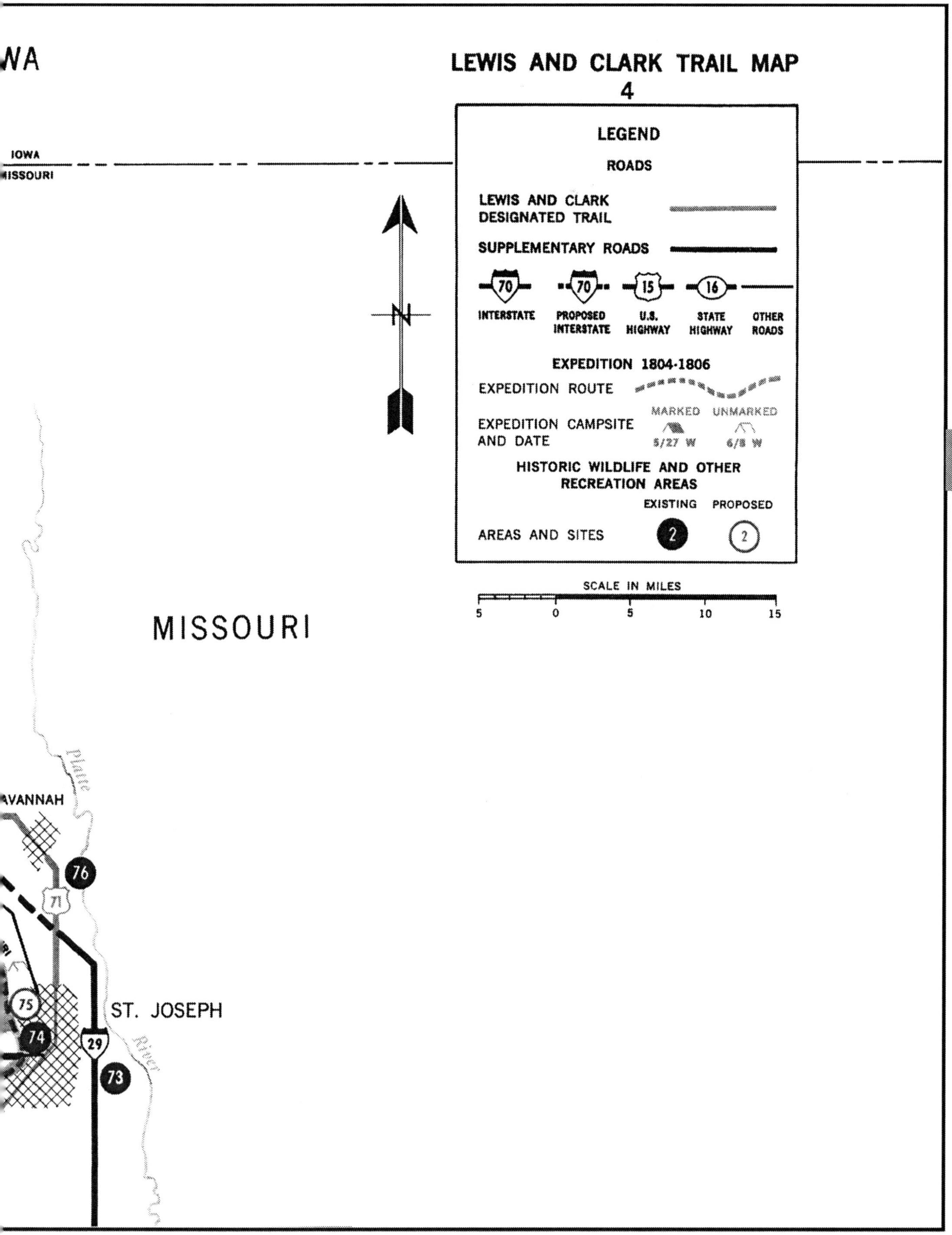

WA
LEWIS AND CLARK TRAIL MAP
4
LEGEND
ROADS
LEWIS AND CLARK DESIGNATED TRAIL
SUPPLEMENTARY ROADS
70
70
15
16
INTERSTATE
PROPOSED INTERSTATE
U.S. HIGHWAY
STATE HIGHWAY
OTHER ROADS
EXPEDITION 1804-1806
EXPEDITION ROUTE
EXPEDITION CAMPSITE AND DATE
MARKED
UNMARKED
5/27 W
6/8 W
HISTORIC WILDLIFE AND OTHER RECREATION AREAS
EXISTING
PROPOSED
AREAS AND SITES
2
2
SCALE IN MILES
5
0
5
10
15
IOWA
MISSOURI
N
MISSOURI
Platte
AVANNAH
76
71
75
74
29
73
ST. JOSEPH
River
4

HISTORIC, WILDLIFE and OTHER

Area Number		Ownership*	Administration*	Recreation Use			Recreation Activities and Attractions															Total Land and Water Acreage
				Day	Overnight	Vacation	Camping	Picnicking	Boating	Water Skiing	Swimming	Hunting	Fishing	Hiking	Horse Trails	Sightseeing	Nature Study	Winter Sports	Historic	Archeologic	Geologic	
	MISSOURI (Continued)																					
73	Pigeon Hill Wildlife Area	S	S	▲								●										200
74	St. Joseph Historic Sites	M	M	▲															●			—
75	St. Michael's Prairie ~	C	C	▲	▲		●	●	●	●	●		●	●		●	●		●			—
76	Rochester Falls Access Area	S	S	▲								●	●									14
77	Honey Creek Wildlife Area	S	S	▲	▲							●	●	●			●					1,448
78	Mill Creek ~	S	S	▲	▲							●	●	●			●					9
79	Squaw Creek National Wildlife Refuge	F	F	▲								●	●	●			●					6,809
80	Big Lake State Park	S	S	▲	▲		●	●	●	●	●		●	●		●	●					111
81	Public Use Area (Unnamed) ~	F	F	▲	▲		●	●	●	●	●		●	●								—
82	Public Use Area (Unnamed) ~	F	F	▲	▲		●	●	●	●	●		●									—
83	Public Use Area (Unnamed) ~	F	F	▲	▲		●	●	●	●	●		●									—
84	Public Use Area (Unnamed) ~	F	F	▲	▲		●	●	●	●	●		●									1,217
85	Brickyard Hill Wildlife Area	S	S	▲	▲		●	●				●	●									1,217
86	Public Use Area (Unnamed) ~	F	F	▲	▲		●	●	●	●	●		●									—
	Kansas (Continued)																					
22	Independence ~	F	F	▲	▲	▲	●	●	●	●	●		●	●	●	●	●		●			—
23	Atchison County State Lake	S	S	▲	▲		●	●	●	●	●		●	●		●	●					248
24	Mission Lake	M	M	▲	▲		●	●	●	●	●		●				●					175
25	Kickapoo Indian Reservation	P	P	▲															●			—
26	Prehistoric Kansa Indian Village	P	P	▲															●	●		—
27	Peevey's Prairie Public Use Area ~	M	M	▲	▲		●	●	●	●	●		●	●	●	●	●		●			35
28	Park Area (Unnamed) ~	P	S	▲	▲	▲	●	●	●	●	●		●	●		●	●		●			3,500
29	Historic Kansa Indian Village	P	P	▲			●	●	●	●	●		●	●		●	●		●	●		4,000
30	Recreation Area (Unnamed) ~	P	S	▲	▲	▲	●	●	●	●	●		●	●		●	●		●			4,000
30	Wolf Camp Recreation Area ~	F	S		▲		●	●	●	●	●		●	●		●	●		●			17

* P - Private   C - County
   Q - Quasi-public   S - State
   M - Municipal   - F - Federal

~Proposed Site

RECREATION AREAS (EXISTING and PROPOSED)

AREA NUMBER		OWNERSHIP*	ADMINISTRATION*	RECREATION USE			RECREATION ACTIVITIES AND ATTRACTIONS															TOTAL LAND AND WATER ACREAGE
				Day	Overnight	Vacation	Camping	Picnicking	Boating	Water Skiing	Swimming	Hunting	Fishing	Hiking	Horse Trails	Sightseeing	Nature Study	Winter Sports	Historic	Archeologic	Geologic	
	KANSAS (Continued)																					
32	*Yellow Clay ~*	M	M	▲	▲	▲	•	•	•	•			•			•	•		•			--
33	Iowa, Sac & Fox Presbyterian Mission	S	S	▲															•	•		--
34	Irwin Hall, Highland Junior College	P	P	▲															•			189
35	Brown County State Lake	S	S	▲	▲		•	•	•	•	•		•			•	•					508
36	Iowa, Sac & Fox Reservations	P	P	▲															•			--
37	Sabetha City Lake	M	M	▲				•	•							•			•	•		120
	NEBRASKA																					
1	Leary Indian Village Site	P	P	▲																•		--
2	*Public Use Area (Unnamed) ~*	F	F	▲	▲		•	•	•	•	•											75
3	Verdon Lake Recreation Area	S	S	▲	▲		•	•			•		•									2,900
4	*Indian Cove State Park ~*	S	S	▲	▲	▲	•	•	•	•	•	•	•	•	•	•						--
5	*Public Use Area (Unnamed) ~*	F	F	▲	▲		•	•	•	•	•											--
6	*Public Use Area (Unnamed) ~*	F	F	▲	▲	▲	•	•	•	•	•											24
7	Brownville Recreation Area	S	S	▲	▲		•	•	•		•											--
8	Historic Brownville	M	M	▲															•			--
9	*Public Use Area (Unnamed) ~*	F	F	▲	▲		•	•	•	•	•		•									--
10	Otoe County Court House	C	C	▲															•			--
11	Arbor Lodge Historical Park	S	S	▲				•					•						•			65
12	Nebraska City Marina	S	S	▲	▲		•	•	•				•									16
	IOWA																					
1	*Southern Border Brigade ~*	P		▲			•	•	•	•	•		•	•		•	•		•			--
2	*State Line Island ~*	S	S	▲	▲		•	•	•	•	•	•	•									110
3	*Public Use Area (Unnamed) ··*	F	F	▲	▲	▲	•	•	•	•	•	•	•									--
4	*Otoe Bend Island ~*	S	S	▲	▲		•	•	•		•	•	•		•							550
5	Waubonsie State Park	S	S	▲	▲	▲	•	•						•		•	•					1,129
6	Riverton Game Management Area	S	S	▲								•	•									941
7	*Capeland Bend Island ~*	S	S	▲	▲	▲	•	•	•		•	•	•	•		•						1,400

~Proposed Site

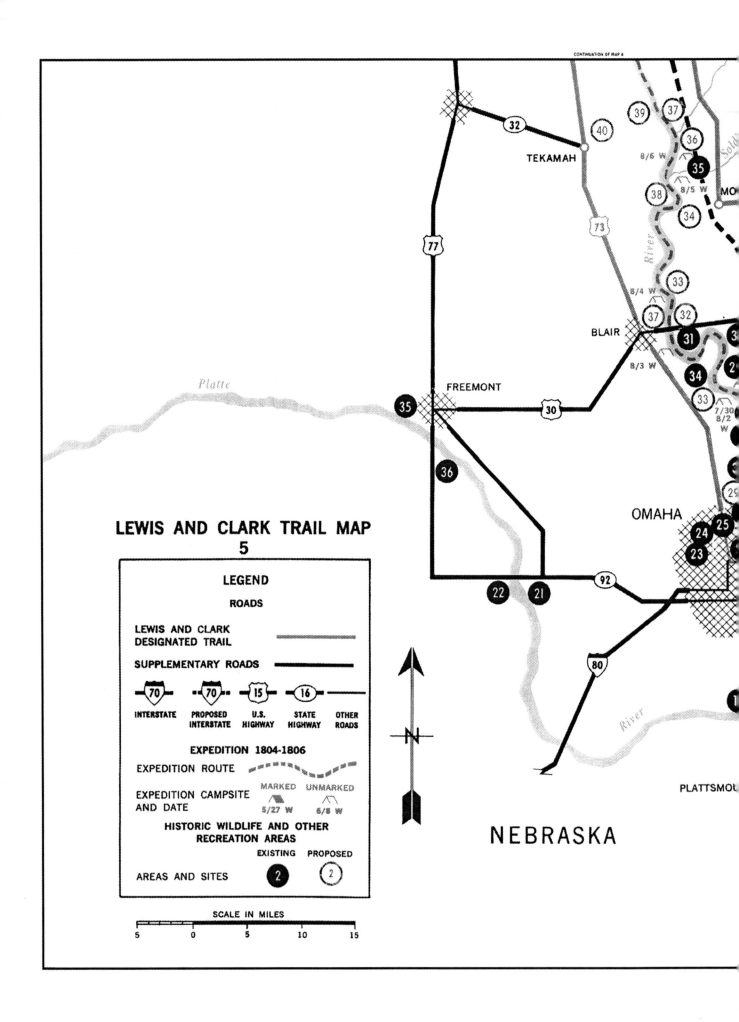

LEWIS AND CLARK TRAIL MAP
5

LEGEND

ROADS

LEWIS AND CLARK
DESIGNATED TRAIL

SUPPLEMENTARY ROADS

70	70	15	16	
INTERSTATE	PROPOSED INTERSTATE	U.S. HIGHWAY	STATE HIGHWAY	OTHER ROADS

EXPEDITION 1804-1806

EXPEDITION ROUTE

EXPEDITION CAMPSITE
AND DATE

MARKED UNMARKED
5/27 W 6/8 W

**HISTORIC WILDLIFE AND OTHER
RECREATION AREAS**

EXISTING PROPOSED

AREAS AND SITES 2 2

SCALE IN MILES

5   0   5   10   15

TEKAMAH

BLAIR

FREEMONT

OMAHA

PLATTSMOU

NEBRASKA

Platte

N

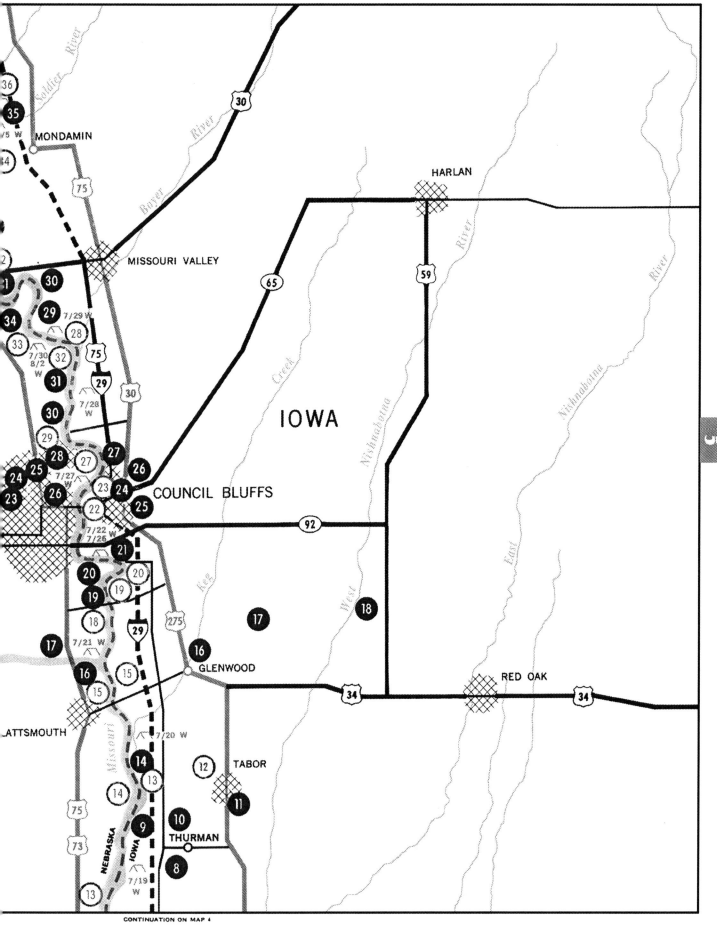

CONTINUATION ON MAP 4

Area Number		Ownership*	Administration*	Recreation Use			Recreation Activities and Attractions															Total Land and Water Acreage
				Day	Overnight	Vacation	Camping	Picnicking	Boating	Water Skiing	Swimming	Hunting	Fishing	Hiking	Horse Trails	Sightseeing	Nature Study	Winter Sports	Historic	Archeologic	Geologic	
	NEBRASKA (Continued)																					
13	*Public Use Area (Unnamed) ~*	F	F	▲	▲		•	•	•	•	•											--
14	*Yellow Wolf ~*	F		▲	▲		•	•			•											33
15	*Plattsmouth Area ~*	F		▲				•	•													10
16	Plattsmouth Waterfowl Management Area	S	S	▲								•						•				1,400
17	Oto Indian Mission	P	P	▲															•			-
18	*Bellevue Landing ~*	F		▲				•	•													15
19	Historic Bellevue	M	M	▲															•	•		-
20	Fontenelle Forest	Q	Q	▲										•			•	•				1,300
21	Two Rivers Recreation Area	Q S	Q S	▲	▲		•	•			•		•									933
22	Yutan Indian Village Site	P	P	▲																•		-
23	Benson Park	M	M	▲				•														218
24	Elmwood Park	M	M	▲				•														216
25	Riverview Park	M	M	▲				•														155
26	Joslyn Art Museum	P M	Q	▲															•			-
27	*River Park ~*	M	M	▲	▲		•															1,000
28	Old Florence & Mormon Cemetery	Q	Q	▲															•			221
29	*Mormon Bridge Area ~*	F		▲				•	•													6
30	Cabanne Trading Post	P	P	▲															•			-
31	Lisa Trading Post	P	P	▲															•			-
32	*Boyer Chute Area ~*	F		▲				•	•	•												14
33	*Fort Atkinson Historical Park ~*	S	S	▲														•	•	•		-
34	Historic Council Bluffs	S	S	▲															•			-
35	Fremont Lakes Recreation Area	S	S	▲	▲	▲	•	•	•	•	•		•									800
36	Pawnee Indian Village	P	P	▲															•	•		-
37	*Blair Recreation Area ~*	S	S	▲					•				•									-
38	*Herman Area ~*	F		▲	▲		•	•	•													36
39	*Pelican Area ~*	F		▲	▲		•	•	•													36
40	*Tekamah Recreation Area ~*	S	S	▲				•	•								•					--

* P - Private   C - County
   Q - Quasi-public   S - State
   M - Municipal   F - Federal

~ *Proposed Site*

RECREATION AREAS (EXISTING and PROPOSED)

Area Number		Ownership*	Administration*	Recreation Use			Recreation Activities and Attractions															Total Land and Water Acreage
				Day	Overnight	Vacation	Camping	Picnicking	Boating	Water Skiing	Swimming	Hunting	Fishing	Hiking	Horse Trails	Sightseeing	Nature Study	Winter Sports	Historic	Archeologic	Geologic	
	IOWA (Continued)																					
8	Plum Creek	S	S	▲								•	•									400
9	Auldon Bar Island	S	S	▲								•	•			•						750
10	Forney's Lake	S	S	▲								•	•									1,069
11	John Brown and Underground Railroad	M	M	▲															•			–
12	Waubonsie's Village ~	P		△															○			10
13	Bartlett Landing ~	F	S	△	△		○	○	○													10
14	Nottleman Island	S		▲									•			•						1,550
15	Glenwood Area ~	F		△	△		○	○														22
16	Mills County Historical Building	C	C	▲															•			–
17	Stagecoach House Silver City	P	P	▲															•			–
18	Willow Slough Wildlife Area	S	S	▲								•										597
19	Trader's Point ~	P		△															○			–
20	Gifford Area ~	F		△				○	○													13
21	Lake Manawa State Park	S	S	▲	▲		•	•	•	•	•	•	•									919
22	Dodge Park Area ~	F		△				○	○							○						22
23	Narrows Area ~	F		△				○	○													7
24	Council Bluffs Historic Sites	Q	Q	▲															•			–
25	Gifford Wildlife Sanctuary	S	S	▲													•		•			40
26	Smith Wildlife Refuge	S	S	▲													•		•			201
27	Carters Lake	S	S	▲				•	•		•											–
28	Rand Bar Recreation Area ~	S	S	▲	▲							○	○									60
29	Wilson Island Recreation Area	S	S	▲	▲		•	•	•			•	•									3
30	Nobels Lake	S	S	▲								•	•									232
31	DeSota National Wildlife Refuge	F S	F S	▲								•	•									7,800
32	California Bend Recreation Area ~	S		△									○				○					550
33	Tyson Bend Recreation Area ~	S	S	△									○									1,100
34	Sandy Point Area ~	F		△	△			○	○		○											35
35	Round Lake Recreation Area	S	S	▲								•	•									393
36	River Stone Area ~	F		△	△			○	○		○											18
37	Deer Island Recreation Area ~	S	S	△	△			○	○													512

~Proposed Site

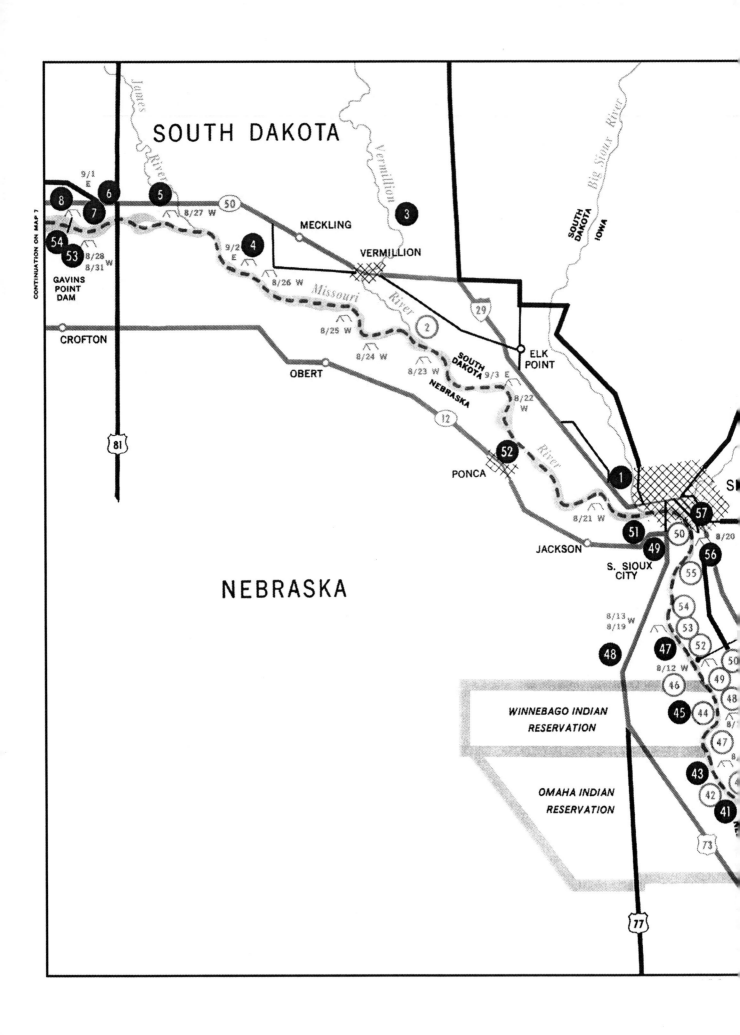

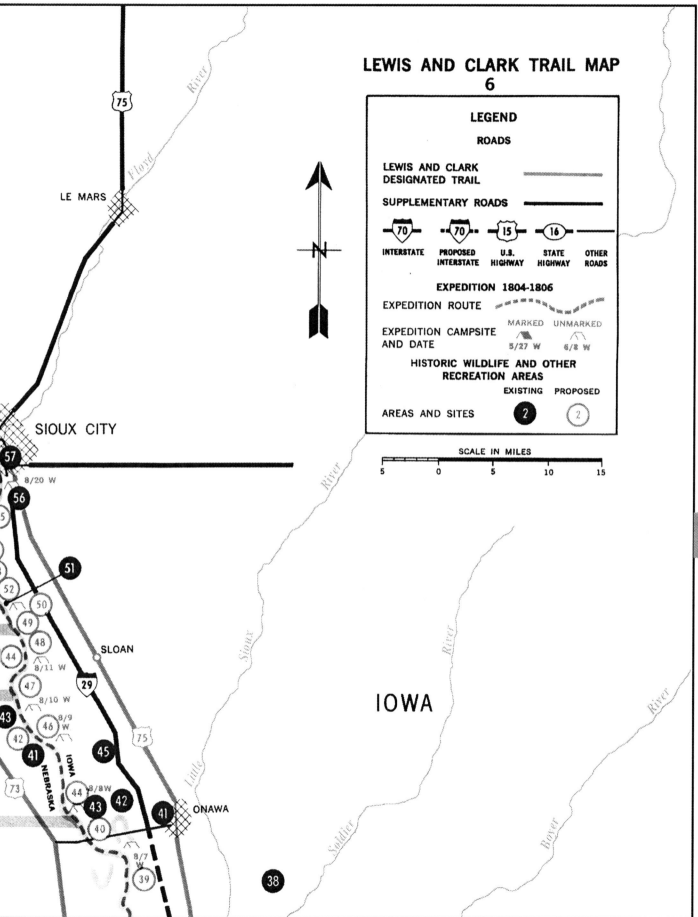

LEWIS AND CLARK TRAIL MAP
6

LEGEND
ROADS

LEWIS AND CLARK DESIGNATED TRAIL

SUPPLEMENTARY ROADS

70	70	15	16	
INTERSTATE	PROPOSED INTERSTATE	U.S. HIGHWAY	STATE HIGHWAY	OTHER ROADS

EXPEDITION 1804-1806

EXPEDITION ROUTE

EXPEDITION CAMPSITE AND DATE

MARKED 5/27 W   UNMARKED 6/8 W

HISTORIC WILDLIFE AND OTHER RECREATION AREAS

EXISTING   PROPOSED

AREAS AND SITES   2   2

SCALE IN MILES

5   0   5   10   15

LE MARS

SIOUX CITY

57

8/20 W

56

51

52

50

49

48

SLOAN

44

8/11 W

47

8/10 W

29

43

46 8/9 W

42

41

45

73

IOWA
NEBRASKA

44 8/8W

43

42

41

ONAWA

40

75

IOWA

8/7 W

39

38

CONTINUATION ON MAP 5

HISTORIC, WILDLIFE and OTHER

AREA NUMBER		OWNERSHIP*	ADMINISTRATION*	RECREATION USE			RECREATION ACTIVITIES AND ATTRACTIONS															TOTAL LAND AND WATER ACREAGE
				Day	Overnight	Vacation	Camping	Picnicking	Boating	Water Skiing	Swimming	Hunting	Fishing	Hiking	Horse Trails	Sightseeing	Nature Study	Winter Sports	Historic	Archeologic	Geologic	
	IOWA (Continued)																					
38	Preparation Canyon Recreation Area	S	S	▲	▲		●	●								●						187
39	*Pickle City Area ~*	F	F	▲	▲		●	●	●				●									18
40	*Blackbird Area ~*	F	F	▲	▲		●	●	●		●		●									22
41	Lewis and Clark State Park	S	S	▲	▲		●	●			●		●									286
42	Blue Lake	S	S	▲								●	●									941
43	Onawa Access Recreation Area	S	S	▲	▲							●	●									6
44	*Recreation Area (6 Sites) ~*	S S	S	▲							●	●	●									1,270
45	Decatur Access Recreation Area	S	S	▲	▲		●					●	●									6
46	*Rabbit Island Recreation Area ~*	P	P	▲									●			●	●					420
47	*Omaha Mission Bend Area ~*	F	F	▲	▲		●	●	●				●									43
48	*Snyder Bend Recreation Area ~*	S	S	▲								●	●						●			1,000
49	*Omandi Bend Recreation Area ~*	S S	S	▲	▲		●	●	●			●	●									400
50	*Glovers Point Bend Recreation Area ~*	S	S	▲	▲		●	●	●	●	●	●	●	●	●	●	●					350
51	Brown's Lake State Park	S S	S	▲	▲		●	●	●	●	●	●	●									783
52	*Winnebago Bend Recreation Area ~*	S	S	▲	▲		●	●	●		●	●	●	●								1,050
53	*Snyder Bend Area ** ~*	F		▲	▲		●	●	●													22
54	*Dakota Bend Wildlife Refuge ~*	S	S	▲								●	●									250
55	*Floyd Bend Area ** ~*	F		▲	▲		●	●	●													17
56	Sergeant Floyd Monument	Q	Q	▲																●	●		—
57	Sioux City Historic Sites	M	M	▲																●	●		—

* P - Private   C - County   ** Inundated historical site, interpretative
   Q - Quasi-public   S - State   marker to be erected on shore
   M - Municipal   F - Federal

~Proposed Site

RECREATION AREAS (EXISTING and PROPOSED)

AREA NUMBER		OWNERSHIP*	ADMINISTRATION*	RECREATION USE			RECREATION ACTIVITIES AND ATTRACTIONS															TOTAL LAND AND WATER ACREAGE
				Day	Overnight	Vacation	Camping	Picnicking	Boating	Water Skiing	Swimming	Hunting	Fishing	Hiking	Horse Trails	Sightseeing	Nature Study	Winter Sports	Historic	Archeologic	Geologic	
	NEBRASKA (Continued)																					
41	Blackbird Hill	P	P	▲															●			–
42	*Ordway Area ~*	F		▲	▲		●	●	●	●	●		●	●		●			●			16
43	Chief Big Elk Recreation Area	P	P	▲	▲		●	●	●				●									1,000
44	*Hole-In-The-Rock Area ~*	F	F	▲	▲		●	●	●	●	●		●	●		●						130
45	Big Bear Hollow Recreation Area	P	P	▲	▲		●	●	●					●								6,000
46	*Fort Charles Historical Park ~*	S	S	▲															●			–
47	Omadi Bend Recreation Area	S	S	▲	▲		●	●	●				●									30
48	Omaha Indian Village	P		▲															●			–
49	Historic Dakota City	M	M	▲															●			–
50	*South Sioux City Area ~*	F			▲		●	●	●	●	●		●	●		●			●			15
51	Crystal Lake Wayside Recreation Area	S	S	▲	▲		●	●					●									20
52	Ponca State Park	S	S	▲	▲	▲	●	●	●		●			●		●	●	●				495
53	Calumet Bluff Council Site	F	F	▲															●			–
54	Gavins Point Dam & Downstream Rec. Areas	F	F	▲	▲		●	●	●		●		●				●	●	●			–
	SOUTH DAKOTA																					
1	Elk Point River Desert	P	P	▲				●								●	●		●			60
2	*Vermillion Trading Post ~*	P	P	▲															●			–
3	Spirit Mound	P	P	▲															●			–
4	Custer Camp Site	P	P	▲															●			20
5	James River Recreation Area	P	P	▲				●											●			–
6	Historic Yankton	M	M	▲															●			–
7	Gavins Point National Fish Hatchery	F	F	▲													●		●			230
8	Gavins Point Dam & Recreation Areas	F	SF	▲	▲	▲	●	●	●	●	●		●	●		●	●		●			325

~Proposed Site

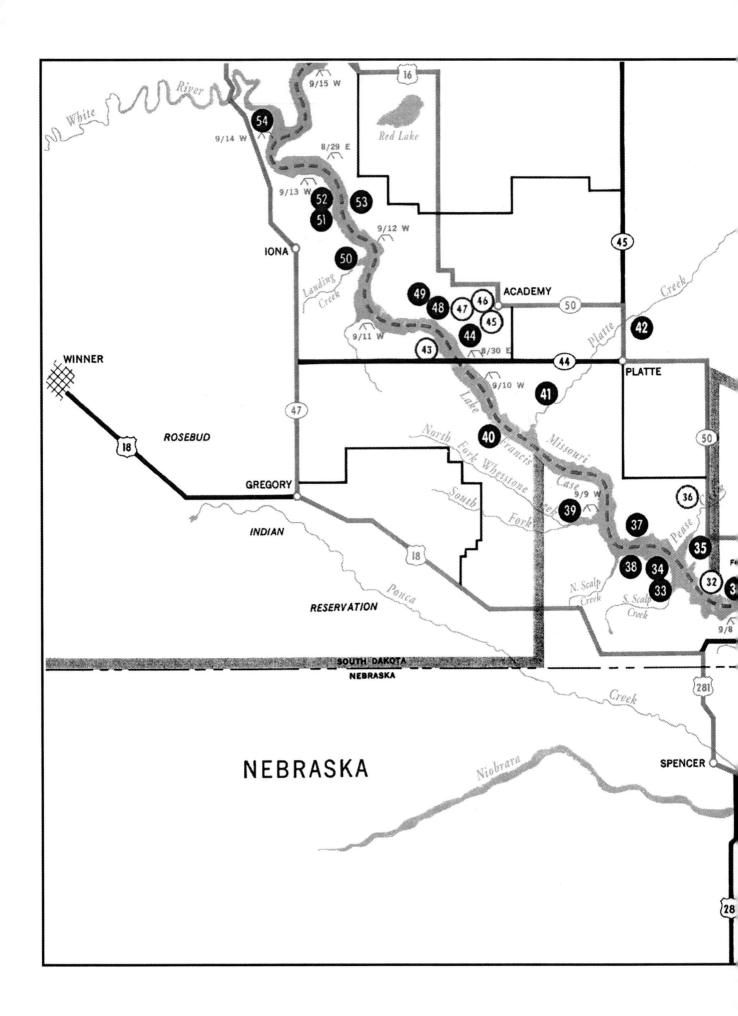

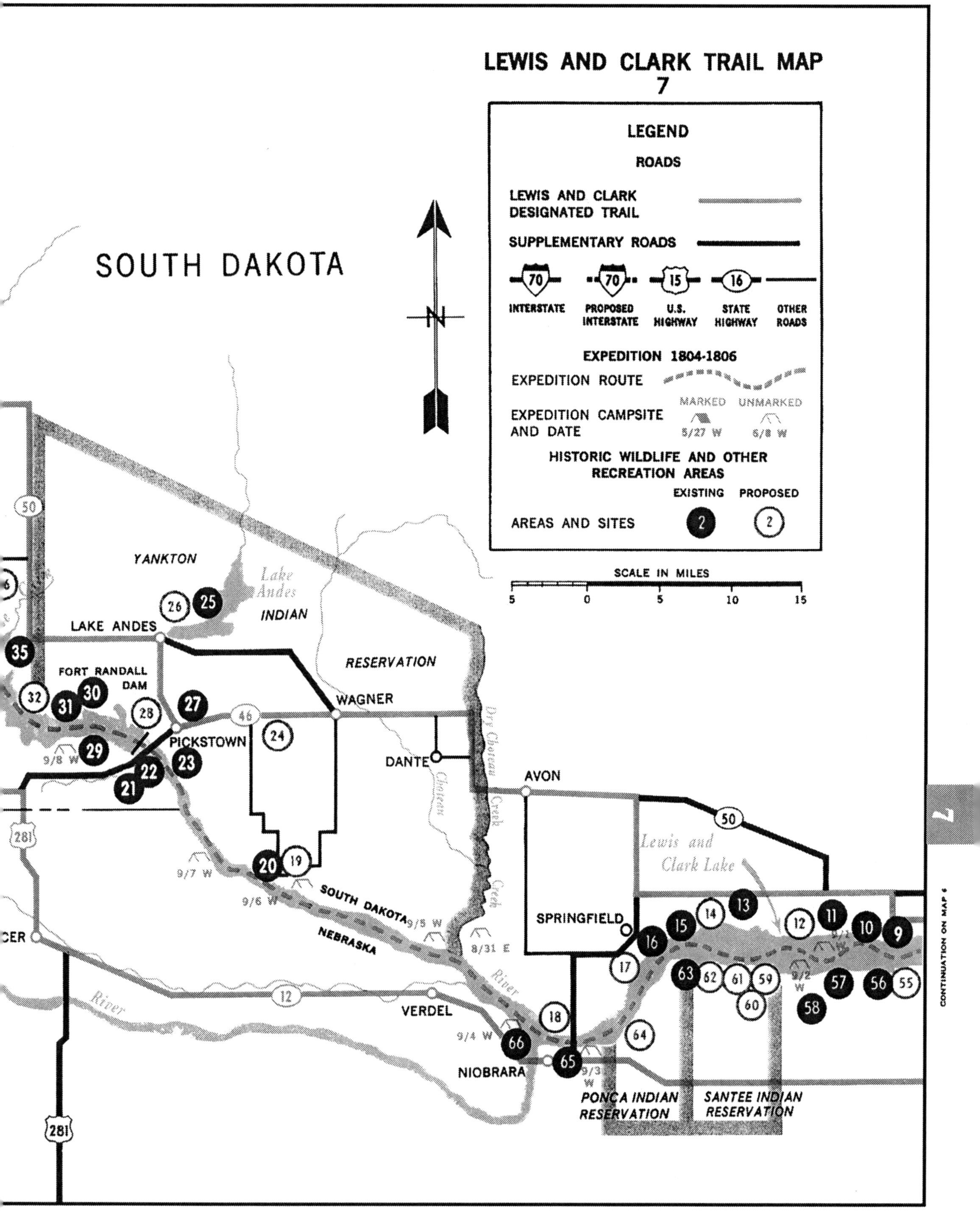

LEWIS AND CLARK TRAIL MAP
7

LEGEND

ROADS

LEWIS AND CLARK DESIGNATED TRAIL

SUPPLEMENTARY ROADS

70	70	15	16	
INTERSTATE	PROPOSED INTERSTATE	U.S. HIGHWAY	STATE HIGHWAY	OTHER ROADS

EXPEDITION 1804-1806

EXPEDITION ROUTE

EXPEDITION CAMPSITE AND DATE — MARKED 5/27 W — UNMARKED 6/8 W

HISTORIC WILDLIFE AND OTHER RECREATION AREAS

AREAS AND SITES — EXISTING 2 — PROPOSED 2

SCALE IN MILES
5 0 5 10 15

SOUTH DAKOTA

N

YANKTON

Lake Andes

INDIAN

RESERVATION

LAKE ANDES

FORT RANDALL DAM

PICKSTOWN

WAGNER

DANTE

AVON

50

Lewis and Clark Lake

SPRINGFIELD

SOUTH DAKOTA

NEBRASKA

9/8 W

9/7 W

9/6 W

9/5 W

8/31 E

VERDEL

12

9/4 W

NIOBRARA

9/3 W

PONCA INDIAN RESERVATION

SANTEE INDIAN RESERVATION

Dry Choteau Creek

Choteau Creek

River

River

281

281

46

24

50

35 32 31 30 28 27 26 25 29 22 23 21 20 19 16 17 15 14 13 12 11 10 9 63 62 61 59 57 56 55 60 58 18 66 65 64

9/2 W

CONTINUATION ON MAP 6

7

HISTORIC, WILDLIFE and OTHER

Area Number		Ownership*	Administration*	Day	Overnight	Vacation	Camping	Picnicking	Boating	Water Skiing	Swimming	Hunting	Fishing	Hiking	Horse Trails	Sightseeing	Nature Study	Winter Sports	Historic	Archeologic	Geologic	Total Land and Water Acreage
	SOUTH DAKOTA (Continued)																					
9	White Bear Cliff	F	F	▲															•			–
10	Lesterville Recreation Area	F	FS	▲									•									70
11	Tabor Recreation Area	F	S	▲	▲		•	•	•													120
12	*Charley Creek Recreation Area ~*	F	F	▲	▲		•	•	•													–
13	Bon Homme Community	P	P	▲															•			–
14	*Snatch Creek Recreation Area ~*	F	F	▲									•									60
15	Sand Creek Recreation Area	FM	S	▲				•	•				•									45
16	Historic Springfield	M	M	▲				•	•										•			–
17	*Emanuel Creek Recreation Area ~*	F	F	▲									•									285
18	*Running Water Recreation Area ~*	F	F	▲																		10
19	*Greenwood Recreation Area ~*	P	P	▲									•									20
20	Yankton Indian Agency	P	P	▲															•			–
21	Old Fort Randall	F	F	▲															•			–
22	Randall Creek Recreation Area	F	F	▲	▲		•	•	•							•			•			466
23	Trudeau Cabin	P	P	▲															•			5
24	*Chalk Rock Colony Recreation Area ~*	P	P	▲											•	•		•			–
25	Lake Andes National Wildlife Refuge	F	F	▲									•			•	•				850
26	*Lake Andes Recreation Area ~*	P	P	▲									•									40
27	Fort Randall Dam and Recreation Area	FP	SF	▲	▲		•	•	•	•	•	•	•									–
28	*Trudeau Recreation Area ~*	P	P	▲															•			80
29	South Shore Recreation Area	F	S	▲				•	•				•									169
30	North Point Public Use Area	F	S	▲	▲		•	•	•	•	•											895
31	Spring Creek Public Use Area	F	S	▲									•									85
32	*St. Phillips Bay Public Use Area ~*	F	S	▲									•									97
33	South Scalp Creek Public Use Area	F	S	▲									•									760
34	North Scalp Creek	F	S	▲									•			•						190
35	Pease Creek Public Use Area	F	S	▲								•	•									474
36	*Recreation Area (Unnamed) ~*	S	S	▲									•			•						40
37	North Wheeler Public Use Area	F	S	▲				•	•				•						•			78
38	South Wheeler Public Use Area	F	S	▲				•	•								•					210

* P - Private C - County
  Q - Quasi-public S - State
  M - Municipal F - Federal

~ Proposed Site

RECREATION AREAS (EXISTING and PROPOSED)

Area Number		Ownership*	Administration*	Recreation Use			Recreation Activities and Attractions															Total Land and Water Acreage
				Day	Overnight	Vacation	Camping	Picnicking	Boating	Water Skiing	Swimming	Hunting	Fishing	Hiking	Horse Trails	Sightseeing	Nature Study	Winter Sports	Historic	Archeologic	Geologic	
	SOUTH DAKOTA (Continued)																					
39	Whetstone Creek Public Use Areas	F	S	▲					●		●		●				●					408
40	Stricker Bottom Public Use Area	F	S	▲	▲		●	●					●									39
41	Platte Creek Public Use Area	F	S	▲					●	●			●									143
42	Platte Public Recreation Area	F	S	▲									●									605
43	*Westbridge Public Use Area ~*	*F*	*F*	▲					●	●			●									266
44	Snake Creek Public Use Area	F	S	▲									●				●					220
45	*Public Use Area (Unnamed) ~*	*F*	*F*	▲								●				●					40
46	*Public Use Area (Unnamed) ~*	*F*	*F*	▲								●				●					80
47	*Public Use Area (Unnamed) ~*	*F*	*F*	▲								●				●					80
48	Turgeon Bottom Public Use Area	F	S	▲									●				●					95
49	Turgeon Well Public Use Area	F	F	▲									●									18
50	Landing Creek Public Use Area	F	F	▲	▲		●	●					●									330
51	Elm Creek Public Use Area	F	F	▲									●									230
52	Waterhole Creek Public Use Area	F	S	▲					●	●			●									253
53	Five Mile Public Use Area	F	S	▲									●									390
54	White River Recreation Areas	S	S	▲													●					897
	NEBRASKA (Continued)																					
55	*Deep Water Recreation Area ~*	*F*	*F*	▲									●									70
56	Weigand Recreation Area	S	S	▲	▲		●	●	●		●		●									340
57	Bloomfield Recreation Area	F	S	▲	▲		●	●	●				●									120
58	Miller Creek Recreation Area	F	S	▲					●		●											45
59	*Devil's Nest Recreation Area ~*	*F*	S	▲									●									140
60	*Lindy Recreation Area ~*	*F*	S	▲									●									30
61	*Sand Island Recreation Area ~*	*F*	S	▲					●	●												70
62	*Knox Recreation Area ~*	*F*	S	▲									●									50
63	Santee Recreation Area	F	S	▲					●				●					●			60
64	*Lost Creek Recreation Area ~*	*F*	S	▲									●									225
65	Niobrara Recreation Area	F	S	▲					●	●												26
66	Niobrara State Park	S	S	▲	▲	▲	●	●	●	●	●		●	●		●				●		408

~Proposed Site

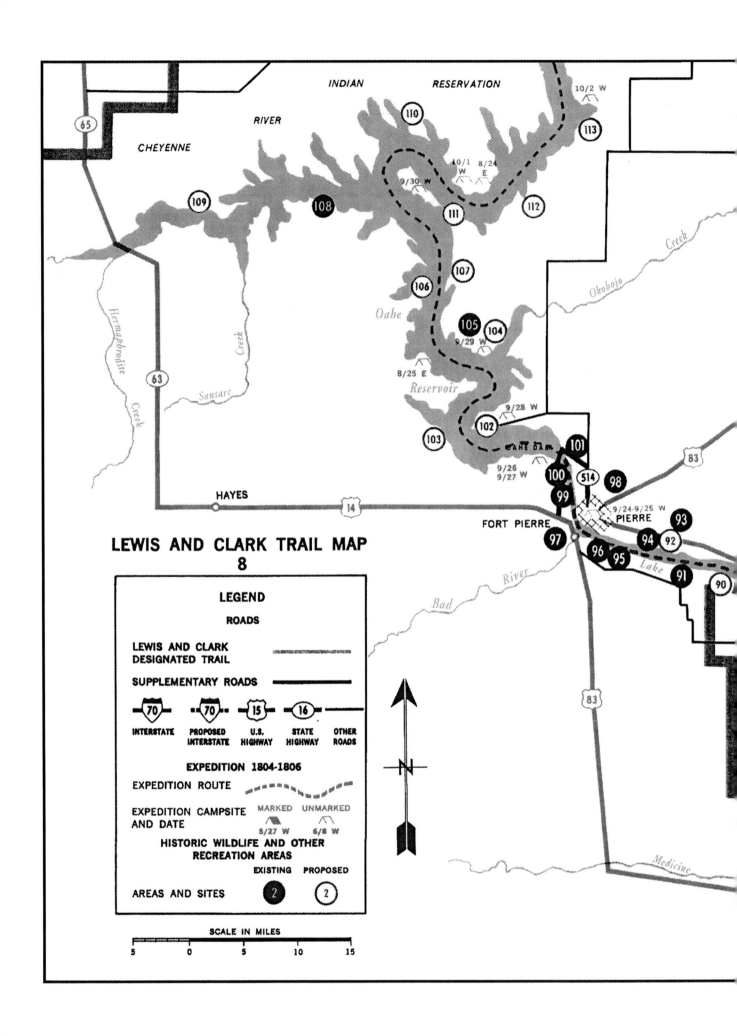

INDIAN RESERVATION

RIVER

CHEYENNE

Creek

Okobojo Creek

Hermaphrodite Creek

Sansarc Creek

Oahe

Reservoir

10/2 W

9/30 W
10/1 W
8/24 E

9/29 W

8/25 E

9/28 W

OAHE DAM

9/26 W
9/27 W

9/24-9/25 W

HAYES

FORT PIERRE

PIERRE

Bad River

Lake

Medicine

LEWIS AND CLARK TRAIL MAP
8

LEGEND
ROADS

LEWIS AND CLARK
DESIGNATED TRAIL

SUPPLEMENTARY ROADS

70	70	15	16	
INTERSTATE	PROPOSED INTERSTATE	U.S. HIGHWAY	STATE HIGHWAY	OTHER ROADS

EXPEDITION 1804-1806

EXPEDITION ROUTE

EXPEDITION CAMPSITE   MARKED   UNMARKED
AND DATE
                     5/27 W   6/8 W

**HISTORIC WILDLIFE AND OTHER
RECREATION AREAS**

                     EXISTING   PROPOSED

AREAS AND SITES   2   2

SCALE IN MILES

5   0   5   10   15

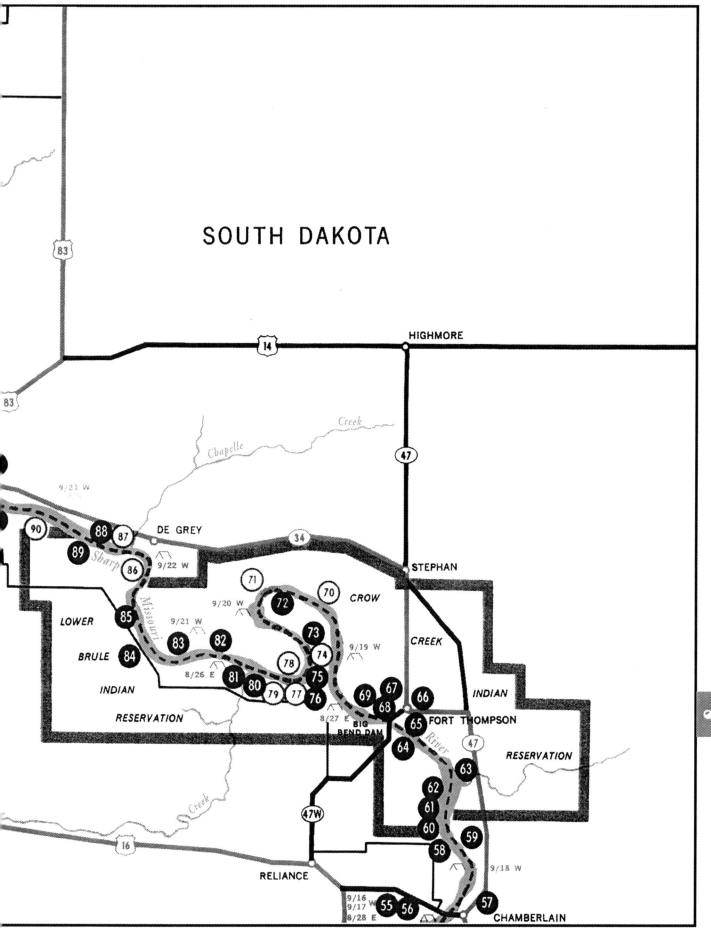

SOUTH DAKOTA

HIGHMORE

Creek

Chapelle

DE GREY

34

STEPHAN

90 88 87
89 Sharp
86 9/22 W

9/23 W

71 CROW 70

9/20 W 72

LOWER 85 9/21 W 73 CREEK

BRULE 84 83 82 74 9/19 W

INDIAN 81 80 78 75 INDIAN

79 77 76

RESERVATION 8/26 E 69 67 66

8/27 E 68 FORT THOMPSON

BIG 65 RESERVATION
BEND DAM 64 River 47

62 63

61

47W 60 59

58

RELIANCE 9/18 W

9/16 55 56 57
9/17 W CHAMBERLAIN
8/28 E

CONTINUATION ON MAP 7

Area Number		Ownership	Administration	Recreation Use			Recreation Activities and Attractions															Total Land and Water Acreage
				Day	Overnight	Vacation	Camping	Picnicking	Boating	Water Skiing	Swimming	Hunting	Fishing	Hiking	Horse Trails	Sightseeing	Nature Study	Winter Sports	Historic	Archeologic	Geologic	
	SOUTH DAKOTA (Continued)																					
55	Old Lower Brule Indian Agency	F	F	▲															•			—
56	Chamberlain – West Bank Rec. Area	F	S	▲					•				•									119
57	Chamberlain – American Creek Rec. Area	F	F	▲					•				•									37
58	Kiowa Unit Recreation Area	F	S	▲								•	•									105
59	Brule Bottom Wildlife Area	F	S	▲									•				•					310
60	Military Fort Lookout	P	P	▲														•			10
61	Fur Post, Ft. Lookout (Fort Kiowa)	F	F	▲												•		•			10
62	Old Fort Hale	P	P	▲														•			1
63	Crow Creek Indian Village	F	F	▲															•		10
64	Tailwaters Public Use Area	F	F	▲									•			•					95
65	Big Bend Dam and Recreation Areas	F	F	▲					•				•			•					—
66	Fort Thompson – Crow Creek Agency	F	F	▲														•			—
67	Fort Thompson Recreation Area	PF	P	▲	▲	▲	•	•	•	•	•	•										—
68	Soldier Creek Public Use Area	F	F	▲									•								170
69	Big Bend Overlook	P	F	▲												•					10
70	*East Bend Recreation Area* ~	*F*	*F*	△				○	○		○		○									*90*
71	*North Bend Recreation Area* ~	*F*	*F*	△				○	○		○		○									*100*
72	Jiggs Thompson Indian Village	F	F	▲																•	—
73	Lanadeau Indian Village	F	F	▲																•	—
74	*Narrows Recreation Area* ~	*F*	*F*	△				○					○									*1,100*
75	Counselor Creek	F	F	▲					•												250
76	Lower Brule Indian Agency	F	F	▲													•			40
77	*Fort Defiance* ~	*P*	*F*	△													○			1
78	*Little Bend Grand View Point Rec. Area* ~	*F*	*F*	△											○	○		○			*1*
79	*Lower Brule Recreation Area* ~	*F*	*F*	△				○	○				○								*45*
80	Red Cloud Agency Recreation Area	F	F	▲	▲		•	•					•								20
81	Iron Nation Public Use Area	F	F	▲					•												700
82	West Bend Public Use Area	F	F	▲					•				•								160
83	Joe Creek Public Use Area	F	F	▲					•				•								160
84	Cedar Creek Public Use Area	F	F	▲					•												250

* P - Private   C - County
   Q - Quasi-public   S - State
   M - Municipal   F - Federal

~Proposed site

RECREATION AREAS (EXISTING and PROPOSED)

AREA NUMBER		OWNERSHIP*	ADMINISTRATION*	RECREATION USE			RECREATION ACTIVITIES AND ATTRACTIONS															TOTAL LAND AND WATER ACREAGE
				Day	Overnight	Vacation	Camping	Picnicking	Boating	Water Skiing	Swimming	Hunting	Fishing	Hiking	Horse Trails	Sightseeing	Nature Study	Winter Sports	Historic	Archeologic	Geologic	
	SOUTH DAKOTA (Continued)																					
85	Loisel's Post	F	F	▲															●			–
86	*Fort George Public Use Area* ~	F	F	▲															●			—
87	*Rousseau Public Use Area* ~	F	F	▲					●	●												200
88	De Grey Public Use Area	F	F	▲					●				●									360
89	Chapelle Creek Overlook	P	P	▲															●			–
90	*LaRoche Public Use Area* ~	F	F	▲					●	●												50
91	Antelope Creek Public Use Area	F	F	▲	▲				●	●		●										300
92	*Hipple Lake Public Use Area* ~	F	F	▲				●	●	●			●									300
93	Prehistoric Indian Village	P	P	▲															●	●		60
94	Fort Sully I	P	P	▲															●			10
95	Farm Island Recreation Park	F	F	▲															●			1,000
96	LaFrambois Island	F	F	▲					●	●												30
97	Verendrye Plaque Discovery Site	S	S	▲															●			–
98	Snake Butte Mosaic	P	P	▲																●	●	6
99	Ft. Pierre Chouteau	PS	PS	▲															●	●		2,000
100	Oahe Dam and Recreation Areas	F	F	▲	▲	▲	●	●	●	●	●		●	●		●	●		●	●		–
101	Oahe Mission Chapel	S	S	▲															●			1
102	*Oahe Mission Recreation Area* ~	F	F	▲					●	●			●									60
103	*Chantier Creek Public Use Area* ~	F	F	▲					●	●			●									110
104	*Okobojo Creek Public Use Area* ~	F	F	▲					●	●			●									80
105	Sully Indian Village	F	F	▲															●	●		60
106	*Fort Bennett* **																		●			
107	*Fort Sully II* **																		●			
108	Little Bend Overlook	P	P	▲												●						50
109	*Cheyenne River Public Use Area* ~	F	F	▲					●	●			●									170
110	*North Heart Butte Bay Recreation Area* ~	F	F	▲					●	●			●									40
111	*Little Bend Public Use Area* ~	F	F	▲					●	●												—
112	*Recreation Area (Unnamed)* ~	F	F	▲					●	●		●					●					320
113	*Sutton Bay Public Use Area* ~	F	F	▲					●	●												150

**Inundated historical site, interpretative
marker to be erected on shore

~Proposed site

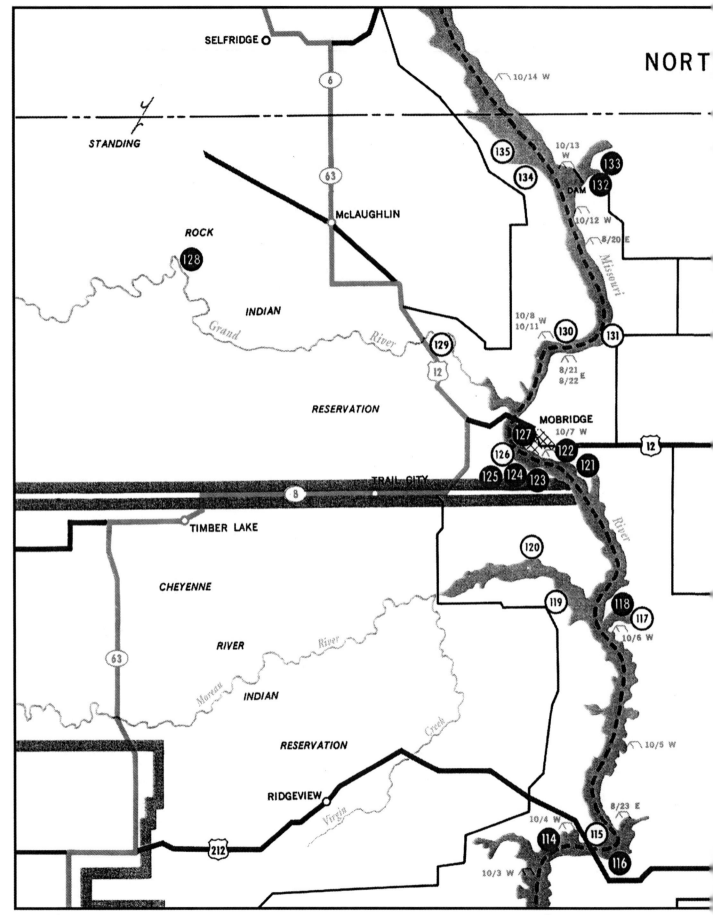

SELFRIDGE O

NORT

STANDING

10/14 W

6

ROCK

135

134

133

DAM

132

63

McLAUGHLIN

10/13 W

128

10/12 W

8/20 E

INDIAN

Missouri

Grand

River

129

10/8 W
10/11

130

131

12

RESERVATION

8/21 E

8/22 E

MOBRIDGE

127

10/7 W

122

12

126

121

125 124 123

River

TRAIL CITY

8

TIMBER LAKE

120

CHEYENNE

119

118

117

RIVER

River

10/6 W

63

Moreau

INDIAN

RESERVATION

10/5 W

RIDGEVIEW

Virgin

Creek

8/23 E

10/4 W

115

212

114

116

10/3 W

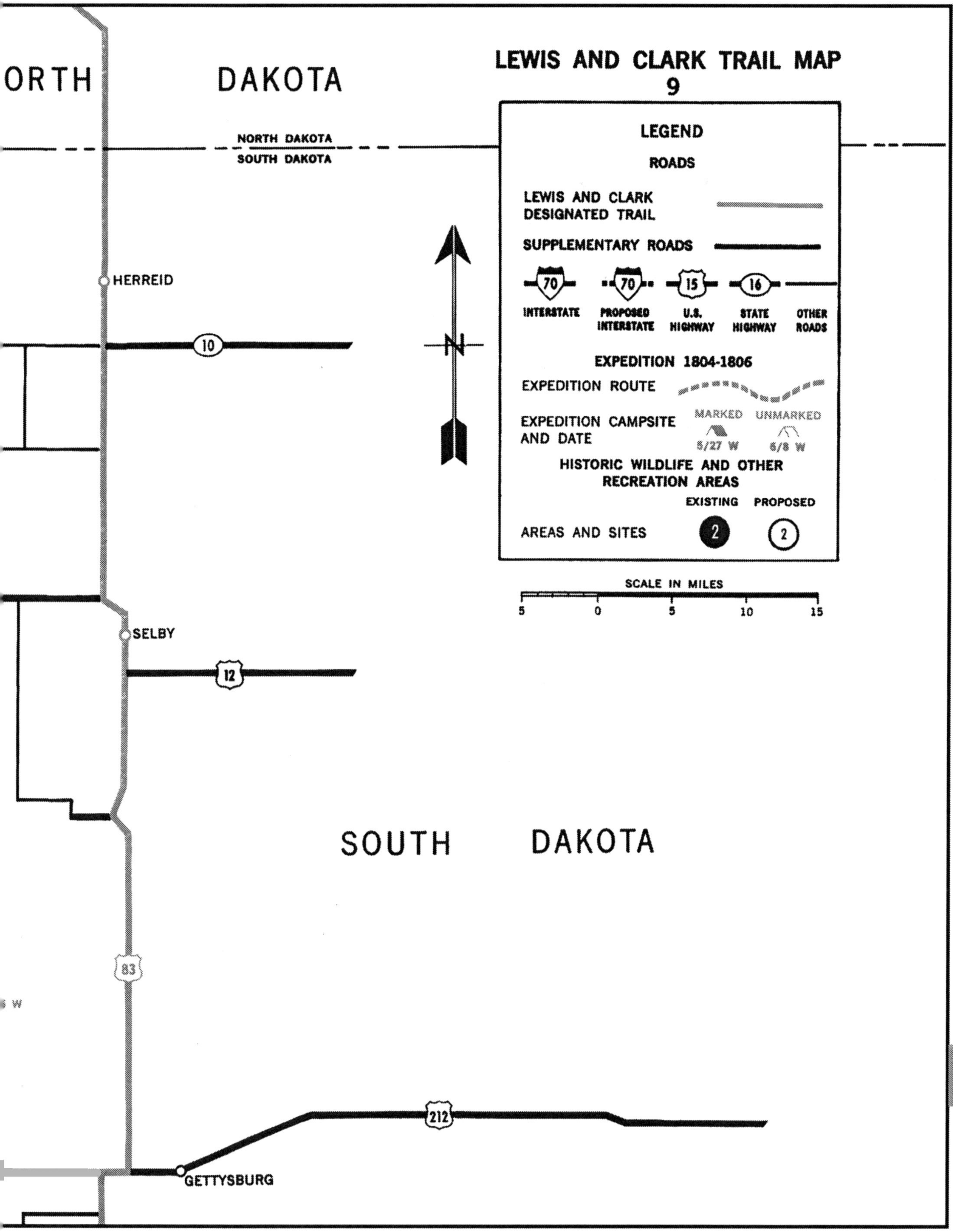

ORTH
DAKOTA
LEWIS AND CLARK TRAIL MAP
9
NORTH DAKOTA
SOUTH DAKOTA
LEGEND
ROADS
LEWIS AND CLARK DESIGNATED TRAIL
SUPPLEMENTARY ROADS
70
INTERSTATE
70
PROPOSED INTERSTATE
15
U.S. HIGHWAY
16
STATE HIGHWAY
OTHER ROADS
EXPEDITION 1804-1806
EXPEDITION ROUTE
EXPEDITION CAMPSITE AND DATE
MARKED
5/27 W
UNMARKED
6/8 W
HISTORIC WILDLIFE AND OTHER RECREATION AREAS
EXISTING
PROPOSED
AREAS AND SITES
2
2
SCALE IN MILES
5
0
5
10
15
N
HERREID
10
SELBY
12
SOUTH DAKOTA
83
212
GETTYSBURG

Area Number		Ownership*	Administration*	Recreation Use			Recreation Activities and Attractions															Total Land and Water Acreage
				Day	Overnight	Vacation	Camping	Picnicking	Boating	Water Skiing	Swimming	Hunting	Fishing	Hiking	Horse Trails	Sightseeing	Nature Study	Winter Sports	Historic	Archeologic	Geologic	
	SOUTH DAKOTA (Continued)																					
114	Cheyenne River Agency Overlook	F	F	▲															●			1
115	*Forest City Public Use Area ~*	F	F	▲				●	●													250
116	Whitlocks Bay Public Use Area	F	F	▲				●	●				●									250
117	*Swan Creek Public Use Area ~*	F	F	▲	▲		●	●	●				●									50
118	Indian Creek Public Use Area	F	F	▲												●						280
119	*Moreau River Public Use Areas (2 units) ~*	F	F	▲				●	●													170
120	*(See No. 19) ~*																					
121	Prehistoric Indian Village	F	F	▲															●			–
122	Sitting Bull Gallery & Museum	M	M	▲															●			10
123	LeCompte Creek Indian Village			▲															●	●		10

* P - Private   C - County
   Q - Quasi - public   S - State
   M - Municipal   F - Federal

~ *Proposed Site*

RECREATION AREAS (EXISTING and PROPOSED)

AREA NUMBER		OWNERSHIP*	ADMINISTRATION*	RECREATION USE			RECREATION ACTIVITIES AND ATTRACTIONS															TOTAL LAND AND WATER ACREAGE
				Day	Overnight	Vacation	Camping	Picnicking	Boating	Water Skiing	Swimming	Hunting	Fishing	Hiking	Horse Trails	Sightseeing	Nature Study	Winter Sports	Historic	Archeologic	Geologic	
	SOUTH DAKOTA (Continued)																					
124	Sakakawea Monument	P	P	▲															•			–
125	Sitting Bull Memorial	P	P	▲															•			–
126	Old Bridge Public Use Area ~	F	F	▲				•	•													20
127	Indian Memorial Public Use Area	F	F	▲				•	•													60
128	Sitting Bull's Home	P	P	▲															•			–
129	Grand River Public Use Area ~	F	F	▲				•	•													90
130	Aricara-Leavenworth Battle ** ~																		•			
131	Locke Creek Public Use Area ~	F	F	▲				•	•													90
132	Pocasse National Wildlife Refuge	F	F	▲	▲		•	•	•	•	•		•			•	•					2,520
133	Lake Pocasse Public Use Area	F	M	▲				•	•	•	•	•	•									20
134	Kenel Public Use Area ~	F	F	▲				•	•													60
135	Fort Manuel Lisa ** ~																		•			

**Inducted historical site, interpretative marker to be erected on shore

~Proposed Site

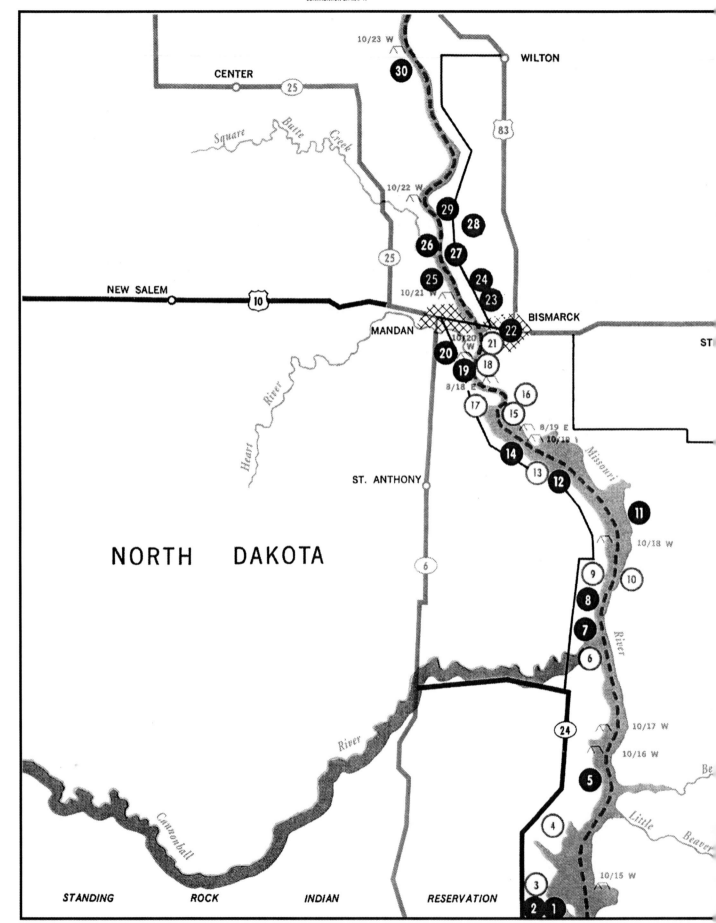

CENTER

WILTON

10/23 W

30

10/22 W

29

28

26

27

25

24

23

NEW SALEM

10

10/21 W

BISMARCK

MANDAN

22

21

10/20 W

20

18

19

8/18 E

16

17

15

8/19 E

10/19

14

13

12

11

10/18 W

St. ANTHONY

9

8

10

NORTH DAKOTA

7

6

River

Heart River

Missouri River

6

24

10/17 W

10/16 W

5

4

Cannonball River

3

10/15 W

2 1

STANDING   ROCK   INDIAN   RESERVATION

Square Butte Creek

Little Beaver

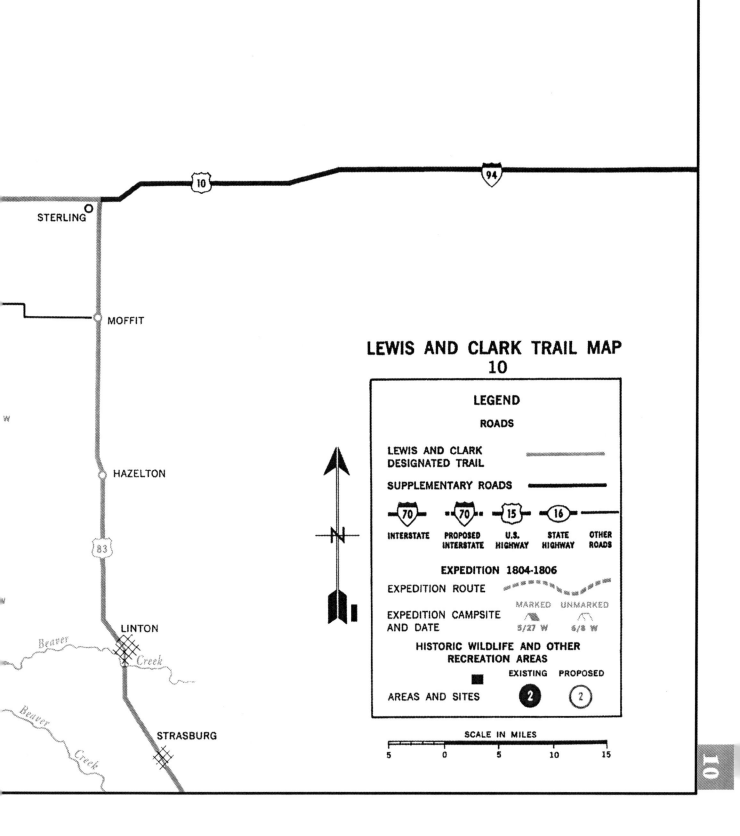

LEWIS AND CLARK TRAIL MAP
10

STERLING

MOFFIT

W

HAZELTON

83

LINTON

Beaver Creek

Beaver Creek

STRASBURG

10

94

LEGEND

ROADS

LEWIS AND CLARK
DESIGNATED TRAIL

SUPPLEMENTARY ROADS

70	70	15	16	
INTERSTATE	PROPOSED INTERSTATE	U.S. HIGHWAY	STATE HIGHWAY	OTHER ROADS

EXPEDITION 1804-1806

EXPEDITION ROUTE

EXPEDITION CAMPSITE
AND DATE

MARKED UNMARKED
5/27 W   6/8 W

**HISTORIC WILDLIFE AND OTHER
RECREATION AREAS**

EXISTING PROPOSED

AREAS AND SITES   2   2

N

SCALE IN MILES

5   0   5   10   15

HISTORIC, WILDLIFE and OTHER

Area Number		Ownership	Administration	Recreation Use			Recreation Activities and Attractions															Total Land and Water Acreage
				Day	Overnight	Vacation	Camping	Picnicking	Boating	Water Skiing	Swimming	Hunting	Fishing	Hiking	Horse Trails	Sightseeing	Nature Study	Winter Sports	Historic	Archeologic	Geologic	
	NORTH DAKOTA																					
1	Ft. Yates & Standing Rock Indian Agency	S	S	▲															●			—
2	Sitting Bull Monument	S	S	▲															●			5
3	Fort Yates Public Use Area ~	F	F	▲				●	●													30
4	Porcupine Creek Recreation Area ~			▲																●		—
5	Cretaceous Sandstone Outcrops	P	P	▲																	●	—
6	Cannonball Public Use Area ~	F	F	▲				●	●													40
7	North Cannonball Indian Village Site			▲																●		12
8	Fort Rice Historic Site	S	S	▲															●			7
9	Fort Rice Public Use Area ~	F	F	▲				●	●													10
10	Hazelton Public Use Area ~	F	F	▲				●	●													90
11	Shermer Indian Village			▲																●		15
12	Huff Indian Village Site	S	S	▲																●		8
13	Huff Village Public Use Area ~	F	F	▲				●	●													25
14	Eagle Nose Indian Village	PC		▲																●		3
15	Wildlife Management Area (Unnamed) ~	F	F	▲								●	●									15

RECREATION AREAS (EXISTING and PROPOSED)

Area Number		Ownership*	Administration*	Recreation Use			Recreation Activities and Attractions															Total Land and Water Acreage
				Day	Overnight	Vacation	Camping	Picnicking	Boating	Water Skiing	Swimming	Hunting	Fishing	Hiking	Horse Trails	Sightseeing	Nature Study	Winter Sports	Historic	Archeologic	Geologic	
	NORTH DAKOTA (Continued)																					
16	*Sibley Island Public Use Area (3 Units)* ~	F	CF	▲					•													750
17	*(See No. 16)* ~																					
18	*(See No. 16)* ~																					
19	Slant Indian Village Site	S	S	▲															•	•		8
20	Fort Lincoln State Park	S	S	▲	▲		•	•	•				•	•	•	•			•	•		740
21	*City of Bismark Recreation Area* ~	CF	CF	▲	▲		•	•	•	•	•		•	•	•				•			340
22	Camp Hancock Museum	C	C	▲															•			–
23	Outcrops of Cannonball Formation	P		▲																	•	–
24	Ward Indian Village Site	S	S	▲																•		6
25	Rock Haven Historical Site			▲															•			–
26	Boley Indian Village Site			▲															•	•		10
27	Double Ditch Indian Village Site	S	S	▲															•	•		12
28	Lignite Beds – Fossil Shells	P	P	▲																	•	–
29	Larson Indian Village Site			▲																•		8
30	Molander Indian Village Site	S	S	▲														•	•	•		12

~Proposed Site

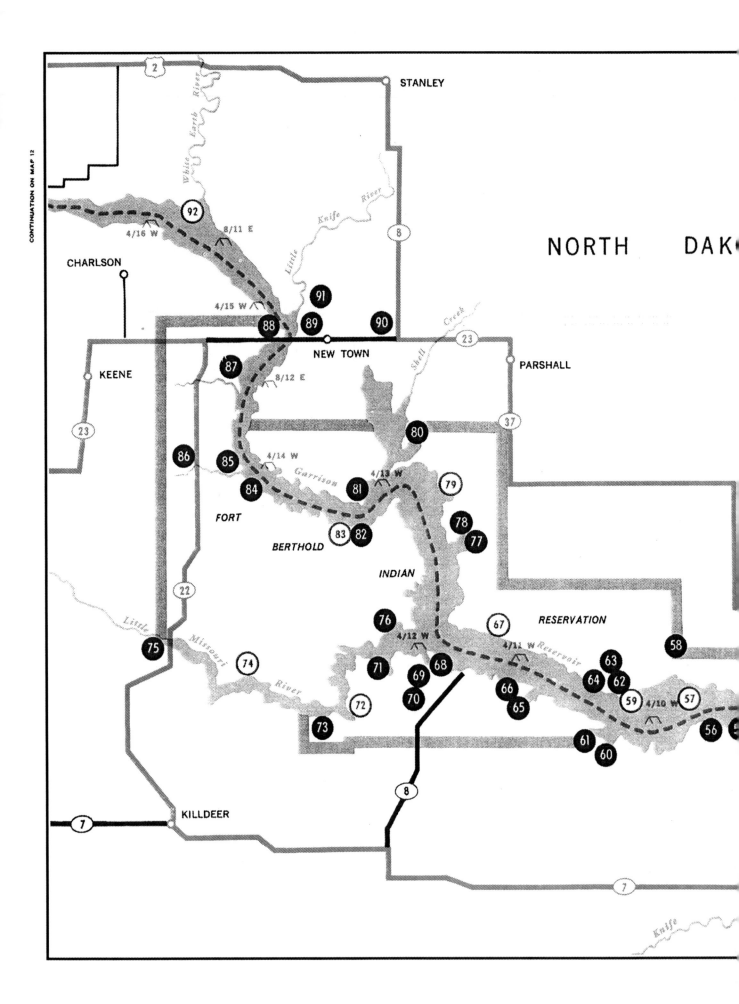

CONTINUATION ON MAP 12

STANLEY

NORTH   DAKO

CHARLSON

(2)

92

4/16 W

8/11 E

(8)

91

4/15 W

88   89

90

23

NEW TOWN

KEENE

87

PARSHALL

8/12 E

23

37

86   85

4/14 W

Garrison

80

84

81   4/13 W

79

FORT

BERTHOLD

83   82

78

77

INDIAN

76

RESERVATION

58

67

4/12 W

4/11 W   Reservoir

75

71   68

63

74

69

64   62

72

70

66   59   4/10 W   57

73

65

56

8

61

60

KILLDEER

7

8

7

Knife

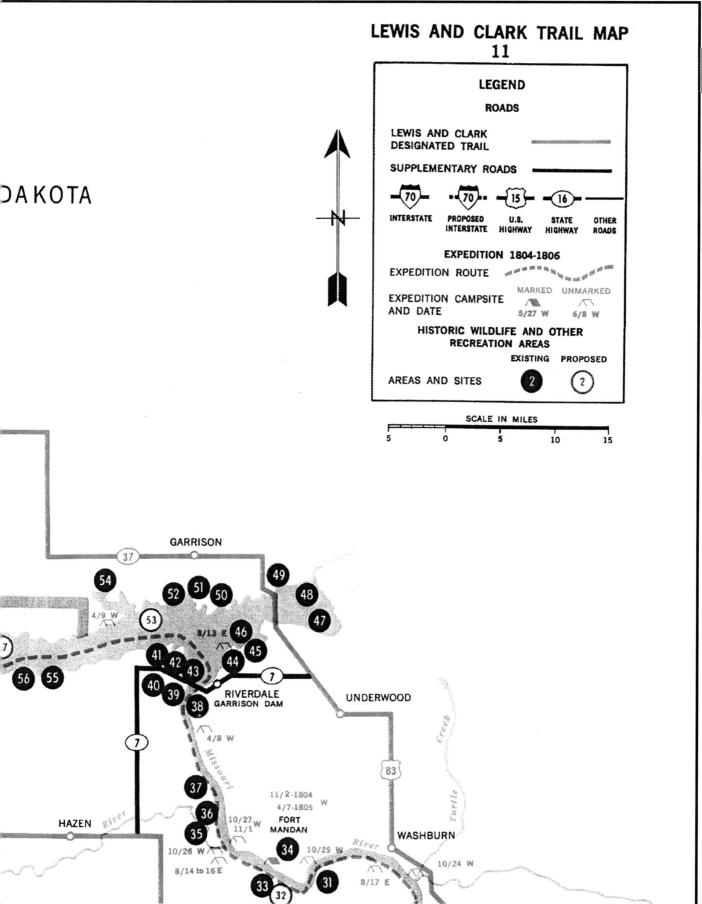

LEWIS AND CLARK TRAIL MAP
11

LEGEND

ROADS

LEWIS AND CLARK
DESIGNATED TRAIL

SUPPLEMENTARY ROADS

INTERSTATE	PROPOSED INTERSTATE	U.S. HIGHWAY	STATE HIGHWAY	OTHER ROADS
70	70	15	16	

EXPEDITION 1804-1806

EXPEDITION ROUTE

EXPEDITION CAMPSITE AND DATE

MARKED 5/27 W   UNMARKED 6/8 W

HISTORIC WILDLIFE AND OTHER RECREATION AREAS

EXISTING 2   PROPOSED 2

AREAS AND SITES

SCALE IN MILES

5   0   5   10   15

DAKOTA

GARRISON

54 52 51 50 49 48 47

4/9 W 53 8/13 E 46 45 44 41 42 43

56 55 40 39 38

RIVERDALE
GARRISON DAM

7

UNDERWOOD

4/8 W

Missouri

7

37

11/2-1804
4/7-1805 W

FORT MANDAN

83

Turtle

Creek

HAZEN

River

36 35

10/27 W
11/1

10/26 W

8/14 to 16 E

34 10/25 W River WASHBURN

10/24 W

33 32 31 8/17 E

CONTINUATION ON MAP 10

HISTORIC, WILDLIFE and OTHER

Area Number		Ownership *	Administration *	Day	Overnight	Vacation	Camping	Picnicking	Boating	Water Skiing	Swimming	Hunting	Fishing	Hiking	Horse Trails	Sightseeing	Nature Study	Winter Sports	Historic	Archeologic	Geologic	Total Land and Water Acreage
	NORTH DAKOTA (Continued)																					
31	Mandan Lake	S		▲								•	•									–
32	*Fort Clark State Park* ~	S	S	▲												•			•			150
33	Big White & Black Cat Indian Village Site			▲															•	•		15
34	Fort Mandan	S	P	▲															•	•		30
35	Lower Hidatsa Village Site	P	P	▲															•	•		8
36	Sakakawea Village Site	P	P	▲															•	•		8
37	Big Hidatsa Village Site	F	F	▲															•	•		15
38	Riverdale Game Management Area	F	S	▲	▲		•	•				•	•				•	•				2,015
39	Garrison Dam National Fish Hatchery	F	F	▲									•				•					88
40	Outlet Channel Fishing Camp	F	F	▲									•				•					10
41	Garrison Dam Downstream Public Use Area	F	F	▲	▲		•	•	•				•	•								210
42	Garrison Reservoir State Park	S	S	▲	▲		•	•	•	•	•	•	•	•			•	•				616
43	Garrison Dam	F	F	▲									•				•					–
44	Exposed Coal Beds in Tongue Formation	F	F	▲																	•	–
45	Wolf Creek Public Use Area	F	F	▲	▲		•	•	•				•									20
46	Wolf Creek Game Management Area	F	S	▲								•	•									4,500
47	Snake Creek National Wildlife Refuge	F	F	▲								•	•				•					13,498
48	Snake Creek Game Management Area	F	S	▲	▲		•	•	•			•	•									11,285
49	Totten Trail State Park	S	S	▲	▲		•	•	•				•	•								116
50	Fort Stevenson Public Use Area	F	M	▲	▲		•	•	•				•									438
51	Garrison Game Management Area	F	S	▲								•	•				•					340
52	Douglas Creek Public Use Area	F	F	▲	▲		•	•	•				•									210
53	*Fort Stevenson* ** ~																	•				
54	Douglas Creek Game Management Area	F	S	▲	▲		•					•	•									1,080
55	Hille Game Management Area	F	S	▲								•	•									1,201
56	Beulah Bay Public Use Area	F	F	▲	▲		•	•					•									103
57	*Fort Berthold* ** ~																		•			
58	Custer's Ree Scouts' Cemetery	P	P	▲				•									•		•	•		3
59	*Arikara Winter Village Site* ** ~																		•			
60	Beaver Creek Game Management Area	F	S	▲								•	•				•	•				539

* P - Private Q - Quasi-public M - Municipal C - County S - State F - Federal

** Inundated historical site, interpretative marker to be erected on shore

~ Proposed site

Area Number		Ownership*	Administration*	Recreation Use			Recreation Activities and Attractions															Total Land and Water Acreage
				Day	Overnight	Vacation	Camping	Picnicking	Boating	Water Skiing	Swimming	Hunting	Fishing	Hiking	Horse Trails	Sightseeing	Nature Study	Winter Sports	Historic	Archeologic	Geologic	
	NORTH DAKOTA (Continued)																					
61	Beaver Creek Fishing Camp	F	F	▲				•					•									40
62	*Night Walks Village in the Bull Pasture~*	P	P	▲				•								•			•			10
63	Little Shell Creek Fishing Camp	F	F	▲				•					•									30
64	Nishu Bay Fishing Camp	F	F	▲				•		•	•											20
65	Twin Buttes Recreational Area	F	F	▲				•					•									51
66	Hidatsa Village Site	P	P	▲	▲		•									•			•			10
67	*Elbowoods Bay ~*	P	P	▲				•								•						10
68	Red Butte Bay Public Use Area	F	F	▲	▲		•		•	•												80
69	Mandan "Big Canoe" Shrine	P	P	▲												•			•			–
70	Seven Rocks	P	P	▲												•			•			1
71	Halliday Public Use Area	M	M	▲	▲		•	•	•				•									80
72	*Hans Creek Bay Recreation Site ~*	P	P	▲	▲		•	•					•									–
73	Little Missouri Public Use Area	F	F	▲	▲		•	•	•				•									140
74	*Jacobson Village Site ~*	P	P	▲	▲		•									•			•			–
75	Lost Bridge Picnic Area	P	P	▲	▲		•	•								•		•	•			40
76	Saddle Butte Bay Recreation Area	P	P	▲	▲		•						•									–
77	Deepwater Creek Game Management Area	F	S	▲								•	•									1,880
78	Deepwater Creek Public Use Area	F	F	▲	▲		•	•					•									25
79	*Spotted Wolf Bay ~*	P	P	▲	▲		•				•		•									–
80	Van Hook Game Management Area	F	S	▲								•	•									5,102
81	Shell Creek Bay	PM	M	▲	▲		•	•	•		•		•									–
82	Skunk Creek Fishing Camp	F	F	▲				•					•									20
83	*Skunk Creek Bay Recreation Area ~*	P	P	▲	▲		•	•			•		•									80
84	Reunion Point Fishing Camp	F	F	▲				•					•									20
85	Two Moon Bay	F	P	▲				•					•									20
86	Bear Den Recreation Area	P	P	▲	▲		•	•					•									35
87	Hunts Along Bay	F	P	▲				•	•				•									10
88	Four Bears Park	P	P	▲	▲		•	•	•	•	•		•	•	•	•			•			136
89	New Town Fishing Camp	F	F	▲					•	•			•									90
90	Hall's Trading Post Fishing Camp	F	F	▲					•				•									20
91	Crow Flies High Butte	S	S	▲												•			•			3
92	*Kipp's Trading Post ** ~*																		•			

** Inundated historical site, interpretative
marker to be erected on shore

~Proposed site

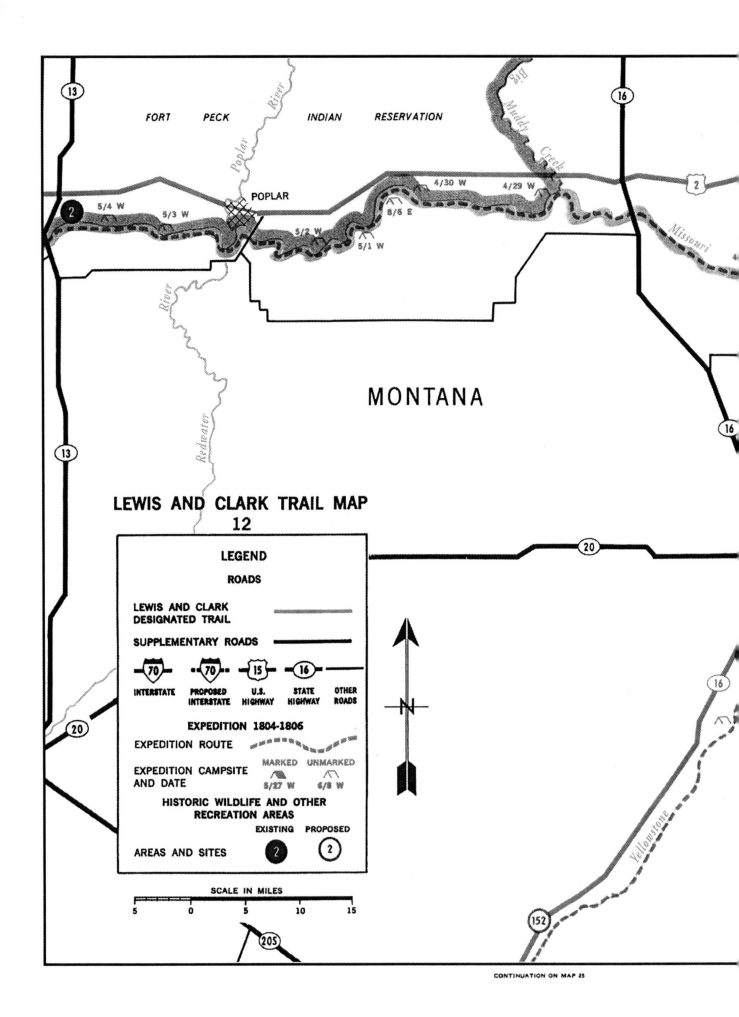

FORT PECK INDIAN RESERVATION

POPLAR

5/4 W 5/3 W 5/2 W 5/1 W 5/5 E 4/30 W 4/29 W

MONTANA

LEWIS AND CLARK TRAIL MAP
12

LEGEND

ROADS

LEWIS AND CLARK
DESIGNATED TRAIL

SUPPLEMENTARY ROADS

70	70	15	16	
INTERSTATE	PROPOSED INTERSTATE	U.S. HIGHWAY	STATE HIGHWAY	OTHER ROADS

EXPEDITION 1804-1806

EXPEDITION ROUTE

EXPEDITION CAMPSITE AND DATE

MARKED UNMARKED
5/27 W 6/8 W

HISTORIC WILDLIFE AND OTHER RECREATION AREAS

EXISTING PROPOSED

AREAS AND SITES   2   2

SCALE IN MILES

5 0 5 10 15

CONTINUATION ON MAP 25

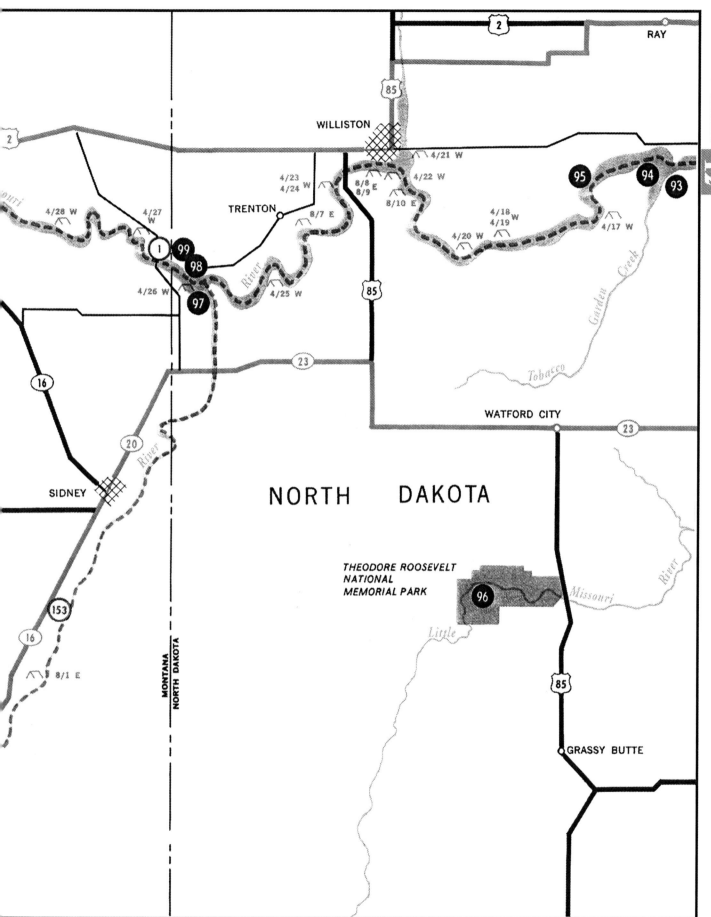

HISTORIC, WILDLIFE and OTHER

Area Number		Ownership*	Administration*	Recreation Use			Recreation Activities and Attractions															Total Land and Water Acreage
				Day	Overnight	Vacation	Camping	Picnicking	Boating	Water Skiing	Swimming	Hunting	Fishing	Hiking	Horse Trails	Sightseeing	Nature Study	Winter Sports	Historic	Archeologic	Geologic	
	NORTH DAKOTA (Continued)																					
93	Tobacco Garden Creek Public Use Area	F	F	▲	▲		•	•	•				•									239
94	Tobacco Garden Game Management Area	F	S	▲								•	•									780
95	Lewis and Clark Public Use Area	F	F	▲	▲		•	•	•		•		•									349
96	Theo. Roosevelt Nat'l Mem. Park (N. Unit)	F	F	▲	▲	▲	•	•						•	•	•	•		•		•	24,062
97	Henry's Post			▲															•			–
98	Fort Buford Historic Park	S	S	▲				•								•			•			60
99	Fort Union Historic Site	S	S	▲															•			10

* P - Private   C - County
   Q - Quasi-public   S - State
   M - Municipal   F - Federal

RECREATION AREAS (EXISTING and PROPOSED)

AREA NUMBER		OWNERSHIP*	ADMINISTRATION*	RECREATION USE			RECREATION ACTIVITIES AND ATTRACTIONS															TOTAL LAND AND WATER ACREAGE
				Day	Overnight	Vacation	Camping	Picnicking	Boating	Water Skiing	Swimming	Hunting	Fishing	Hiking	Horse Trails	Sightseeing	Nature Study	Winter Sports	Historic	Archeologic	Geologic	
	MONTANA																					
1	*Nohly Bridge Resreation Site ~*	F	F	▲					●				●									22
2	Lewis & Clark Memorial Park	M	M	▲	▲		●	●	●		●	●	●	●								40
152	*Schaffer Island Recreation Site ~*	F	F	▲	▲			●	●			●	●									194
153	*Crane Island Recreation Site ~*	F	F	▲	▲		●	●	●			●						●				83

~Proposed Site

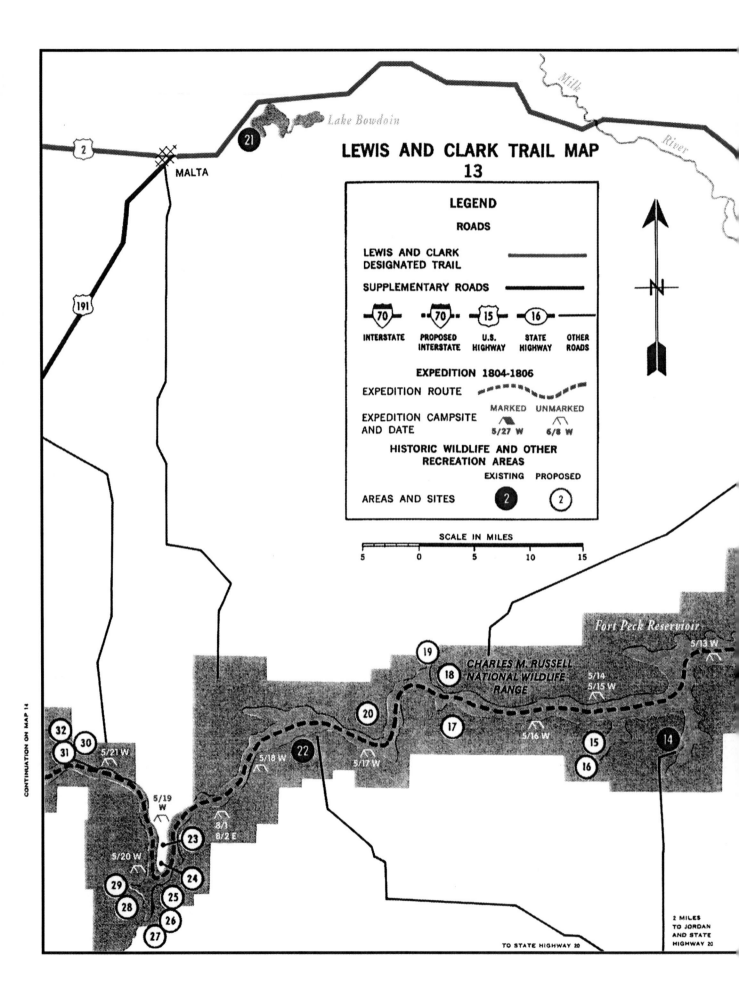

LEWIS AND CLARK TRAIL MAP
13

LEGEND

ROADS

LEWIS AND CLARK
DESIGNATED TRAIL

SUPPLEMENTARY ROADS

| 70 | 70 | 15 | 16 |
| INTERSTATE | PROPOSED INTERSTATE | U.S. HIGHWAY | STATE HIGHWAY | OTHER ROADS |

EXPEDITION 1804-1806

EXPEDITION ROUTE

EXPEDITION CAMPSITE
AND DATE

MARKED 5/27 W   UNMARKED 6/8 W

HISTORIC WILDLIFE AND OTHER RECREATION AREAS

EXISTING   PROPOSED

AREAS AND SITES   2   2

SCALE IN MILES

5   0   5   10   15

Milk River

Lake Bowdoin

2

MALTA

191

21

CHARLES M. RUSSELL NATIONAL WILDLIFE RANGE

Fort Peck Reservoir

5/13 W

19
18
5/14
5/15 W
20
17
5/16 W
15
16
14
5/17 W
22
5/18 W
32
30
31
5/21 W
5/19 W
23
8/1 8/2 E
5/20 W
24
29
25
28
26
27

CONTINUATION ON MAP 14

TO STATE HIGHWAY 20

2 MILES
TO JORDAN
AND STATE
HIGHWAY 20

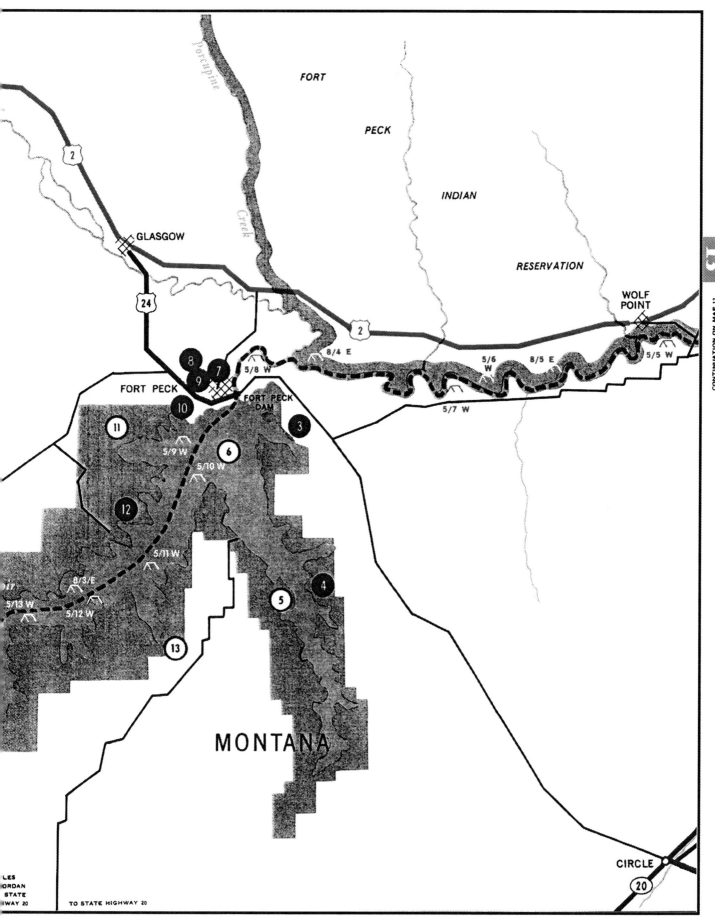

FORT

PECK

INDIAN

RESERVATION

GLASGOW

WOLF
POINT

8/4 E

5/8 W

5/6
W

8/5 E

5/5 W

5/7 W

FORT PECK

FORT PECK
DAM

10

3

11

5/9 W

6

5/10 W

12

5/11 W

8/3/E

5/13 W

5/12 W

4

5

13

MONTANA

CIRCLE

20

LES
ORDAN
STATE
WAY 20

TO STATE HIGHWAY 20

Area Number		Ownership *	Administration *	Recreation Use			Recreation Activities and Attractions															Total Land and Water Acreage
				Day	Overnight	Vacation	Camping	Picnicking	Boating	Water Skiing	Swimming	Hunting	Fishing	Hiking	Horse Trails	Sightseeing	Nature Study	Winter Sports	Historic	Archeologic	Geologic	
	MONTANA (Continued)																					
3	Bear Creek Public Use Area	F	F	▲				•	•				•									345
4	Rock Creek State Park	F	S	▲	▲	▲	•	•	•	•	•		•									340
5	Box Creek Public Use Area ~	F	F	▲				•	•				•									360
6	York Island Public Use Area ~	F	F	▲				•	•				•									160
7	Fort Peck Downstream Public Use Area	F	F	▲	▲	▲	•	•	•	•	•		•						•			820
8	Fort Peck Game Station	F	F	▲	▲		•		•				•				•					160
9	Fort Peck Exhibition Pasture	F	F	▲													•					160
10	Fort Peck Public Use Area	F	F	▲	▲	▲	•	•	•				•				•					910
11	Duck Creek Waterfowl Area ~	F	F	▲								•	•				•					3,000
12	The Pines Public Use Area	F	F	▲	▲	▲	•	•	•				•									900
13	Gilbert Creek Waterfowl Area ~	F	F	▲								•	•		•		•					1,500
14	Hell Creek State Park	F	S	▲	▲		•	•	•	•	•		•									113
15	Snow Creek Public Use Area ~	F	F	▲					•	•			•									360
16	Snow Creek Waterfowl Area ~	F	F	▲	▲		•					•	•				•					1,500
17	Billy Creek Bighorn Sheep Pasture ~	F	F	▲								•	•				•					15,000

* P - Private   C - County
   Q - Quasi-public   S - State
   M - Municipal   F - Federal

~ Proposed Site

RECREATION AREAS (EXISTING and PROPOSED)

Area Number		Ownership*	Administration*	Day	Overnight	Vacation	Camping	Picnicking	Boating	Water Skiing	Swimming	Hunting	Fishing	Hiking	Horse Trails	Sightseeing	Nature Study	Winter Sports	Historic	Archeologic	Geologic	Total Land and Water Acreage
	MONTANA (Continued)																					
18	Timber Creek Public Use Area ~	F	F	▲					●				●									630
19	Timber Creek Waterfowl Area ~	F	F	▲	▲		●					●	●				●					1,500
20	Burnt Lodge Wild Area ~	F	F	▲	▲	▲	●					●	●	●		●	●				●	13,386
21	Bowdoin National Wildlife Refuge	F	F	▲								●	●			●	●					15,500
22	Devil's Creek Public Use Area	F	F	▲	▲		●	●				●	●									370
23	U.L. Bend Public Use Area ~	F	F	▲								●	●				●					490
24	U.L. Bend Game Station ~	F	F	▲													●		●			160
25	Musselshell Recreation Area ~	F	F	▲	▲		●					●	●				●					160
26	Musselshell Game Station ~	F	F	▲													●					160
27	Musselshell Waterfowl Area ~	F	F	▲								●	●				●					3,600
28	Crooked Creek Public Use Area ~	F	F	▲								●	●				●					650
29	Fort Musselshell Recreation Site ~	F	F	▲				●				●	●									80
30	Beauchamp Waterfowl Area ~	F	F	▲									●				●					1,200
31	Fort Hawley Recreation Site ~	F	F	▲	▲		●					●	●									80
32	Beauchamp Creek Public Use Area ~	F	F	▲				●	●			●					●					900

~Proposed Site

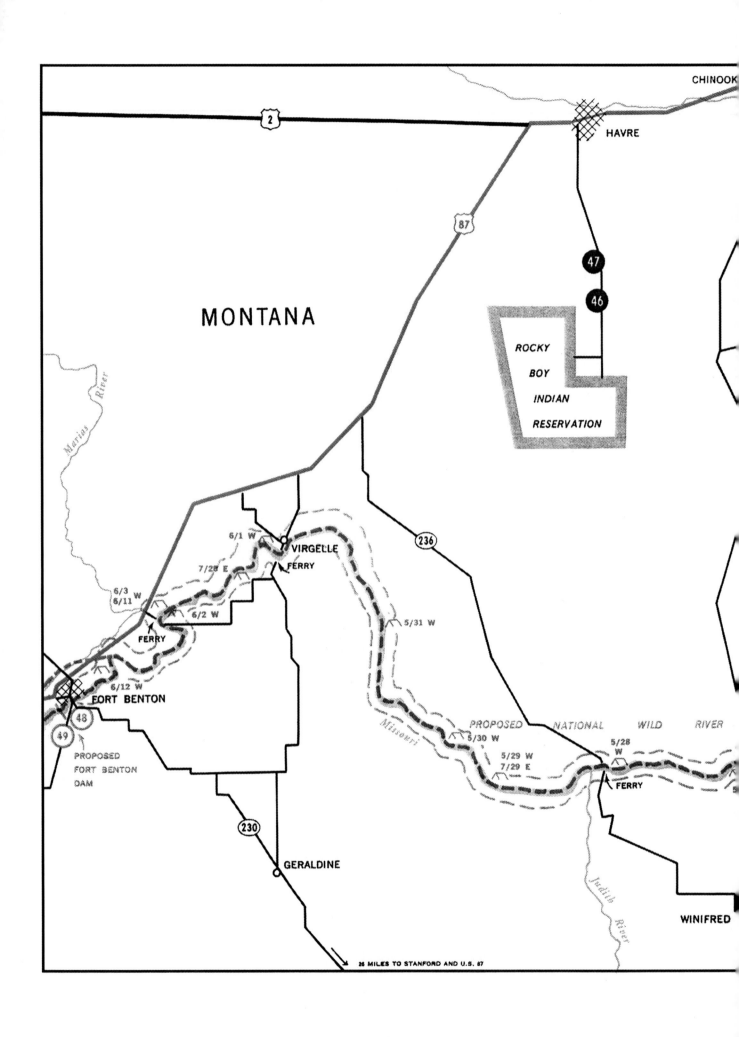

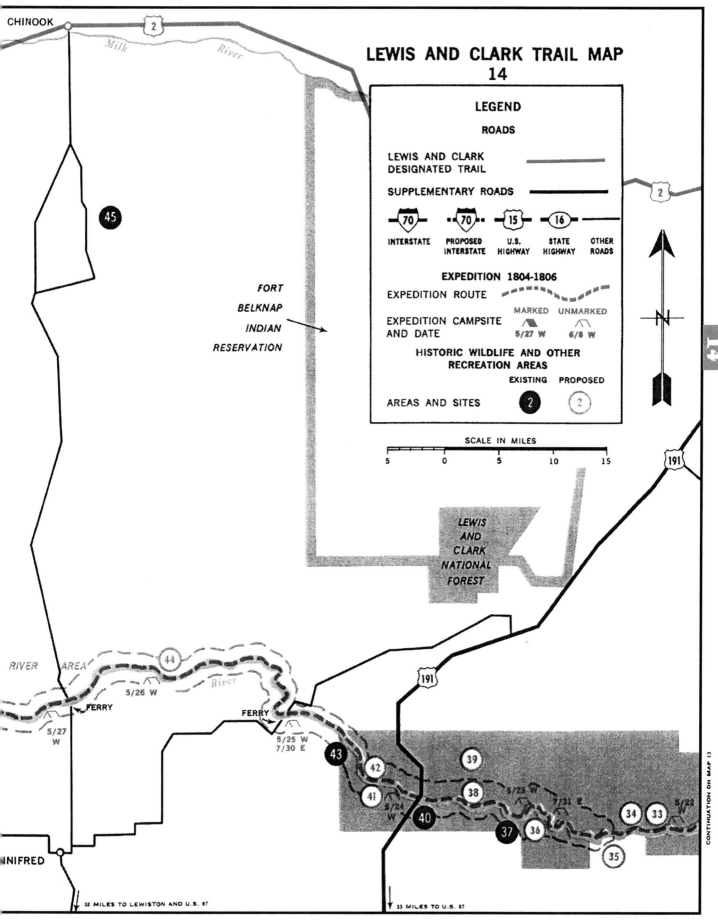

LEWIS AND CLARK TRAIL MAP
14

LEGEND

ROADS

LEWIS AND CLARK
DESIGNATED TRAIL

SUPPLEMENTARY ROADS

70	70	15	16	
INTERSTATE	PROPOSED INTERSTATE	U.S. HIGHWAY	STATE HIGHWAY	OTHER ROADS

EXPEDITION 1804-1806

EXPEDITION ROUTE

EXPEDITION CAMPSITE AND DATE — MARKED 5/27 W — UNMARKED 6/8 W

HISTORIC WILDLIFE AND OTHER RECREATION AREAS

EXISTING 2 — PROPOSED 2

AREAS AND SITES

SCALE IN MILES
5 0 5 10 15

CHINOOK

Milk River

FORT
BELKNAP
INDIAN
RESERVATION

LEWIS
AND
CLARK
NATIONAL
FOREST

N

45

RIVER AREA

44

5/26 W

River

FERRY

5/27 W

FERRY

5/25 W
7/30 E

43

42

41

5/24 W

40

37

39

38

5/23 W

7/31 E

36

35

34

33

5/22 W

191

191

NIFRED

CONTINUATION ON MAP 13

32 MILES TO LEWISTON AND U.S. 87

33 MILES TO U.S. 87

HISTORIC, WILDLIFE and OTHER

AREA NUMBER		OWNERSHIP *	ADMINISTRATION *	RECREATION USE			RECREATION ACTIVITIES AND ATTRACTIONS															TOTAL LAND AND WATER ACREAGE
				Day	Overnight	Vacation	Camping	Picnicking	Boating	Water Skiing	Swimming	Hunting	Fishing	Hiking	Horse Trails	Sightseeing	Nature Study	Winter Sports	Historic	Archeologic	Geologic	
	MONTANA (Continued)																					
33	O K Creek Waterfowl Area ~	F	F	▲								●					●					640
34	Tracts 33 & 36 Waterfowl Area ~	F	F	▲	▲							●	●				●					1,500
35	Fort Carroll Recreation Site ~	F	F	▲	▲		●	●				●	●	●			●					40
36	Rocky Point Recreation Area ~	F	F	▲	▲		●	●	●			●	●				●					80
37	Slippery Ann Game Station	F	F	▲	▲									●			●					160
38	Slippery Ann Recreation Site ~	F	F	▲	▲		●	●	●				●				●					20
39	C.M. Russell Buffalo Range ~	F	F	▲	▲	▲	●	●	●							●						40,000
40	James Kipp State Park	F	S	▲	▲	▲	●	●	●							●						465
41	Two Calf Island Recreation Site ~	F	F	▲	▲		●	●	●			●	●									30
42	Chief Joseph's Parade Ground Rec. Site ~	F	F	▲				●				●	●						●			80

RECREATION AREAS (EXISTING and PROPOSED)

Area Number		Ownership*	Administration*	Recreation Use			Recreation Activities and Attractions															Total Land and Water Acreage
				Day	Overnight	Vacation	Camping	Picnicking	Boating	Water Skiing	Swimming	Hunting	Fishing	Hiking	Horse Trails	Sightseeing	Nature Study	Winter Sports	Historic	Archeologic	Geologic	
	MONTANA (Continued)																					
43	Bighorn Sheep Pasture	F	F	▲									●			●					2,220
44	*Lewis & Clark Nat'l Wilderness Waterway ~*	PSF	F	▲	▲	▲	●	●	●			●	●	●	●	●	●		●	●	●	186,000
45	Chief Joseph Battlefield State Mon.	S	S	▲												●		●			160
46	Beaver Creek Park	C	C	▲	▲		●	●				●	●			●					10,000
47	Bear Paw Lake Fishing Site	S	S	▲									●								140
48	*Fort Benton Downstream Public Use Area ~*	F	F	▲	▲	▲	●	●	●		●	●	●	●		●	●					200
49	*Ft. Benton South Shore Public Use Area ~*	F	F	▲	▲	●	●	●	●		●	●	●	●		●	●					300

~Proposed Site

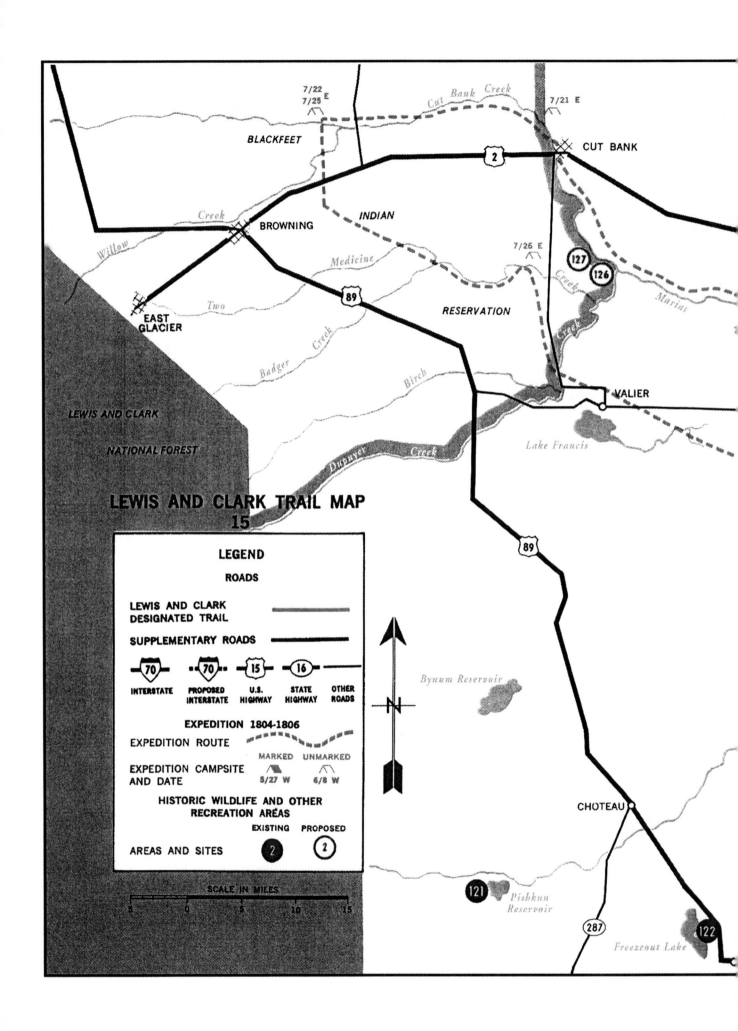

LEWIS AND CLARK TRAIL MAP
15

BLACKFEET

Cut Bank Creek

7/22 E
7/25

7/21 E

CUT BANK

2

INDIAN

Creek

BROWNING

Willow

Medicine

127

126

Marias

7/26 E

EAST
GLACIER

Two

Badger Creek

RESERVATION

Creek

Birch Creek

VALIER

LEWIS AND CLARK

NATIONAL FOREST

Dupuyer Creek

Lake Francis

89

LEGEND

ROADS

LEWIS AND CLARK
DESIGNATED TRAIL

SUPPLEMENTARY ROADS

70 INTERSTATE

70 PROPOSED INTERSTATE

15 U.S. HIGHWAY

16 STATE HIGHWAY

OTHER ROADS

Bynum Reservoir

EXPEDITION 1804-1806

EXPEDITION ROUTE

MARKED 5/27 W

UNMARKED 6/8 W

EXPEDITION CAMPSITE
AND DATE

HISTORIC WILDLIFE AND OTHER
RECREATION AREAS

EXISTING 2

PROPOSED 2

AREAS AND SITES

N

89

CHOTEAU

SCALE IN MILES
5 0 5 10 15

121

Pishkun Reservoir

287

122

Freezeout Lake

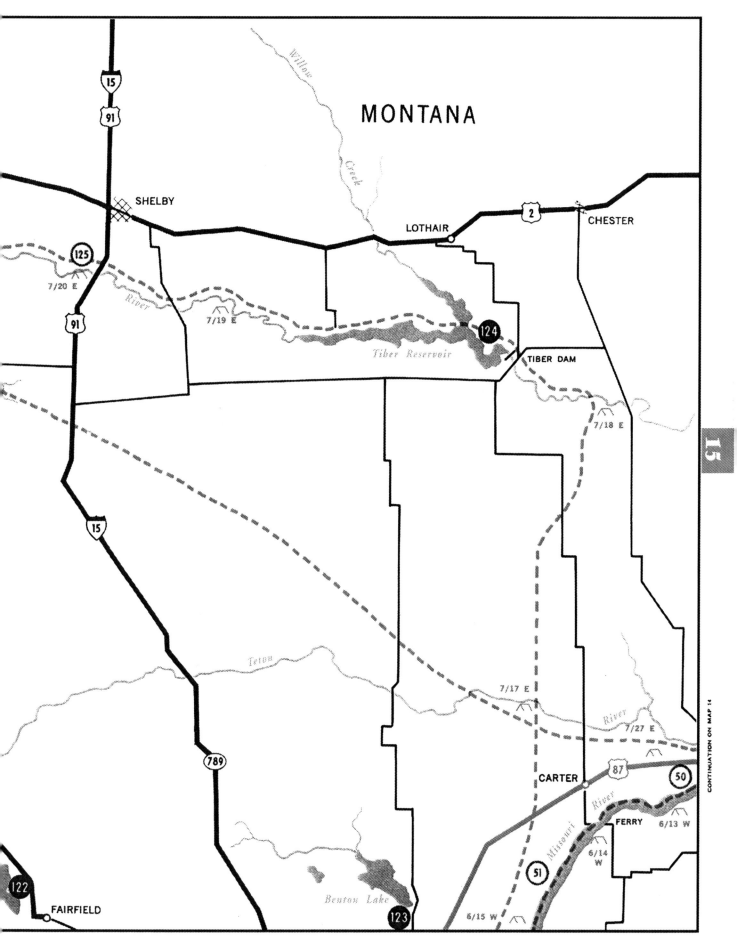

MONTANA

SHELBY

LOTHAIR

2 CHESTER

15
91

125
7/20 E

River

91
7/19 E

Tiber Reservoir

124

TIBER DAM

7/18 E

15

789

Teton

7/17 E

River

7/27 E

87

CARTER

50

FERRY
6/13 W

Missouri River

51

6/14 W

122

FAIRFIELD

Benton Lake

123

6/15 W

Willow Creek

HISTORIC, WILDLIFE and OTHER

AREA NUMBER		OWNERSHIP *	ADMINISTRATION *	RECREATION USE			RECREATION ACTIVITIES AND ATTRACTIONS															TOTAL LAND AND WATER ACREAGE
				Day	Overnight	Vacation	Camping	Picnicking	Boating	Water Skiing	Swimming	Hunting	Fishing	Hiking	Horse Trails	Sightseeing	Nature Study	Winter Sports	Historic	Archeologic	Geologic	
	MONTANA (Continued)																					
50	*Ft. Benton North Shore Public Use Area* ~	F	F	▲	▲	▲	●	●	●	●	●	●	●	●		●	●	●	●	●	●	300
51	*Ryan Coulee Public Use Area* ~	F	F	▲	▲	▲	●	●	●	●	●	●	●	●		●	●	●	●	●	●	200
121	Pishkun National Wildlife Refuge	F	F	▲	▲		●	●	●			●					●					8,195
122	Freezeout Lake	S	S	▲								●										11,000
123	Benton Lake National Wildlife Refuge	F	F	▲													●					12,383

* P - Private   C - County
  Q - Quasi-public   S - State
  M - Municipal   F - Federal

~ Proposed Site

RECREATION AREAS (EXISTING and PROPOSED)

AREA NUMBER		OWNERSHIP*	ADMINISTRATION*	RECREATION USE			RECREATION ACTIVITIES AND ATTRACTIONS															TOTAL LAND AND WATER ACREAGE
				Day	Overnight	Vacation	Camping	Picnicking	Boating	Water Skiing	Swimming	Hunting	Fishing	Hiking	Horse Trails	Sightseeing	Nature Study	Winter Sports	Historic	Archeologic	Geologic	
	MONTANA (Continued)																					
124	Tiber Reservoir Recreation Area	F	S	▲	▲		●	●	●	●	●	●	●	●								38,834
125	*Marias River Access Sites*	F	F	~	~		~		~			~	~						~			1,726
126	*Cut Bank River Recreation Site No. 1*	F	F	~			~					~	~									117
127	*Cut Bank River Recreation Site No. 2*	F	F	~			~					~	~									50

~Proposed Site

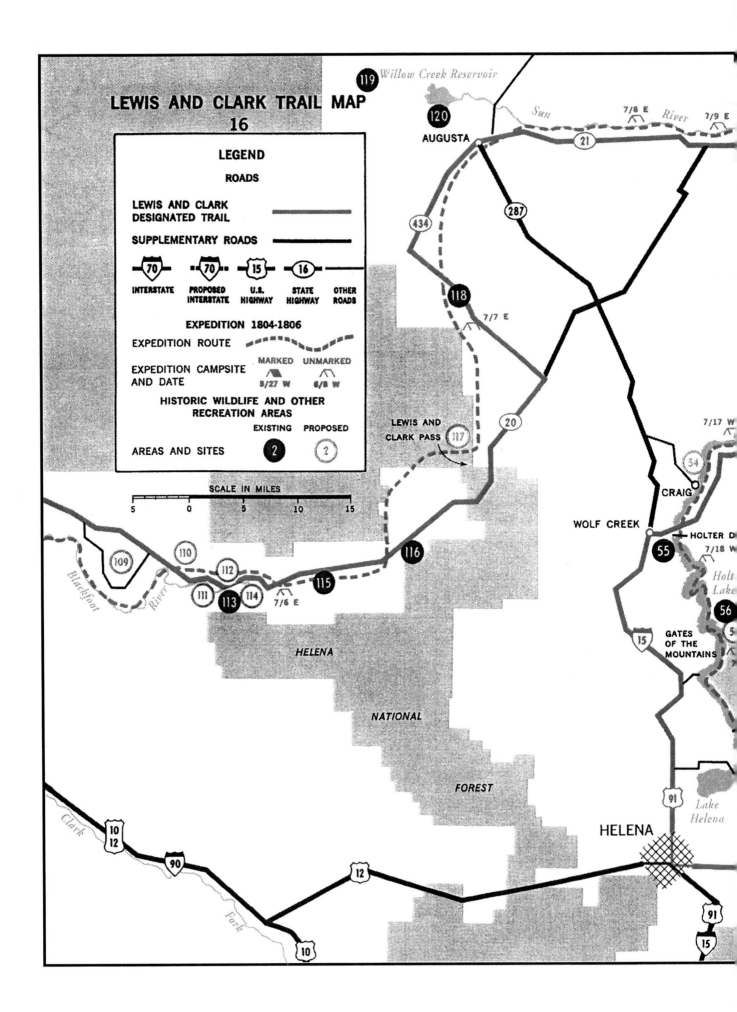

LEWIS AND CLARK TRAIL MAP
16

LEGEND

ROADS

LEWIS AND CLARK
DESIGNATED TRAIL

SUPPLEMENTARY ROADS

70	70	15	16	
INTERSTATE	PROPOSED INTERSTATE	U.S. HIGHWAY	STATE HIGHWAY	OTHER ROADS

EXPEDITION 1804-1806

EXPEDITION ROUTE

EXPEDITION CAMPSITE
AND DATE

MARKED   UNMARKED
5/27 W   6/8 W

HISTORIC WILDLIFE AND OTHER
RECREATION AREAS

EXISTING   PROPOSED

AREAS AND SITES   2   2

SCALE IN MILES
5   0   5   10   15

Willow Creek Reservoir

119

120

AUGUSTA

Sun   River   7/8 E   7/9 E

21

287

434

118

7/7 E

20

LEWIS AND
CLARK PASS   117

7/17 W

34

CRAIG

WOLF CREEK

HOLTER D

7/18 W

55

Holte
Lake

116

115

7/6 E

112

110

109

111   113   114

Blackfoot   River

HELENA

NATIONAL

56

GATES
OF THE
MOUNTAINS

15

FOREST

91

Lake
Helena

HELENA

Clark

10
12

90

12

91

Fork

10

15

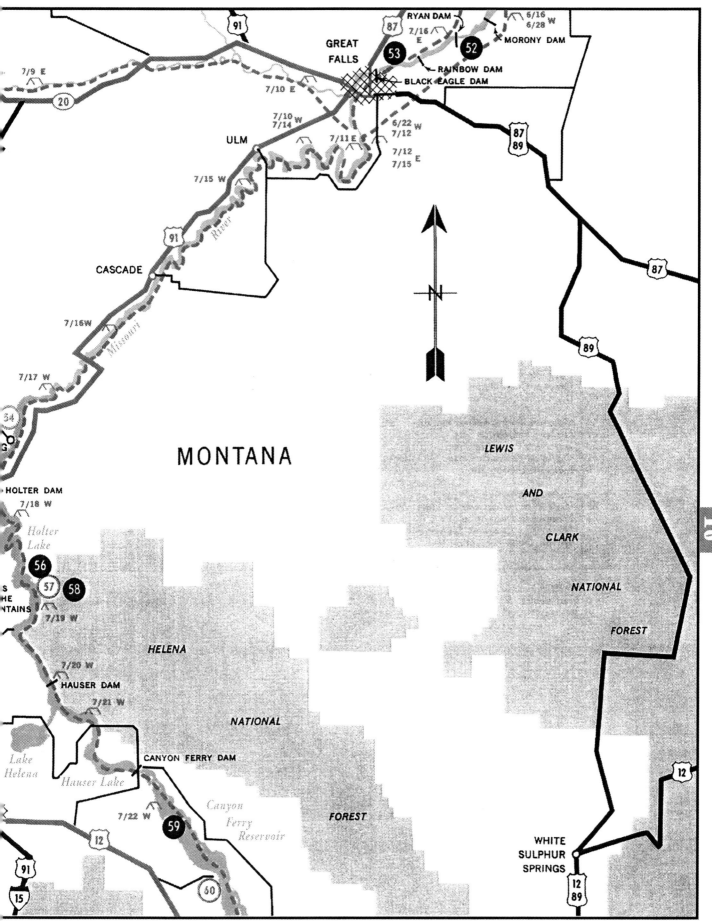

91

7/9 E

20

GREAT
FALLS

RYAN DAM

87

7/16
E

53

52

6/16 W
6/28 W

MORONY DAM

RAINBOW DAM

7/10 E

BLACK EAGLE DAM

7/10 W
7/14

87
89

ULM

6/22 W
7/12

7/11 E

7/12 E
7/15

7/15 W

87

91

River

CASCADE

Missouri

7/16 W

89

7/17 W

54

G

MONTANA

LEWIS

HOLTER DAM

7/18 W

AND

Holter
Lake

CLARK

56

NATIONAL

S

57

58

HE
NTAINS

7/19 W

FOREST

16

HELENA

7/20 W

HAUSER DAM

7/21 W

NATIONAL

Lake
Helena

Hauser Lake

CANYON FERRY DAM

FOREST

12

Canyon
Ferry
Reservoir

7/22 W

59

12

WHITE
SULPHUR
SPRINGS

91

12

15

60

12
89

CONTINUATION ON MAP 17

HISTORIC, WILDLIFE and OTHER

AREA NUMBER		OWNERSHIP *	ADMINISTRATION *	RECREATION USE			RECREATION ACTIVITIES AND ATTRACTIONS															TOTAL LAND AND WATER ACREAGE
				Day	Overnight	Vacation	Camping	Picnicking	Boating	Water Skiing	Swimming	Hunting	Fishing	Hiking	Horse Trails	Sightseeing	Nature Study	Winter Sports	Historic	Archeologic	Geologic	
	MONTANA (Continued)																					
52	Ryan Island Picnic Area	P	P	▲				●														4
53	Giant Spring Picnic Area	M	M	▲				●					●									5
54	Craig Island Recreation Area ~	F	F	△	△		●					●	●						●			15
55	Holter Lake Picnic Area	P	P	▲				●	●													3
56	Meriwether Picnic Area	F	F	▲				●	●							●			●			–
57	Gates of the Mountain Recreation Area ~	F	F	△					●							●						363
58	Gates of the Mountain Wilderness	F	F	▲	▲	▲	●	●	●	●	●	●	●	●	●	●			●			28,562
59	Canyon Ferry Recreation Area	F	S	△	▲		●	●	●	●	●	●	●	●		●	●	●	●			42,827
60	Canyon Ferry Recreation Areas 1,2,& 3 ~	F	F	△	△		●	●	●	●	●	●	●	●		●	●		●			1,840
109	Kleinschmidt Lake Recreation Area ~	F	F	△	△		●	●				●	●									160

* P - Private   C - County
   Q - Quasi-public   S - State
   M - Municipal   F - Federal

~ Proposed Site

RECREATION AREAS (EXISTING and PROPOSED)

AREA NUMBER		OWNERSHIP*	ADMINISTRATION*	RECREATION USE			RECREATION ACTIVITIES AND ATTRACTIONS															TOTAL LAND AND WATER ACREAGE
				Day	Overnight	Vacation	Camping	Picnicking	Boating	Water Skiing	Swimming	Hunting	Fishing	Hiking	Horse Trails	Sightseeing	Nature Study	Winter Sports	Historic	Archeologic	Geologic	
	MONTANA (Continued)																					
110	*Markham Mtn. Recreation Site ~*	F	F	▲	▲		●	●				●	●									160
111	*Blue Smoke Recreation Site ~*	F	F	▲	▲		●	●					●						●			80
112	*Arrasta Creek Recreation Site ~*	F	F	▲	▲		●	●					●			●			●			120
113	Blackfoot Campground	F	F	▲	▲		●	●					●									-
114	*Big Blackfoot Recreation Site ~*	F	F	▲	▲		●	●					●			●			●			560
115	Hooper State Park	S	S	▲	▲		●	●					●									17
116	Aspen Grove Campground	F	F	▲	▲		●	●					●									-
117	*Lewis and Clark Pass Historical Site ~*	F	F	▲												●			●			-
118	Bean Lake Fishing Access	S	S	▲	▲		●	●	●				●									17
119	Sun River Game Range	S	S	▲								●										21,000
120	Willow Creek National Wildlife Refuge	F	F	▲	▲		●	●	●				●				●					3,119

~Proposed Site

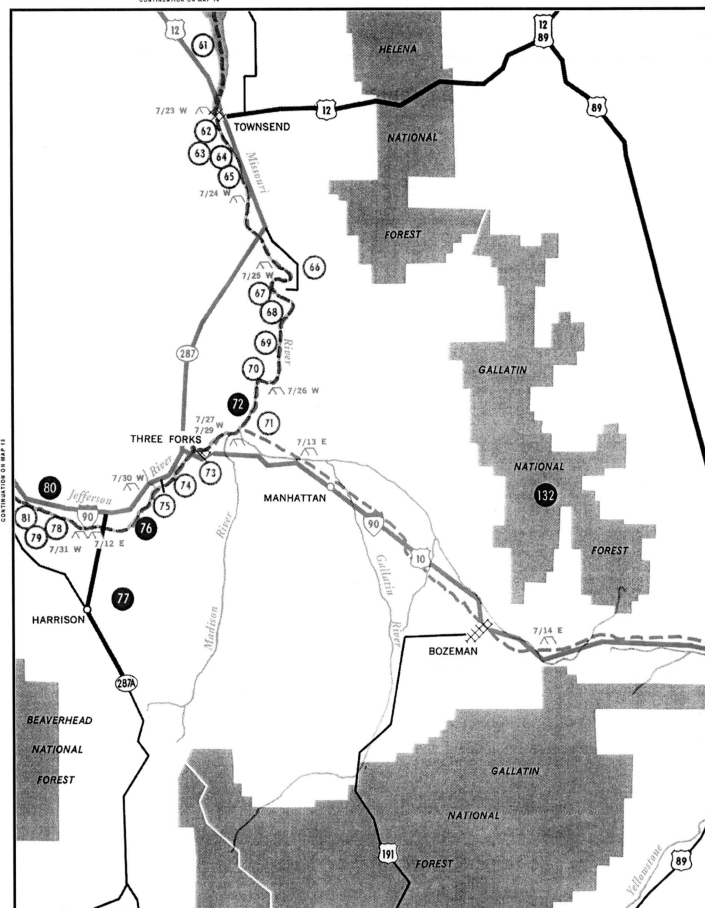

CONTINUATION ON MAP 18

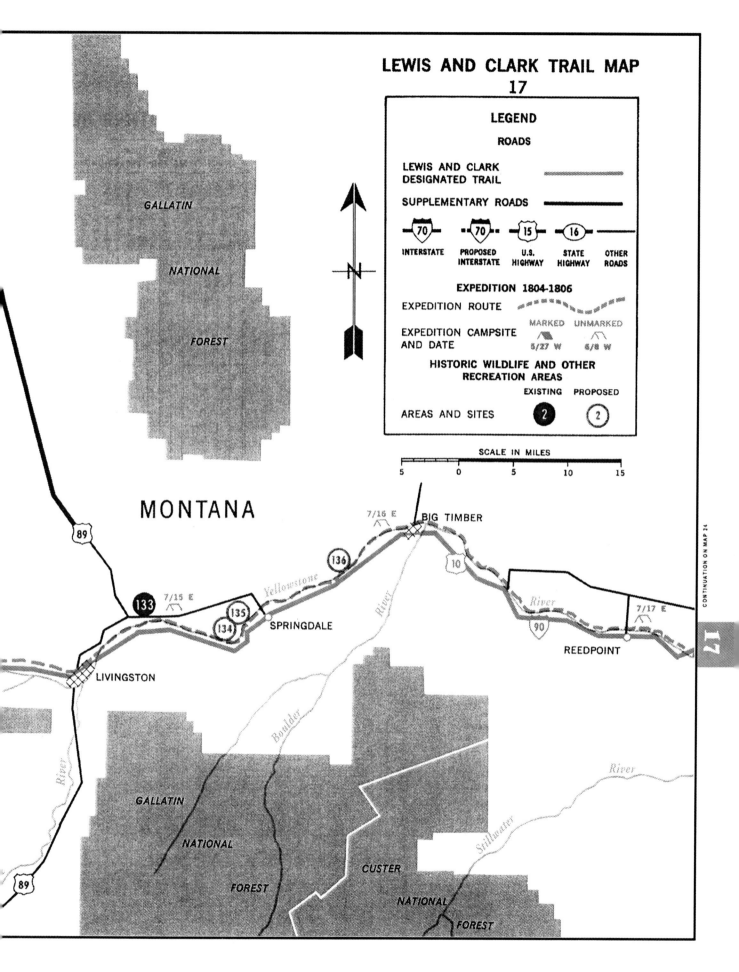

LEWIS AND CLARK TRAIL MAP
17

LEGEND

ROADS

LEWIS AND CLARK DESIGNATED TRAIL

SUPPLEMENTARY ROADS

70	70	15	16	
INTERSTATE	PROPOSED INTERSTATE	U.S. HIGHWAY	STATE HIGHWAY	OTHER ROADS

EXPEDITION 1804-1806

EXPEDITION ROUTE

EXPEDITION CAMPSITE AND DATE

MARKED 6/27 W   UNMARKED 6/8 W

HISTORIC WILDLIFE AND OTHER RECREATION AREAS

EXISTING   PROPOSED

AREAS AND SITES   2   2

SCALE IN MILES
5 0 5 10 15

GALLATIN

NATIONAL

FOREST

MONTANA

89

136

7/16 E   BIG TIMBER

7/15 E   10

133   135   90

134   SPRINGDALE   REEDPOINT   7/17 E

LIVINGSTON

Yellowstone   River   River   River

89   Boulder   Stillwater

GALLATIN

NATIONAL   CUSTER

FOREST   NATIONAL

FOREST

CONTINUATION ON MAP 24

17

HISTORIC, WILDLIFE and OTHER

Area Number		Ownership *	Administration *	Recreation Use			Recreation Activities and Attractions															Total Land and Water Acreage
				Day	Overnight	Vacation	Camping	Picnicking	Boating	Water Skiing	Swimming	Hunting	Fishing	Hiking	Horse Trails	Sightseeing	Nature Study	Winter Sports	Historic	Archeologic	Geologic	
	MONTANA (Continued)																					
61	*Winston Roadside Park ~*	F	F	▲				●								●			●			640
62	*Townsend Recreation Site ~*	F	F	▲				●					●			●			●			153
63	*Deep Creek Recreation Site ~*	F	F	▲				●					●			●			●			187
64	*Greyson Creek Recreation Site ~*	F	F	▲	▲		●	●	●		●	●	●						●			130
65	*Dry Creek Recreation Site ~*	F	F	▲	▲		●	●				●	●						●			60
66	*Mammoth Spring Recreation Site ~*	F	F	▲	▲		●	●	●		●		●	●		●	●		●			451
67	*Lombard Recreation Site ~*	F	F	▲	▲		●	●	●		●		●						●			174
68	*Lone Pine Recreation Site ~*	F	F	▲	▲		●	●					●						●			320
69	*Clarkson Recreation Site ~*	F	F	▲	▲		●	●			●		●						●			57
70	*Eustis Recreation Site ~*	F	F	▲	▲		●	●			●		●			●			●			129
71	*Trident Recreation Site ~*	F	F	▲	▲		●	●					●			●			●			297
72	*Missouri River Headwaters State Mon.*	S	S	▲	▲		●	●					●						●			9
73	*Three Forks Recreation Site ~*	F	F	▲	▲		●	●					●						●			16
74	*Three Forks Overlook Recreation Site ~*	F	F	▲				●					●		●	●			●			411
75	*Willow Creek Recreation Site ~*	F	F	▲	▲		●	●					●						●			40

* P - Private   C - County
   Q - Quasi-public   S - State
   M - Municipal   F - Federal

~ Proposed Site

RECREATION AREAS (EXISTING and PROPOSED)

AREA NUMBER		OWNERSHIP*	ADMINISTRATION*	RECREATION USE			RECREATION ACTIVITIES AND ATTRACTIONS															TOTAL LAND AND WATER ACREAGE
				Day	Overnight	Vacation	Camping	Picnicking	Boating	Water Skiing	Swimming	Hunting	Fishing	Hiking	Horse Trails	Sightseeing	Nature Study	Winter Sports	Historic	Archeologic	Geologic	
	MONTANA (Continued)																					
76	Willow Creek Fishing Access Site	S	S	▲									●									2
77	Harrison Lake Access Site	S	S	▲	▲		●		●				●									40
78	River Bend Recreation Site ~	F	F	▲	▲		●	●					●						●			17
79	Canyon Recreation Site ~	F	F	▲	▲		●	●					●			●			●			36
80	Lewis and Clark Caverns State Park	S	S	▲	▲		●	●					●			●					●	2,770
81	South Boulder Recreation Site ~	F	F	▲	▲		●	●					●						●			164
132	Bridger Bowl Ski Area	SF	PF	▲														●				–
133	Sheep Mountain Fishing Access	S	S	▲				●					●									4
134	Buffalo Hump Recreation Site ~	F	F	▲	▲		●	●					●									24
135	McAdow's Canyon Recreation Site ~	F	F	▲				●					●									176
136	Yellowstone Bridge Recreation Site ~	F	F	▲	▲		●	●	●				●									45

~Proposed Site

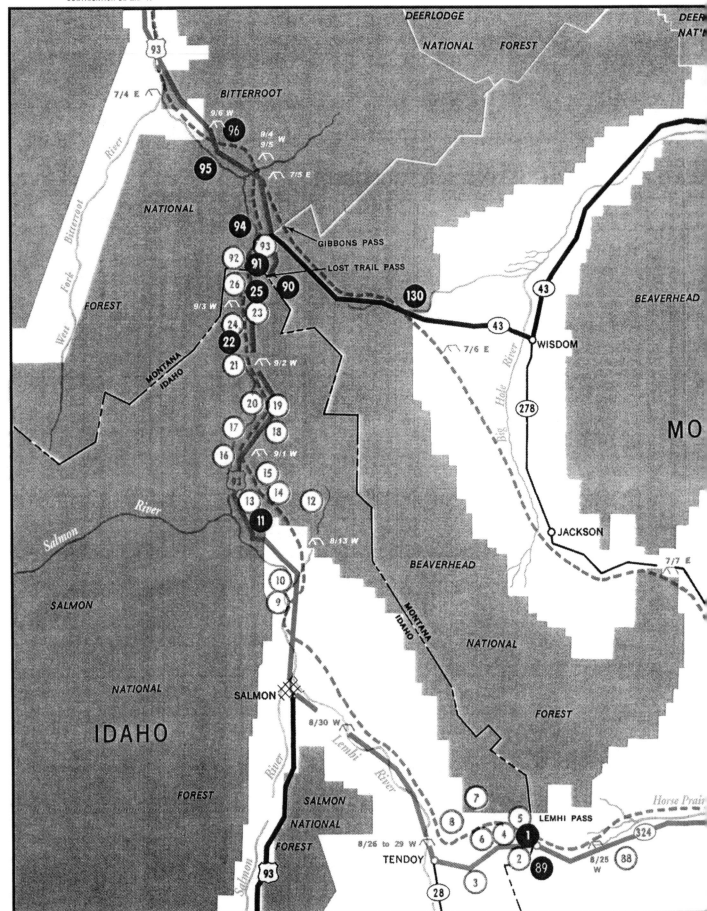

CONTINUATION ON MAP 19

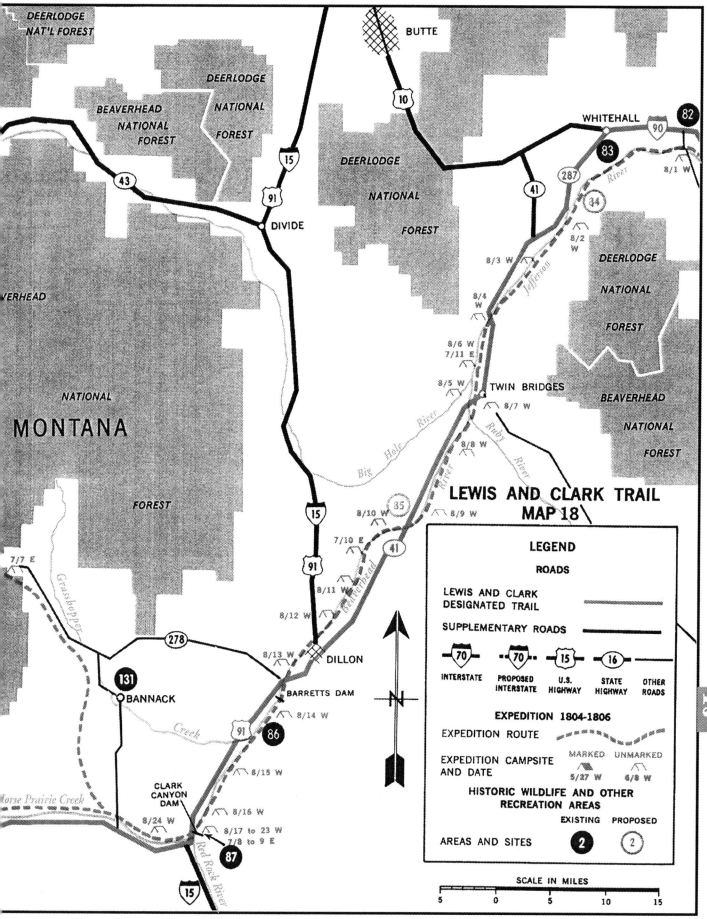

LEWIS AND CLARK TRAIL
MAP 18

CONTINUATION ON MAP 17

18

DEERLODGE
NAT'L FOREST

BUTTE

BEAVERHEAD
NATIONAL
FOREST

DEERLODGE
NATIONAL
FOREST

WHITEHALL

82

90

83

8/1 W

10

15

91

DIVIDE

43

DEERLODGE

NATIONAL

FOREST

41

287

34

8/2
W

8/3 W

DEERLODGE

NATIONAL

FOREST

Jefferson

8/4
W

VERHEAD

MONTANA

NATIONAL

FOREST

8/6 W
7/11 E

8/5 W

TWIN BRIDGES

BEAVERHEAD

NATIONAL

FOREST

8/7 W

8/8 W

Big Hole River

Ruby River

85

8/10 W

8/9 W

7/10 E

41

15

8/11 W

Beaverhead

7/7 E

Grasshopper

8/12 W

278

8/13 W

DILLON

BARRETTS DAM

131

BANNACK

8/14 W

Creek

91

86

8/15 W

CLARK
CANYON
DAM

8/16 W

Horse Prairie Creek

8/24 W

8/17 to 23 W
7/8 to 9 E

87

Red Rock River

15

N

LEGEND

ROADS

LEWIS AND CLARK
DESIGNATED TRAIL

SUPPLEMENTARY ROADS

70	70	15	16	
INTERSTATE	PROPOSED INTERSTATE	U.S. HIGHWAY	STATE HIGHWAY	OTHER ROADS

EXPEDITION 1804-1806

EXPEDITION ROUTE

EXPEDITION CAMPSITE
AND DATE

MARKED
8/27 W

UNMARKED
8/8 W

HISTORIC WILDLIFE AND OTHER
RECREATION AREAS

EXISTING   PROPOSED

AREAS AND SITES   2   2

SCALE IN MILES

5   0   5   10   15

MONTANA (Continued)

Area Number		Ownership*	Administration*	Day	Overnight	Vacation	Camping	Picnicking	Boating	Water Skiing	Swimming	Hunting	Fishing	Hiking	Horse Trails	Sightseeing	Nature Study	Winter Sports	Historic	Archeologic	Geologic	Total Land and Water Acreage
82	Cardwell Fishing Access Site	S	S	▲									•									6
83	Parrot Castle Fishing Access Site	S	S	▲									•									30
84	Renova Recreation Site ~	F	F	△	△		○	○					○			○			○			179
85	Beaverhead Rock Historic Site ~	F	F	△									○						○			120
86	Barretts Diversion Dam Recreation Area	F	S	▲	▲		•	•					•			•			•			20
87	Clark Canyon Reservoir Recreation Area	F	S	▲	▲		•	•	•		•		•			•			•			9,140
88	Trail Creek Recreation Site ~	F	F	△	△		○	○									○					600
89	Sacajawea Memorial Area	F	F	▲			•	•									•		•			—
90	Lost Trail Visitor Center	F	F	▲														•				—
91	Lost Trail Ski Area	F	F	▲														•				—
92	Lost Trail Ski Area ~	F	F	△														○				—
93	Lost Trail Campground ~	F	F	△	△		○	○														—
94	Indian Tree Campground	F	F	▲	▲		•	•											•			—
95	Warm Springs Campground	F	F	▲	▲		•	•														—
96	Spring Gulch Campground	F	F	▲	▲		•	•														—
128	May Creek Campground ~	F	F	△	△	△	○	○					○	○	○							—
129	Placer Creek Campground ~	F	F	△	△		○	○					○									—
130	Big Hole National Battlefield Monument	F	F	▲															•			656
131	Bannock State Monument	S	S	▲	▲		•	•					•						•			50

*
  P - Private   C - County
  Q - Quasi-public   S - State
  M - Municipal   F - Federal
  ~ Proposed Site

RECREATION AREAS (EXISTING and PROPOSED)

AREA NUMBER		OWNERSHIP*	ADMINISTRATION*	RECREATION USE			RECREATION ACTIVITIES AND ATTRACTIONS															TOTAL LAND AND WATER ACREAGE
				Day	Overnight	Vacation	Camping	Picnicking	Boating	Water Skiing	Swimming	Hunting	Fishing	Hiking	Horse Trails	Sightseeing	Nature Study	Winter Sports	Historic	Archeologic	Geologic	
	IDAHO																					
1	Sacajawea Recreational Area	F	F	▲															●			141
2	Chief Tendoy Recreation Site ~	F	F	▲	▲		●	●														160
3	Agency Creek Recreation Site ~	F	F	▲	▲		●	●														40
4	Flume Creek Recreation Site ~	F	F	▲				●														40
5	Lewis and Clark Trail Historical Area ~	F	F	▲												●			●			415
6	White Creek Recreation Site ~	F	F	▲	▲		●	●														30
7	Gass Recreation Site ~	F	F	▲	▲		●	●											●			160
8	Pattee Creek Recreation Site ~	F	F	▲	▲		●	●														80
9	Bolander's Ranch Recreation Site ~	F	F	▲	▲		●	●						●								9
10	Tower Creek Flat Recreation Site ~	PF	F	▲	▲		●	●						●								200
11	Wagonhammer Spring Picnic Area	F	F	▲				●											●			1
12	Blacktail Campground ~	F	F	▲	▲		●	●														4
13	Big Silverlead Campground ~	F	F	▲	▲		●	●											●			2
14	Rattlesnake Campground ~	F	F	▲	▲		●	●														2
15	Little Silverlead Campground ~	F	F	▲	▲		●	●														2
16	South Fork Hull Creek Campground ~	F	F	▲	▲		●	●														2
17	Humbug Creek Campground ~	F	F	▲	▲		●	●														7
18	Stein Gulch Campground ~	F	F	▲	▲		●	●														2
19	Lick Creek Campground ~	F	F	▲	▲		●	●														11
20	Votler Creek Campground ~	F	F	▲	▲		●	●														3
21	Deep Creek Campground ~	F	F	▲	▲		●	●														5
22	Twin Creeks Campground	F	F	▲	▲		●	●														20
23	Moose Creek Campground ~	F	F	▲	▲		●	●														8
24	North Fork Campground ~	F	F	▲	▲		●	●														4
25	Lost Trail Pass Recreation Area	F	F	▲	▲		●	●														320
26	Lewis and Clark Campground ~	F	F	▲	▲		●	●														28

~Proposed Site

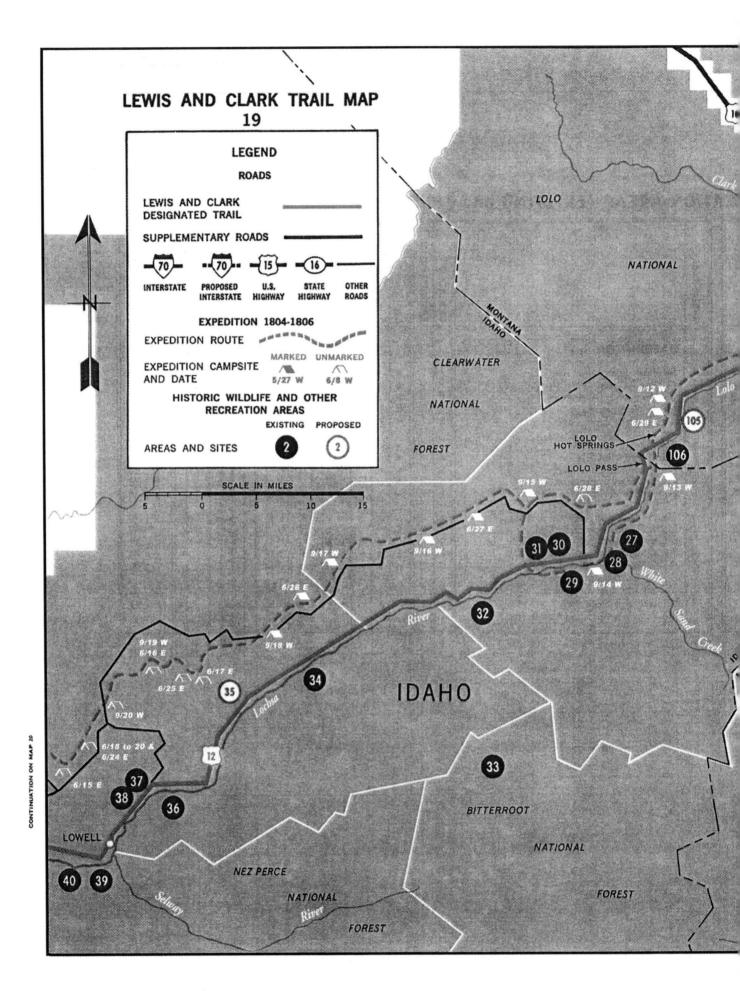

LEWIS AND CLARK TRAIL MAP
19

LEGEND
ROADS

LEWIS AND CLARK DESIGNATED TRAIL

SUPPLEMENTARY ROADS

70	70	15	16	
INTERSTATE	PROPOSED INTERSTATE	U.S. HIGHWAY	STATE HIGHWAY	OTHER ROADS

EXPEDITION 1804-1806

EXPEDITION ROUTE

EXPEDITION CAMPSITE AND DATE

MARKED 5/27 W   UNMARKED 6/8 W

HISTORIC WILDLIFE AND OTHER RECREATION AREAS

EXISTING 2   PROPOSED 2

AREAS AND SITES

SCALE IN MILES

5   0   5   10   15

LOLO

NATIONAL

MONTANA IDAHO

CLEARWATER

NATIONAL

FOREST

Clark

9/12 W
6/29 E

105

LOLO HOT SPRINGS

LOLO PASS

106

9/13 W

9/15 W
6/28 E

27

28

31   30

29
9/14 W

32

White

Sand Creek

9/17 W

6/26 E

9/16 W

9/19 W
6/16 E

9/18 W

6/17 E

6/25 E

35

34

IDAHO

Lochsa

9/20 W

12

33

BITTERROOT

6/15 to 20 & 6/24 E

6/15 E

37

38

36

NATIONAL

FOREST

LOWELL

NEZ PERCE

40   39

Selway

NATIONAL

River

FOREST

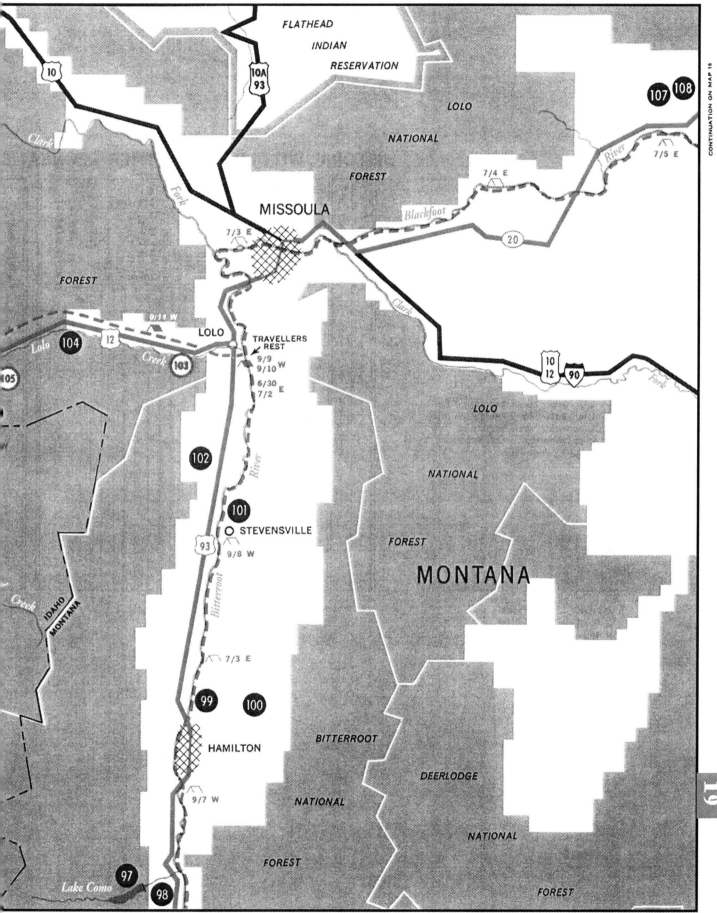

FLATHEAD

INDIAN

RESERVATION

LOLO

NATIONAL

FOREST

10A
93

10

Clark

Fork

MISSOULA

107 108

7/5 E

River

Blackfoot

7/4 E

20

7/3 E

Clark

FOREST

9/11 W

LOLO

LOLO

10
12

90

Lolo

104

12

Creek

103

TRAVELLERS
REST
9/9
9/10 W

6/30 E
7/2

NATIONAL

105

102

FOREST

MONTANA

101

93

O STEVENSVILLE

9/8 W

River

Bitterroot

7/3 E

99

100

BITTERROOT

7/3 E

Creek

IDAHO
MONTANA

HAMILTON

DEERLODGE

NATIONAL

9/7 W

NATIONAL

FOREST

19

97

FOREST

Lake Como

98

AREA NUMBER		OWNERSHIP *	ADMINISTRATION *	RECREATION USE			RECREATION ACTIVITIES AND ATTRACTIONS															TOTAL LAND AND WATER ACREAGE
				Day	Overnight	Vacation	Camping	Picnicking	Boating	Water Skiing	Swimming	Hunting	Fishing	Hiking	Horse Trails	Sightseeing	Nature Study	Winter Sports	Historic	Archeologic	Geologic	
	MONTANA (Continued)																					
97	Lake Como Campground	F	F	▲	▲		•	•	•	•	•						•					1
98	Durland Park		Q	▲			•	•														1
99	Blodgett Park		Q	▲			•	•														
100	Bitterroot Game Range	S	S	▲								•										3,300
101	Fort Owen State Monument	S	S	▲															•			1
102	Bass Creek Recreation Area	F	F	▲	▲		•	•					•						•			–
103	*Lolo Creek Recreation Site* ~	*F*	*F*	▲			•	•														240
104	Lewis and Clark Campground	F	F	▲	▲		•	•														–
105	*Mud Creek Campground* ~	*F*	*F*	▲	▲		•	•														–
106	Lee Creek Campground	F	F	▲	▲		•	•														–
107	Blackfoot-Clearwater Game Range	S	S	▲								•	•									52,000
108	Upsata Lake Fishing Access	S	S	▲									•									11

* P - Private   C - County
Q - Quasi-public   S - State
M - Municipal   F - Federal

~Proposed Site

RECREATION AREAS (EXISTING and PROPOSED)

AREA NUMBER		OWNERSHIP*	ADMINISTRATION*	RECREATION USE			RECREATION ACTIVITIES AND ATTRACTIONS															TOTAL LAND AND WATER ACREAGE
				Day	Overnight	Vacation	Camping	Picnicking	Boating	Water Skiing	Swimming	Hunting	Fishing	Hiking	Horse Trails	Sightseeing	Nature Study	Winter Sports	Historic	Archeologic	Geologic	
	IDAHO (Continued)																					
27	Bernard DeVoto Memorial Grove	F	F	▲															●	●		−
28	Whitesand Campground	F	F	▲	▲		●	●														−
29	Powell Campground	F	F	▲	▲		●	●				●	●									−
30	Whitehouse Campground	F	F	▲	▲	▲	●	●					●									−
31	Wendover Campground	F	F	▲	▲	▲	●	●					●									−
32	Jerry Johnson Campground	F	F	▲	▲		●	●														−
33	Selway–Bitterroot Wilderness	F	F	▲	▲	▲	●					●	●	●	●	●						1,239,840
34	Green Flat Campground	F	F	▲	▲		●						●									−
35	*Boulder Flat Campground ~*	*F*	*F*	▲	▲		●					●	●									50
36	Major Fenn Picnic Ground	F	F	▲				●					●									−
37	Glade Creek Campground	F	F	▲	▲		●	●					●									−
38	Apgar Campground	F	F	▲	▲		●	●					●									−
39	Wild Goose Campground	F	F	▲	▲		●	●			●		●									−
40	Three Devils Picnic Ground	F	F	▲				●			●		●									−

~Proposed Site

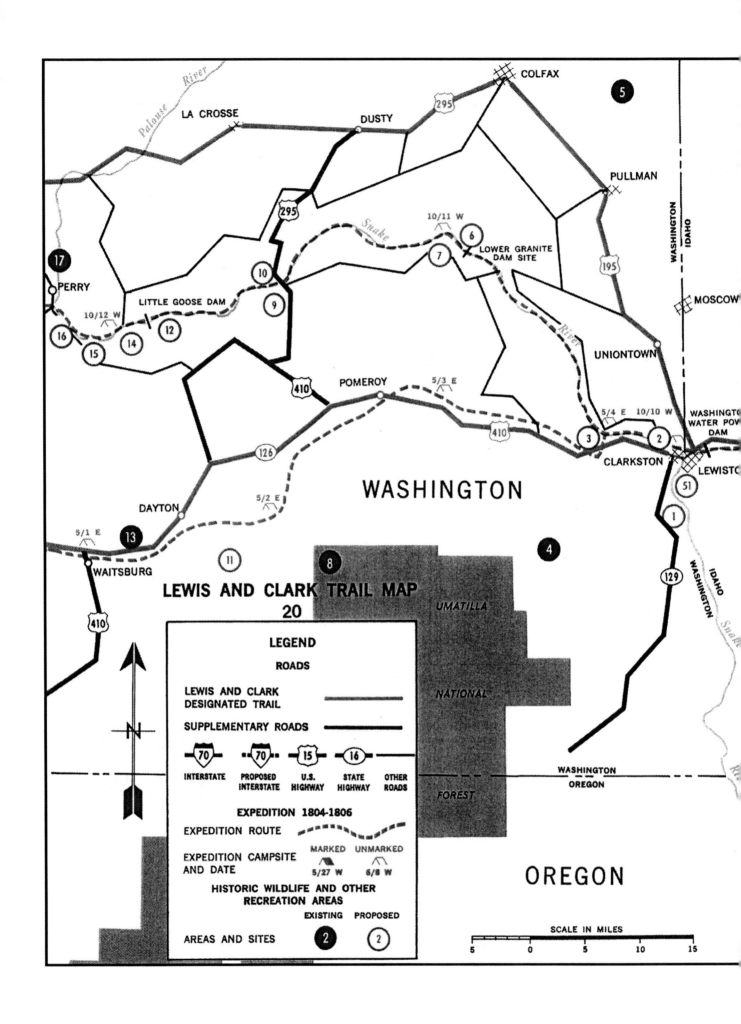

LEWIS AND CLARK TRAIL MAP
20

LEGEND

ROADS

LEWIS AND CLARK
DESIGNATED TRAIL

SUPPLEMENTARY ROADS

70 INTERSTATE
70 PROPOSED INTERSTATE
15 U.S. HIGHWAY
16 STATE HIGHWAY
OTHER ROADS

EXPEDITION 1804-1806

EXPEDITION ROUTE

EXPEDITION CAMPSITE AND DATE
MARKED 5/27 W
UNMARKED 5/8 W

HISTORIC WILDLIFE AND OTHER RECREATION AREAS

AREAS AND SITES
EXISTING 2
PROPOSED 2

SCALE IN MILES
5   0   5   10   15

MOSCOW

Pollatch

River

North Fork Clearwater River

Clearwater

DWORSHAK
DAM SITE

9/26 to 30 &
10/1 to 6 W

5/6 E   10/7 W

10/8 W   5/5 E
10/9

WASHINGTON
WATER POWER
DAM

(48)   (47)   (46)   (45)   (44)   OROFINO

(49) (50)

LEWISTON

5/7 E

5/8 E

9/24 W
9/25

NEZ PERCE

WEIPPE

9/23 W   9/22 W
6/10 to 14
& 6/21 to 23 E

5/9 E

(41)

River

IDAHO
WASHINGTON

Snake

INDIAN

[12] 5/14 to 31 E
6/1 to 9 E

5/13
E

(43) (42)

9/21 W

IDAHO

NEZPERCE

KAMIAH

5/10
5/12 E

Middle   Fork

RESERVATION

KOOSKIA

Clearwater River

[95]

Salmon

River

IDAHO
OREGON

South

NEZ PERCE

NATIONAL

[13]

GRANGEVILLE

FOREST

Clearwater   River

CONTINUATION ON MAP 19

HISTORIC, WILDLIFE and OTHER

Area Number		Ownership *	Administration *	Day	Overnight	Vacation	Camping	Picnicking	Boating	Water Skiing	Swimming	Hunting	Fishing	Hiking	Horse Trails	Sightseeing	Nature Study	Winter Sports	Historic	Archeologic	Geologic	Total Land and Water Acreage
	IDAHO (Continued)																					
41	Brown's Ridge Recreation Site	F	F	▲				●								●			●			20
42	*Nez Perce Nat'l Hist. Pk. (E.Kamiah Unit)* ~	P	F	▲	▲		●	●											●			103
43	Tom Taha Creek Recreation Site	F	F	▲			●	●											●			3
44	Canoe Camp State Park	S	S	▲															●			3
45	*Ahsahka Recreation Site* ~	F	F	▲	▲		●	●														10
46	*Clearwater No. 1 Recreation Site* ~	F	F	▲	▲		●	●														10
47	*Clearwater No. 2 Recreation Site* ~	F	F	▲	▲		●	●														5
48	*Clearwater No. 3 Recreation Site* ~	F	F	▲	▲		●	●														5
49	*Nez Perce Nat'l Hist. Pk. (Hdqt. Unit)* ~	PSF	PSF	▲	▲	▲	●	●								●			●	●		122
50	Spalding State Park	S	S	▲				●											●			19
51	*Snake River Recreation Site* ~	F	F	▲				●	●	●			●									6

*
P - Private   C - County
Q - Quasi-public   S - State
M - Municipal   F - Federal

~ Proposed Site

RECREATION AREAS (EXISTING and PROPOSED)

Area Number		Ownership*	Administration*	Recreation Use			Recreation Activities and Attractions															Total Land and Water Acreage
				Day	Overnight	Vacation	Camping	Picnicking	Boating	Water Skiing	Swimming	Hunting	Fishing	Hiking	Horse Trails	Sightseeing	Nature Study	Winter Sports	Historic	Archeologic	Geologic	
	WASHINGTON																					
1	Swallows Recreation Site ~	F	F	△					○	○	○	○		○									20
2	North Clarkston Recreation Site ~	F	F	△						○				○									4
3	Chief Timothy Recreation Site ~	F	F	△	△		○		○	○	○	○		○									100
4	Asotin Game Range	S	S	▲	▲		●					●											6,357
5	Kamiak Butte State Park	S	S	▲	▲		●	●							●		●						284
6	Boyer Recreation Site ~	F	F	△					○	○				○			○						185
7	Illia Recreation Site ~	F	F	△					○	○				○			○						347
8	W. T. Wooten Game Range	S	S	▲	▲		●					●	●									11,234
9	Central Ferry Recreation Site ~	F	F	△						○				○									58
10	Peyton Recreation Site ~	F	F	△	△		○		○	○	○		○										160
11	Dayton Reservoir Recreation Area ~	F	F	△	△		○		○	○	○	○	○									1,473
12	Little Goose Recreation Site ~	F	F	△			○		○	○	○		○										172
13	Lewis and Clark Trail State Park	S	S	▲	▲		●	●					●									35
14	Texas Rapids Recreation Site ~	F	F	△	△		○		○	○	○		○										74
15	Columbia County Park ~	C	C	△	△		○		○	○	○		○										1,000
16	Lyons Ferry Recreation Site ~	F	F	△	△		○		○	○	○	○		○			○		○	○	○	1,366
17	Palouse Falls State Park	S	S	▲	▲		●	●									●				●	91

~Proposed Site

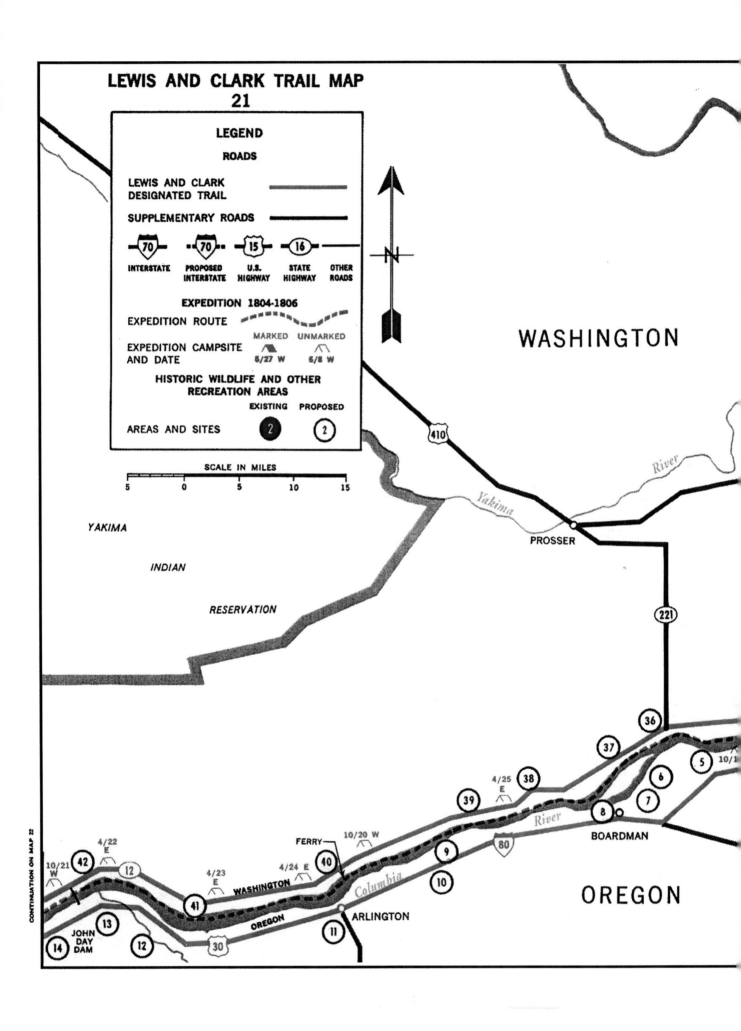

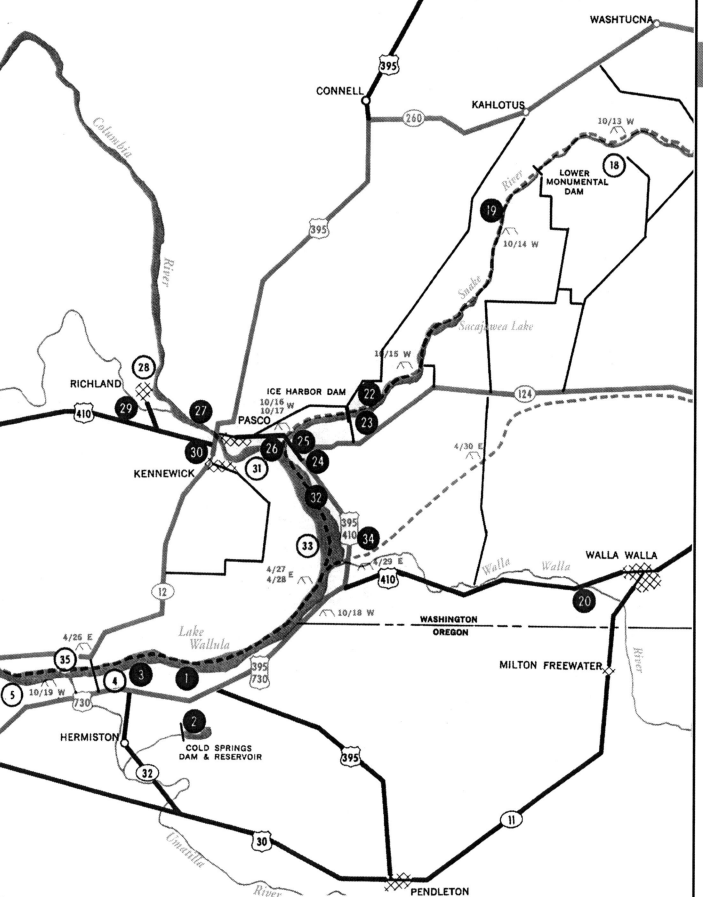

WASHTUCNA

395
CONNELL

260
KAHLOTUS

10/13 W

LOWER
MONUMENTAL
DAM

18

19

395

10/14 W

Snake

River

Sacajawea Lake

Columbia

River

10/15 W

28
RICHLAND

ICE HARBOR DAM
10/16 W
10/17 W

22

124

410
29

27
PASCO

23

30

26 25

31

24

4/30 E

KENNEWICK

32

395
410

34

WALLA WALLA

33

12

4/27
4/28 E

4/29 E

410

Walla

Walla

20

10/18 W

WASHINGTON
OREGON

MILTON FREEWATER

River

Lake
Wallula

395
730

4/26 E

35

4
3

1

395
730

5
10/19 W

730

2

HERMISTON

COLD SPRINGS
DAM & RESERVOIR

395

32

30

Umatilla

11

River

PENDLETON

Area Number		Ownership*	Administration*	Recreation Use			Recreation Activities and Attractions															Total Land and Water Acreage
				Day	Overnight	Vacation	Camping	Picnicking	Boating	Water Skiing	Swimming	Hunting	Fishing	Hiking	Horse Trails	Sightseeing	Nature Study	Winter Sports	Historic	Archeologic	Geologic	
	WASHINGTON (Continued)																					
18	*Ayner Recreation Site ~*	F	F	▲				•	•					•									192
19	Windust Park	F	F	▲				•	•					•									44
20	Whitman Mission National Historic Site	F	F	▲	▲			•								•				•			98
21	Fishhook Park	F	F	▲	▲		•	•	•	•	•		•									287
22	Levey Landing Park	F	F	▲					•	•	•		•									76
23	Charbonneau Park	F	F	▲				•	•	•	•		•									197
24	McNary National Wildlife Refuge	F	F	▲					•				•				•					2,800
25	Hood Park	F	C	▲				•	•	•	•		•									136
26	Sacajawea State Park	SF	SC	▲				•	•				•						•			30
27	Chiawana Park	F	C	▲				•	•		•											90
28	*Nelson Island Recreation Site ~*	F	F	▲				•	•	•	•											210
29	Riverside Park	C	C	▲				•	•													–
30	Columbia Park	F	C	▲	▲		•	•	•	•	•											600
31	*Two Rivers Recreation Site ~*	F	C	▲					•		•											129
32	McNary Game Range	F	S	▲					•			•	•									8,945
33	*Hover Recreation Site ~*	F	C	▲				•	•						•							··
34	Wallula Park	F	F	▲				•	•													323
35	*Plymouth Recreation Site ~*	F	F	▲	▲		•	•	•		•								•			150
36	*Paterson Recreation Site ~*	F	F	▲				•	•													25
37	*Glade Creek Recreation Site ~*	F	F	▲				•	•													15

* P- Private   C- County
Q- Quasi-public   S- State
M- Municipal   F- Federal

~Proposed Site

RECREATION AREAS (EXISTING and PROPOSED)

Area Number		Ownership*	Administration*	Recreation Use			Recreation Activities and Attractions															Total Land and Water Acreage
				Day	Overnight	Vacation	Camping	Picnicking	Boating	Water Skiing	Swimming	Hunting	Fishing	Hiking	Horse Trails	Sightseeing	Nature Study	Winter Sports	Historic	Archeologic	Geologic	
	WASHINGTON (Continued)																					
38	Crow Butte Recreation Site ~	F	F	▲	▲		●	●	●	●	●					●	●					150
39	Alder Creek Recreation Site ~	F	F	▲				●	●	●	●											120
40	Roosevelt Recreation Site ~	F	F	▲				●	●	●	●											125
41	Rock Creek Recreation Site ~	F	F	▲	▲		●	●	●		●					●					●		260
42	North Shore Recreation Site ~	F	F	▲				●	●	●												115
	OREGON																					
1	Hat Rock State Park	SF	S	▲				●	●	●	●		●	●		●			●		●	369
2	Cold Springs National Wildlife Refuge	F	F	▲				●	●			●			●		●					3,000
3	McNary Beach Park	F	F	▲				●		●	●											33
4	Umatilla Recreation Site ~	F	F	▲	▲		●	●	●	●	●											110
5	Irrigon Recreation Site ~	F	F	▲				●	●	●	●											20
6	John Day Waterfowl Management Area ~	F	F	▲								●	●									29,370
7	Dunes Recreation Site ~	F	F	▲				●	●		●											75
8	Boardman Recreation Site ~	F	F	▲				●	●	●	●											35
9	Willows Recreation Site ~	F	F	▲	▲		●	●	●	●	●											790
10	Willow Creek Game Management Area ~	F	F	▲								●	●									–
11	Arlington Recreation Site ~	F	F	▲				●	●		●											10
12	John Day River Game Managemant Area ~	F	F	▲								●	●									–
13	John Day River Recreation Site ~	F	F	▲	▲		●	●	●	●	●		●			●		●				880
14	Rufus Recreation Site ~	F	F	▲				●					●									–

~Proposed Site

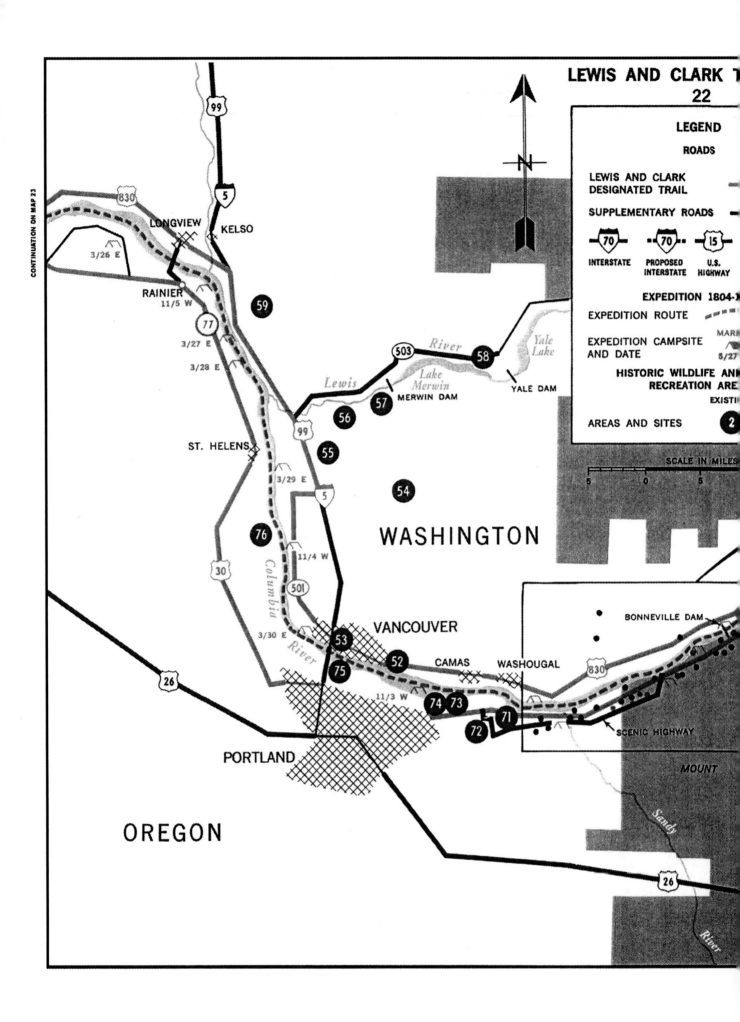

CONTINUATION ON MAP 23

99

830

5

LONGVIEW

KELSO

3/26 E

RAINIER

11/5 W

77

3/27 E

3/28 E

59

503

River

58

Lewis

Yale Lake

Lake Merwin

57

MERWIN DAM

YALE DAM

99

56

ST. HELENS

55

3/29 E

5

54

WASHINGTON

76

11/4 W

30

501

Columbia River

VANCOUVER

3/30 E

53

52

CAMAS

WASHOUGAL

830

BONNEVILLE DAM

75

11/3 W

74 73

71

72

SCENIC HIGHWAY

26

PORTLAND

MOUNT

Sandy

OREGON

26

River

LEGEND

ROADS

LEWIS AND CLARK
DESIGNATED TRAIL

SUPPLEMENTARY ROADS

70 INTERSTATE

70 PROPOSED INTERSTATE

15 U.S. HIGHWAY

EXPEDITION 1804-

EXPEDITION ROUTE

EXPEDITION CAMPSITE
AND DATE

MAR
8/27

HISTORIC WILDLIFE AN
RECREATION ARE

EXISTI

AREAS AND SITES

2

SCALE IN MILES

5   0   5

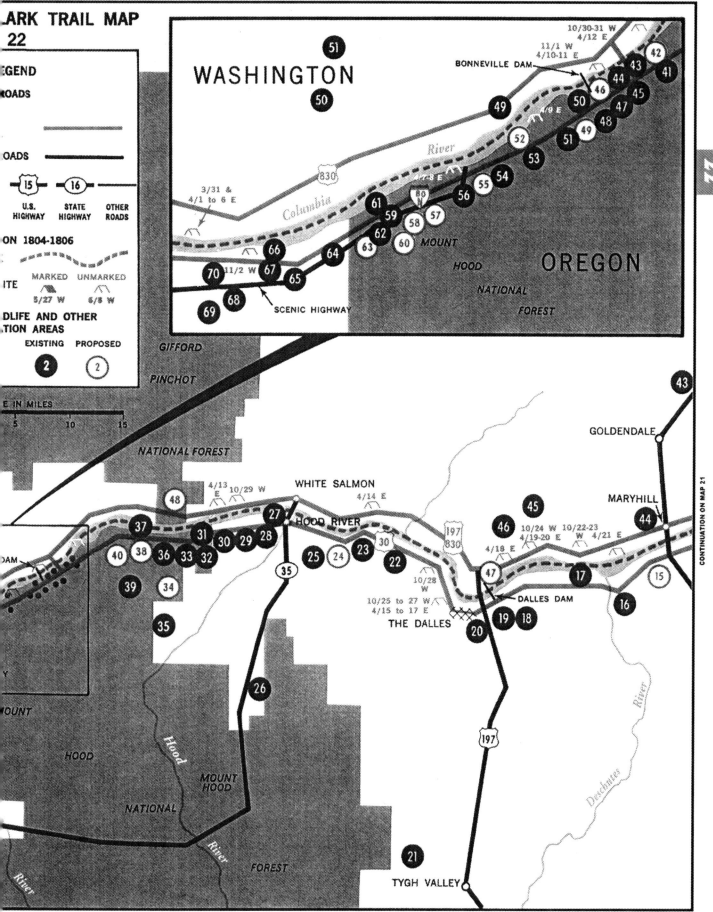

LEGEND

ROADS

ROADS

| 15 | 16 | |
| U.S. HIGHWAY | STATE HIGHWAY | OTHER ROADS |

ON 1804-1806

MARKED   UNMARKED
5/27 W   5/5 W

DLIFE AND OTHER
TION AREAS

EXISTING   PROPOSED

2   2

E IN MILES

5   10   15

WASHINGTON

OREGON

Columbia   River

Mount Hood National Forest

Bonneville Dam

Scenic Highway

Gifford Pinchot

National Forest

White Salmon

Hood River

Goldendale

Maryhill

Dalles Dam

The Dalles

Mount Hood

National Forest

Hood River

River

Deschutes River

Tygh Valley

CONTINUATION ON MAP 21

22

HISTORIC, WILDLIFE and OTHER

Area Number		Ownership*	Administration*	Recreation Use			Recreation Activities and Attractions															Total Land and Water Acreage
				Day	Overnight	Vacation	Camping	Picnicking	Boating	Water Skiing	Swimming	Hunting	Fishing	Hiking	Horse Trails	Sightseeing	Nature Study	Winter Sports	Historic	Archeologic	Geologic	
WASHINGTON (Continued)																						
43	Brooks Memorial State Park	S	S	▲	▲		●											●				734
44	Maryhill Park	F	F	▲				●	●	●	●											8
45	Avery Recreation Area	F	F	▲				●	●	●	●		●									65
46	Horsethief Lake State Park	F	S	▲				●	●	●	●		●									293
47	*Spearfish Lake Recreation Area ~*	F	F	▲									●									*125*
48	*Dog Mountain Observation Site ~*	F	F	▲												●						*1*
49	Beacon Rock State Park	S	S	▲	▲		●	●	●			●	●			●		●		●	4,051
50	Skamania Hatchery	S	S	▲												●						45
51	Washougal Salmon Hatchery	S	S	▲												●						–
52	Vancouver Hatchery	S	S	▲												●						42
53	Fort Vancouver National Historic Site	F	F	▲														●			90
54	Lewisville Park	C	C	▲	▲			●			●											244
55	Paradise Point State Park	S	S	▲	▲		●	●	●		●		●									70
56	Lewis River Salmon Hatchery	S	S	▲												●						–
57	Merwin Park	P	P	▲				●	●		●											25
58	Speelyai Bay Park	P	P	▲				●	●	●	●		●									4
59	Kalama Salmon Hatchery	S	S	▲												●						–
OREGON (Continued)																						
15	*Biggs Recreation Area ~*	F	F	▲									●			●						*2*
16	Deschutes River State Park	S	S	▲									●									35
17	Celilo Park	F	C	▲				●	●	●	●		●			●		●				12
18	The Dalles Viewpoint and Memorial	F	C	▲									●			●		●				–
19	Seufert Park	F	C	▲									●					●	●			30
20	The Dalles Small-Boat Basin	M	M	▲					●													–
21	White River Game Management Area	S	S	▲	▲		●					●	●	●		●		●				12,000
22	Mayer State Park	S	S	▲				●	●	●	●		●			●						333
23	Chatfield-Memaloose Area	S	S	▲				●								●		●				329
24	*Mosier Battlements Recreation Site ~*	P	S	▲				●							●	●		●	●	●	*100*
25	Koberg Beach Wayside	S	S	▲				●		●						●						88
26	Zibe Dimmick State Park	S	S	▲				●	●				●									23
27	Hood River Small-Boat Basin	M	M	▲					●													–
28	Senaca Fouts Memorial State Park	S	S	▲									●	●		●						316
29	Vinzenz Lausmann Memorial State Park	S	S	▲									●	●		●						126
30	Wygant State Park	S	S	▲					●				●			●						691
31	Viento State Park	S	S	▲	▲		●	●					●			●						244
32	Starvation Creek State Park	S	S	▲					●				●			●		●				153
33	Old Wagon Road Historical Area	F	F	▲														●				49
34	*Lindsey Creek Development Site ~*	F	F	▲												●						*16*

RECREATION AREAS (EXISTING and PROPOSED)

AREA NUMBER		OWNERSHIP*	ADMINISTRATION*	RECREATION USE			RECREATION ACTIVITIES AND ATTRACTIONS															TOTAL LAND AND WATER ACREAGE
				Day	Overnight	Vacation	Camping	Picnicking	Boating	Water Skiing	Swimming	Hunting	Fishing	Hiking	Horse Trails	Sightseeing	Nature Study	Winter Sports	Historic	Archeologic	Geologic	
	OREGON (Continued)																					
35	Hood River Trout Hatchery	S	S	▲												●						9
36	Lindsey Creek State Park	S	S	▲				●								●						129
37	Lang State Park	S	S	▲												●						162
38	*Wyeth Development Site ~*	*F*	*F*	▲	▲		●	●								●						5
39	Herman Creek Campground	F	F	▲	▲		●	●					●									1
40	*Herman Creek Development Site ~*	*F*	*F*	▲	▲		●	●					●									2
41	Oxbow Salmon Hatchery	FS	S	▲												●						22
42	*Cascade Locks Small-Boat Basin ~*	*M*	*M*	▲					●													-
43	Cascade Locks Indian Picnic Site	F	FS	▲				●					●			●			●			2
44	Sheridan State Park	S	S	▲				●					●			●			●			12
45	Overlook Picnic Ground	F	F	▲				●								●						4
46	*Eagle Creek Waterfront Development Site ~*	*F*	*FS*	▲					●			●										3
47	Cascade Salmon Hatchery	S	S	▲												●						8
48	Eagle Creek Picnic Ground	F	F	▲	▲		●	●					●									20
49	*Columbia Gorge Scenic Area ~*	*F*	*F*	▲	▲		●	●			●	●	●	●	●	●	●					23,040
50	Bonneville Salmon Hatchery	S	S	▲												●						100
51	Bonneville State Park	S	S	▲												●						51
52	*Eloah Development Site ~*	*F*	*F*	▲	▲		●	●	●				●									9
53	John B. Yeon State Park	S	S	▲									●			●						284
54	McLoughlin State Park	S	S	▲									●			●						162
55	*St. Peter's Dome Mtn. Climbing Area ~*	*F*	*F*	▲												●						280
56	Ainsworth State Park	S	S	▲				●					●			●					●	46
57	*Oneonta Falls Geological Area ~*	*F*	*F*	▲												●					●	180
58	*Horsetail Falls Development Site ~*	*F*	*F*	▲				●								●						2
59	Multnomah Falls Lodge	F	F	▲									●			●						4
60	*Headwater Development Site ~*	*F*	*F*	▲	▲		●					●			●							45
61	Benson State Park	FS	S	▲				●	●		●		●			●						84
62	Wahkeena Falls Picnic Ground	F	F	▲									●			●						6
63	*Bridal Veil Falls State Park ~*	*P*	*S*	▲				●					●			●	●					60
64	Shepperd's Dell State Park	S	S	▲									●			●	●					292
65	George W. Joseph State Park	S	S	▲									●			●	●					150
66	Rooster Rock State Park	S	S	▲				●	●	●	●		●			●		●		●		825
67	Guy W. Talbot State Park	S	S	▲				●					●			●	●					241
68	Crown Point State Park	S	S	▲									●			●						270
69	Oxbow Park	CSF	C	▲	▲		●	●			●		●									800
70	Portland Women's Forum State Park	S	S	▲												●						4
71	Dabney State Park	S	S	▲	▲		●	●	●		●		●			●						79
72	Lewis and Clark State Park	S	S	▲	▲		●	●	●		●		●			●		●				56
73	Blue Lake Park	C	C	▲				●	●		●		●									150
74	Government Island Game Mgt. Area	S	S	▲				●	●			●	●									2,093
75	Oregon Slough Entrance Channel	P	P	▲					●	●			●									-
76	Sauvie Island Game Management Area	S	S	▲				●	●			●	●			●						11,030
77	*Coffin Rock State Park ~*	*P*	*S*	▲				●	●			●	●			●			●			282

~Proposed Site

Pacific   Ocean

N

LEGEND

ROADS

LEWIS AND CLARK
DESIGNATED TRAIL

SUPPLEMENTARY ROADS

INTERSTATE   PROPOSED   U.S.
           INTERSTATE HIGHWAY

EXPEDITION 1804-

EXPEDITION ROUTE

               MARK
EXPEDITION CAMPSITE
AND DATE   5/27

HISTORIC WILDLIFE AN
RECREATION ARE

           EXISTI

AREAS AND SITES   2

SCALE IN MILES

5   0   5

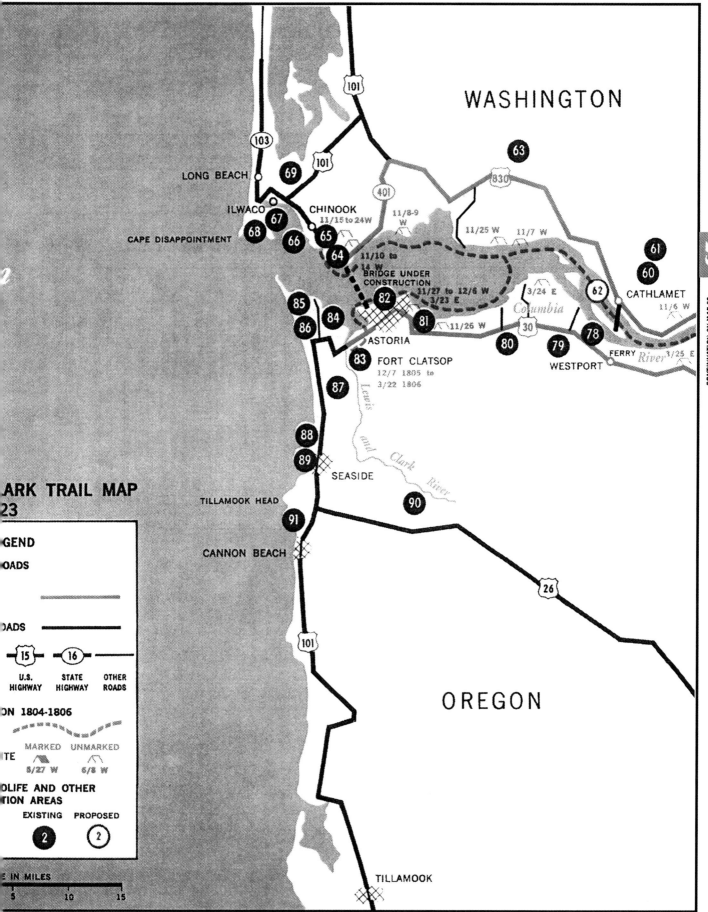

WASHINGTON

101

103

63

830

LONG BEACH

69

101

401

11/8-9 W

ILWACO

CHINOOK
11/15 to 24W

11/25 W

11/7 W

61

67

65

60

68

66

CAPE DISAPPOINTMENT

64

11/10 to
14 W
BRIDGE UNDER
CONSTRUCTION

CATHLAMET

62

11/6 W

85

82

11/27 to 12/6 W
3/23 E

Columbia

3/24 E

81

86

84

11/26 W

30

78

ASTORIA

80

79

FERRY

River 3/25 E

83

FORT CLATSOP
12/7 1805 to
3/22 1806

WESTPORT

87

Lewis

88

and

Clark

89

SEASIDE

River

ARK TRAIL MAP

23

TILLAMOOK HEAD

90

91

26

GEND

CANNON BEACH

OADS

OADS

15   16

U.S.   STATE   OTHER
HIGHWAY   HIGHWAY   ROADS

101

ON 1804-1806

MARKED   UNMARKED

OREGON

TE

3/27 W   6/8 W

DLIFE AND OTHER
TION AREAS

EXISTING   PROPOSED

2   2

E IN MILES

5   10   15

TILLAMOOK

HISTORIC, WILDLIFE and OTHER

Area Number		Ownership*	Administration*	Recreation Use			Recreation Activities and Attractions															Total Land and Water Acreage
				Day	Overnight	Vacation	Camping	Picnicking	Boating	Water Skiing	Swimming	Hunting	Fishing	Hiking	Horse Trails	Sightseeing	Nature Study	Winter Sports	Historic	Archeologic	Geologic	
	WASHINGTON (Continued)																					
60	Beaver Creek Hatchery	S	S	▲													•					45
61	Elokomin Salmon Hatchery	S	S	▲													•					–
62	*Cathlamet Mooring Basin ~*	M	M	▲					•				•									–
63	Grays River Salmon Hatchery	S	S	▲													•					554
64	Fort Columbia State Park	S	S	▲				•					•						•			554
65	Lewis and Clark Campsite State Park	S	S	▲															•			1
66	Chinook Small–Boat Basin	M	M	▲					•				•									–
67	Ilwaco Small–Boat Basin	M	M	▲					•				•									–
68	Fort Canby State Park	S	S	▲	▲		•	•					•			•			•			791
69	Willapa National Wildlife Refuge	F	F	▲								•					•					17,500

* P - Private   C - County
   Q - Quasi-public   S - State
   M - Municipal   F - Federal

~*Proposed Site*

Area Number		Ownership*	Administration*	Recreation Use			Recreation Activities and Attractions															Total Land and Water Acreage
				Day	Overnight	Vacation	Camping	Picnicking	Boating	Water Skiing	Swimming	Hunting	Fishing	Hiking	Horse Trails	Sightseeing	Nature Study	Winter Sports	Historic	Archeologic	Geologic	
	OREGON (Continued)																					
78	Bradley Wayside	S	S	▲				•								•						18
79	Gnat Creek Fish Hatchery	S	S	▲													•					17
80	Big Creek Salmon Hatchery	S	S	▲													•					80
81	John Day River Park	C	C	▲					•				•						•			54
82	Astoria Small-Boat Basin	M	M	▲					•				•									–
83	Fort Clatsop National Memorial	F	F	▲				•											•			125
84	Warrenton Small-Boat Basin	M	M	▲					•				•									–
85	Fort Stevens Game Management Area	S	S	▲					•			•	•			•						1,467
86	Fort Stevens State Park	S	S	▲	▲	▲	•	•	•		•	•	•			•	•					793
87	Cullaby Lake Park	C	C	▲				•	•	•	•		•				•					60
88	Gearhart Ocean Wayside	S	S	▲									•			•	•					286
89	Salt Cairn	P	P	▲															•			–
90	Saddle Mountain State Park	S	S	▲	▲		•	•					•			•	•		•		•	3,054
91	Ecola State Park	S	S	▲				•			•		•	•		•	•		•	•	•	1,147

LEWIS AND CLARK TRAIL MAP
24

LEGEND

ROADS

LEWIS AND CLARK
DESIGNATED TRAIL

SUPPLEMENTARY ROADS

70	70	15	16	
INTERSTATE	PROPOSED INTERSTATE	U.S. HIGHWAY	STATE HIGHWAY	OTHER ROADS

EXPEDITION 1804-1806

EXPEDITION ROUTE

EXPEDITION CAMPSITE AND DATE — MARKED 5/27 W — UNMARKED 6/8 W

HISTORIC WILDLIFE AND OTHER RECREATION AREAS

AREAS AND SITES — EXISTING 2 — PROPOSED 2

SCALE IN MILES
5 0 5 10 15

CONTINUATION ON MAP 17

N

87

Yellowstone

7/24 E

10
312

BILLINGS

141

90

River

LAUREL

10

7/19
7/23 E

COLUMBUS
139

7/18 E

138

137

140

Yellowstone

212
310

Clarks Fork

212

310

212

87
212

CROW

I

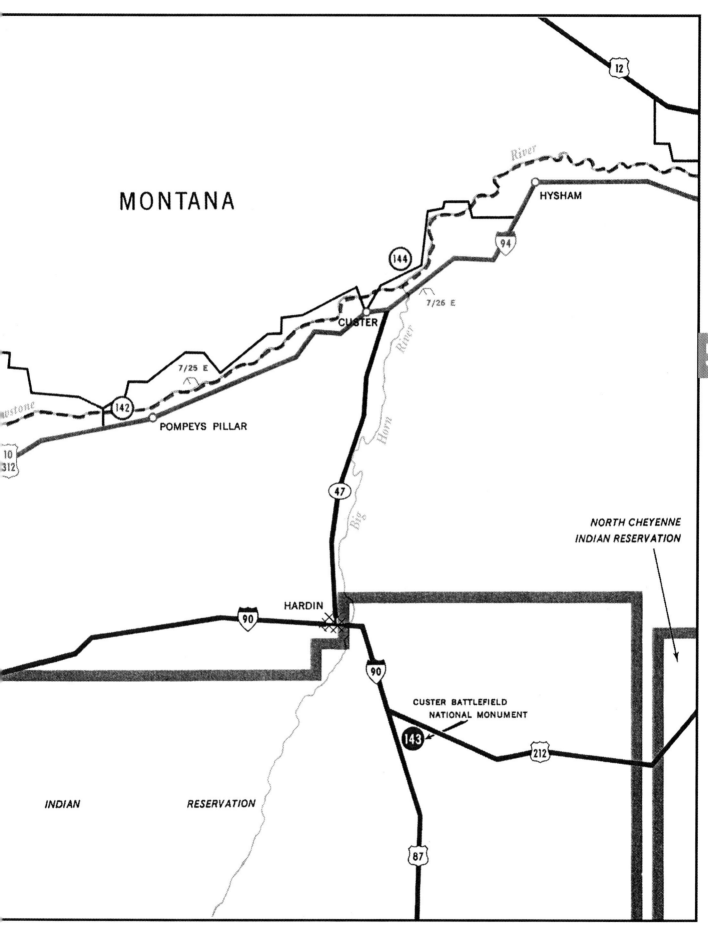

MONTANA

CONTINUATION ON MAP 25

24

HYSHAM

94

144

7/26 E

CUSTER

7/25 E

142

POMPEYS PILLAR

10
312

47

HARDIN

90

90

CUSTER BATTLEFIELD
NATIONAL MONUMENT

143

212

87

NORTH CHEYENNE
INDIAN RESERVATION

INDIAN   RESERVATION

12

HISTORIC, WILDLIFE and OTHER

Area Number		Ownership*	Administration*	Recreation Use			Recreation Activities and Attractions															Total Land and Water Acreage
				Day	Overnight	Vacation	Camping	Picnicking	Boating	Water Skiing	Swimming	Hunting	Fishing	Hiking	Horse Trails	Sightseeing	Nature Study	Winter Sports	Historic	Archeologic	Geologic	
	MONTANA (Continued)																					
137	Swinging Bridge Fishing Access Site	S	S	▲								•	•									4
138	Columbus Fishing Access Site	S	S	▲								•	•									5
139	*East Columbus Recreation Site ~*	F	F	▲	▲								•									25
140	*Tutt Creek Recreation Site ~*	F	F	▲	▲								•									40
141	*Josephine Island Recreation Site ~*	F	F	▲	▲		•		•				•						•			56

*
P - Private   C - County
Q - Quasi-public   S - State
M - Municipal   F - Federal

~Proposed Site

RECREATION AREAS (EXISTING and PROPOSED)

AREA NUMBER		OWNERSHIP*	ADMINISTRATION*	RECREATION USE			RECREATION ACTIVITIES AND ATTRACTIONS															TOTAL LAND AND WATER ACREAGE
				Day	Overnight	Vacation	Camping	Picnicking	Boating	Water Skiing	Swimming	Hunting	Fishing	Hiking	Horse Trails	Sightseeing	Nature Study	Winter Sports	Historic	Archeologic	Geologic	
	MONTANA (Continued)																					
142	*Pompey's Pillar Historic Monument ~*	S	S	▲	▲		◉	◉					◉				◉		◉		◉	320
143	Custer Battlefield National Monument	F	F	▲												●			●	●		765
144	*Big Horn Island Recreation Site ~*	F	F	▲	▲		◉	◉					◉						◉			249

~Proposed Site

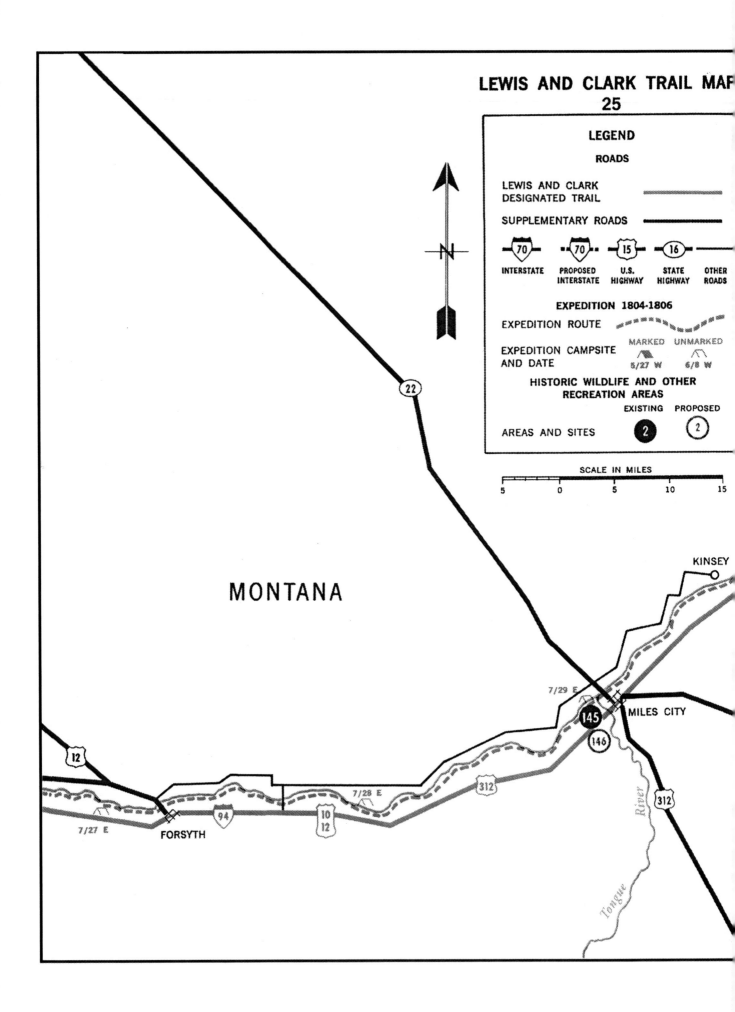

LEGEND

ROADS

LEWIS AND CLARK
DESIGNATED TRAIL

SUPPLEMENTARY ROADS

70 INTERSTATE   70 PROPOSED INTERSTATE   15 U.S. HIGHWAY   16 STATE HIGHWAY   OTHER ROADS

EXPEDITION 1804-1806

EXPEDITION ROUTE

EXPEDITION CAMPSITE AND DATE   MARKED 5/27 W   UNMARKED 6/8 W

HISTORIC WILDLIFE AND OTHER RECREATION AREAS

AREAS AND SITES   EXISTING 2   PROPOSED 2

SCALE IN MILES
5   0   5   10   15

N

MONTANA

KINSEY

22

7/29 E

145

146

MILES CITY

12

312

312

10 12

7/28 E

94

7/27 E

FORSYTH

Tongue

River

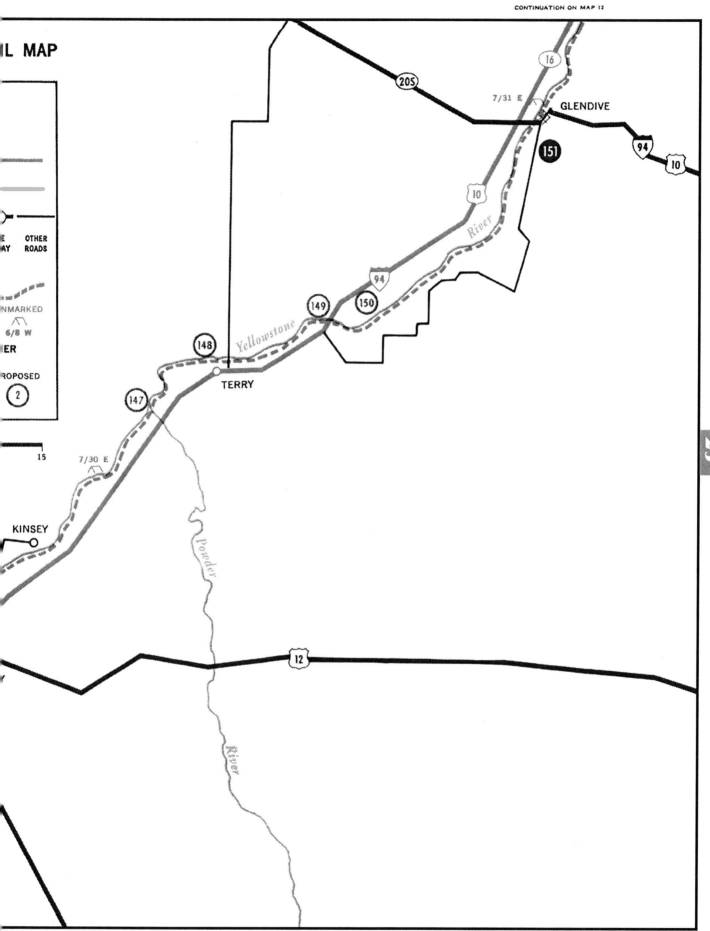

L MAP

OTHER
ROADS

NMARKED

6/8 W
ER

ROPOSED

2

15

7/30 E

KINSEY

20S

16

7/31 E

GLENDIVE

151

10

94

94

10

River

Yellowstone

149

150

148

147

TERRY

Powder

River

12

25

AREA NUMBER		OWNERSHIP *	ADMINISTRATION *	RECREATION USE			RECREATION ACTIVITIES AND ATTRACTIONS															TOTAL LAND AND WATER ACREAGE
				Day	Overnight	Vacation	Camping	Picnicking	Boating	Water Skiing	Swimming	Hunting	Fishing	Hiking	Horse Trails	Sightseeing	Nature Study	Winter Sports	Historic	Archeologic	Geologic	
	MONTANA (Continued)																					
145	Brannum Lake Fishing Access Site	S	S	▲				•					•									68
146	*Miles City Recreation Site ~*	F	F	▲	▲		•	•					•	•								100
147	*P-Y Confluence Recreation Site ~*	F	F	▲	▲		•	•	•				•									19
148	*Scenic View Recreation Site ~*	F	F	▲	▲		•	•				•	•	•		•	•				•	400
149	*Fallon Bridge Recreation Site ~*	F	F	▲	▲		•						•									6

* P - Private   C - County
   Q - Quasi-public   S - State
   M - Municipal   F - Federal

~ *Proposed Site*

RECREATION AREAS (EXISTING and PROPOSED)

AREA NUMBER		OWNERSHIP*	ADMINISTRATION*	RECREATION USE			RECREATION ACTIVITIES AND ATTRACTIONS															TOTAL LAND AND WATER ACREAGE
				Day	Overnight	Vacation	Camping	Picnicking	Boating	Water Skiing	Swimming	Hunting	Fishing	Hiking	Horse Trails	Sightseeing	Nature Study	Winter Sports	Historic	Archeologic	Geologic	
	MONTANA (Continued)																					
150	*Fallon Island Recreation Site ~*	F	F	▲	▲		●	●	●			●	●									147
151	Makoshika State Park	S	S	▲	▲		●	●								●					●	784

~ Proposed Site

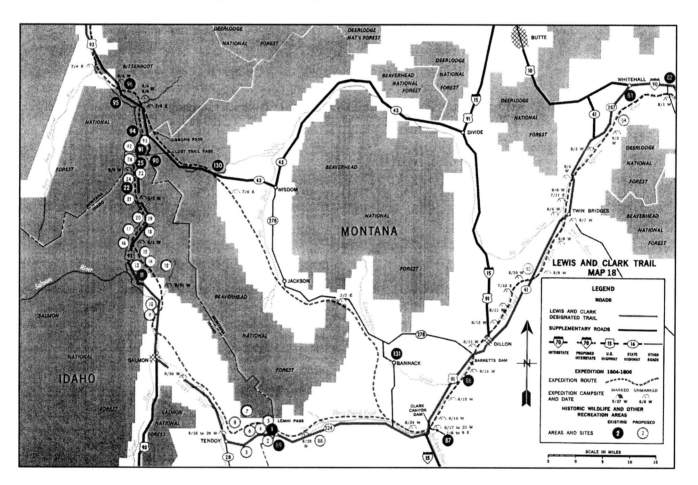

Other Lewis and Clark Titles from DSI

Now back in print
Original Journals of Lewis and Clark
Edited by Reuben Gold Thwaites

Now back in print "Original Journals of The Lewis and Clark Expedition" as published by Dodd Mead in 1904/1905. In preparation for the Bicentennial commemoration of the historic Lewis and Clark Expedition, Digital Scanning, Inc. (DSI) announces the release of their digital reprint edition. The 1903-04 set of **"Original Journals of the Lewis and Clark Expedition"** have been described as the most accurate, work on the expedition. Edited and including an introduction and index by Reuben Gold Thwaites, this set is considered a valuable resource for historians, students and history buffs. This set includes 7 two-part volumes and the Atlas. Illustrated throughout by Karl Bodmer.

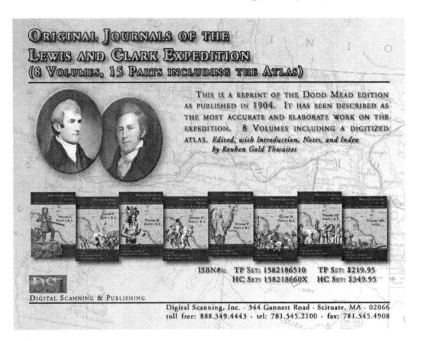

Trade Paper Editions	Hardcover Editions
8 Volume Trade Paper Set 1582186510	8 Volume Hardcover Ser 158218660X
ISBN	ISBN
TP Volume 1 1582186529	HC Volume 1 1582186618
TP Volume 2 1582186537	HC Volume 2 1582186626
TP Volume 3 1582186545	HC Volume 3 1582186634
TP Volume 4 1582186553	HC Volume 4 1582186642
TP Volume 5 1582186561	HC Volume 5 1582186650
TP Volume 6 158218657X	HC Volume 6 1582186669
TP Volume 7 1582186588	HC Volume 7 1582186677
TP Volume 8 1582186596	HC Volume 8 1582186685

Additional Information is available at http://www.Digitalscanning.com or http://www.PDFLibrary.com.

History of The Expedition of Captains Lewis and Clark 1804-1806 by James K. Hosmer

Reprinted from the edition of 1814.

History of the Expedition under the Command of Captains Lewis and Clark is a reprint of the 1814 edition as prepared by Paul Allen, Esquire. This 2-volume set was published in 1903 in preparation for the centennial celebration at that time. The introduction was written by James K. Hosmer past President of the American Library Association.

Volume 1	ISBN	Volume 2	ISBN
Individually		Individually	
Trade paper	1582186979	Trade paper	1582187029
Hardcover	1582186987	Hardcover	1582187037
2 Vol. Sets		**2 Vol. Sets**	
Trade paper	1582186995	Hardcover	1582187045

Information and samples available at:
http://www.digitalscanning.com and http://www.PDFlibrary.com

First Across The Continent By Noah Brooks
As Published in 1901

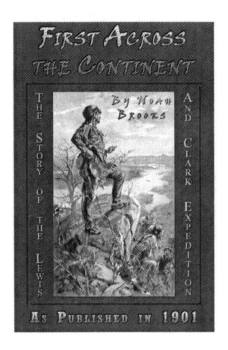

First Across the Continent: The Story of the Lewis and Clark Expedition is presented as a captivating tale. It is drawn from the original journals of the explorers. Noah Brooks uses extensive, carefully selected excerpts from the journals to entice the reader, and then sends the armchair adventurer along on the trek with Lewis and Clark. The detailed description and faithful narratives immerse you in one of the most amazing journeys in history. Originally published in 1901.

Noah Brooks (1830-1903 was a political confidant and personal friend of Abraham Lincoln. A journalist for the *Sacramento Union* during the Lincoln presidency, Brooks was a frequent guest at the White House. After Lincoln's assassination, Brooks moved to the east coast and wrote for other newspapers, including the *New York Tribune* and the *New York Times*.

A great introduction for the young reader, audience 10 to adult.

ISBN TP 1582186820 HC 1582186839 eBook 1582186812

Information and samples available at:
http://www.digitalscanning.com and http://www.PDFlibrary.com

"The Trail of Lewis and Clark" by Olin D. Wheeler
"As Published in 1904"

A Century after Lewis and Clark explored the newly purchased lands west of the Mississippi, Olin D. Wheeler set out on his own epic journey. Using the explorer's journals as a guide, he followed the old trail and recorded the changes to the land and landscape. Wheeler traveled by train, steamboat and pack train accompanied by a photographer. The 2 Volume set contains hundreds of photographs, sketches and maps.

Volume 1	ISBN	Volume 2	ISBN
Individually		Individually	
Trade paper	1582187258	Trade paper	1582187266
Hardcover	1582187274	Hardcover	1582187282
2 Vol. Sets		2 Vol. Sets	
Trade paper	1582187290	Hardcover	1582187304

Information and samples available at:
http://www.digitalscanning.com and http://www.PDFlibrary.com

Breinigsville, PA USA
20 August 2009
222644BV00001B/8/A